Marginal Language and Literature

Badan Riset dan Inovasi Nasional

Edited by

Maman S. Mahayana · Prof. Koh Young Hun

Marginal Language And Literature

Badan Riset dan Inovasi Nasional

Edited by
Maman S. Mahayana
Prof. Koh Young Hun

HUEBOOKs

Introduction

Marginal Language and Literature is a book presented to provide a broader explanation and understanding of language and literature issues considered marginal in society. It is undeniable that marginal language and literature are frequently disregarded and regarded as having no significance. However, marginalized languages and literature have pivotal roles and values that enrich the culture and identity of an ethnic or social group. Marginal language and literature are part of the cultural identity of a social-ethnic group. In addition, marginal language and literature become a medium for expressing feelings, experiences, knowledge, and worldviews that are unique and typical of a social-ethnic group.

This book highlights marginal languages and literature, including regional languages and literature. This book encourages readers to comprehend and recognize why marginal language and literature are pivotal in a social community's life. In addition, this book significantly contributes to the diversity of languages and literature in Indonesia in particular and the world in general.

Reading this book is essential for anyone interested in language and literature, including students, academics, practitioners, and society. This book has 13 titles that discuss marginalized languages and literature in Indonesia. The authors of this book are researchers under the auspices of the Research Center for Language, Literature, and Community, the National Research and Innovation Agency. This book will assist the community, provide enlightenment, and broaden their views regarding language and literature, which are considered marginal in the social community.

Ultimately, we thank all those who have contributed considerably to the success of this book's publication. This book is published with various contributing parties' support and participation.

Head of Research Center for Language,
Literature, and Community

Table of Contents

Prologue
The Political Roots of the Marginalization of Indonesian Language and Litetrature

Maman S. Mahayana(maman_s_mahayana@yahoo.com)

The marginalization of literature and other cultural products is essentially a reaction to the anxiety or arrogance of the ruling group over the emergence of public awareness to produce their own cultural creations or products. Consider, for example, the claim of a high culture to distinguish it from folk culture. This dichotomy was deliberately raised by the royal court to demean cultural products outside their environment. For the royal family, courtiers, nobles, and the elite, there was a kind of privilege attached as their privilege to create culture and even determine people's right to life. They were entitled to create cultural products. People do not have the right to be creative, and are prohibited from thinking. Creation comes from gods, and those who have the right to run it are those who have power. That is why, as we can see in the cultural products by the kings, splendors, luxury, and nobility often become their main characteristics that are impossible for ordinary people to do.

Thus, there was a kind of ambition in the palace circles to achieve greatness and reputation, which made the cultural products they produced a costly, time-consuming, and incalculable workforce, even sacrificing thousands of lives (the common people). The goal was to leave a legacy so that the king or figure was still remembered; during his reign, he once appeared as someone who succeeded in upholding the milestones of spectacular achievements!

Moreover, considering that the fate, life, and death of the people were in the hands of the king, the people had to obey his orders. That is why in the life of a powerful kingdom or empire, there is only one cultural product, namely, that produced by the royal court. It has always been imagined, through various mythologies and legends, that everything that was born in the palace environment represented a message from the gods. This assumption is increasingly firmly rooted because the mythology that gives legitimacy is continuously produced as truth that is passed down by the gods and voiced to the public as facts, belief systems, doctrines, and even the truth itself.

Nevertheless, people who are in marginal, peripheral, and cheap positions have their own desire to express their existence, reveal their identity, and assert their role in society. Therefore, in their own way, they put up a fight: they create and cover up their suffering with entertaining work. Lines of fate may be different, but as human beings, people also have dreams, hopes, ideas, thoughts, and creativity. It cannot be restrained, prohibited, or suppressed. Thus, differences in social status and the line of fate cannot immerse ideas and creativity that are not bound by space and time. It can strike out of nowhere, unexpectedly, and is full of surprise. It was from this movement that cultural products, creative works and various other forms of art were born that originated, grew and developed and are intended for the people themselves. This is where the term folk culture emerged to distinguish it from palace culture. The court created a strict dichotomy, demeaning, to distinguish between high and low cultures. This is the beginning of cultural marginalization, which is essentially the cultural politics of rulers.

After the Industrial Revolution, there was a spirit of commercialization in all areas of life, including cultural products. High cultural products are simplified, reproduced en masse, packaged according to public tastes, and commercialized at low cost. Take, for example, the Monalisa painting by Leonardo da Vinci or other paintings by masters of painting. Considering that the original work is the only one and that the price cannot be afforded by common people, the work is printed and reproduced en masse and sold at a low price. For people who are interested in owning the painting, it is sufficient to buy reproductions that are spread all over the place. The commercialization of high cultural products also applies to all other fields of art and later in the literature.

The use of high culture for commercial purposes has generated many economic benefits. However, it does not contribute to the development or improvement of the high culture itself. This is why some cultural theorists call for the commercialization of a high-culture parasite. It absorbs the existence of a high culture and makes as much profit as possible, giving nothing to it.

The commercialization movement carried out by these capitalists has also penetrated people's cultural products. As a result, various folk arts were reproduced en masse, distributed widely, and sold at low prices. Folk art that was originally created for their own interests and limited to being enjoyed among them suddenly spread to all corners of the world beyond its own cultural area. Commercialization and massization are the main characteristics of this cultural product. From there, theorists call it popular culture, which is populist in nature; there are also those who call it mass culture.

***

The process of the division of three cultures, namely high culture, folk culture, and popular culture in post-Industrial Revolution Europe, can be understood given the role of the empire, the power of the bourgeoisie and aristocrats, the strong influence of church circles, and the philosophical traditions of the intellectuals there since the Greek era. Ancient civilizations have succeeded in building civilizations and cultural development. Of course, the process of growth and formation of culture that occurs in people in the archipelago is different and perhaps even more complicated and problematic. However, the diversity of ethnic backgrounds and their closeness to nature not only creates various belief systems, but also creates cultural expressions that are almost inseparable from the influence of nature. In such an atmosphere of mysticism, the entry of foreign nations brought about major social changes in almost all aspects of the sociocultural lives of the Indonesian people. Even so, respect for nature cannot be ignored.

The first wave of social change was marked by the arrival of the Indians, who brought Hinduism, knowledge of the system of government (kingdom), and forms of writing (Brahmi and Pallawa letters), as well as literature through the Mahabharata and Ramayana epics. The golden age of Hindu kingdoms in Java was a representation of cultural development—the first wave of Nusantara civilization–due to the influx of foreign nations, followed by acculturation and inculturation. Even so, in this early period, culture belonged only to the kingdom, and cultural products, especially art, of the people did not appear on the surface, considering that there were not many records of it. Historic buildings, such as palaces and temples, inscriptions, and ancient books inscribed with Kawi, Sanskrit, or old Javanese characters, are products of palace culture.

The second wave of social change in the archipelago was marked by the arrival of Islam. Just as the Indians introduced a belief system (religion), government (kingdom), and a form of writing, Islamic intellectuals also introduced these three aspects (religion, empire, and writing). Even so, there is a fundamental difference in what Muslim clerics do: they convey their treatises in Malay, which are relatively well known to the people of the Archipelago. Thus, we see that if the influence of Hinduism tends to center on Java, the problem is solely due to language media and writing (Kawi, Sanskrit, or Old Javanese), which are too complicated for non-Javanese people to learn and understand. This is also why the spread of Hinduism and its literature has not widely reached areas outside Java.

The acceptance of Islam into various regions in the archipelago was made possible by at least five of the following factors: (i) The spread through the Malay language as a lingua franca which was relatively well known to the local population, facilitated widespread acceptance of Islam; (ii) The use of Jawi (Arabic-Malay) letters introduced by Hamzah Fansuri is like a bridge connecting the Malay language and Islamic teachings which are relatively well known through the Arabic Al-Quran; (iii) The spirit of Islam which is populist, egalitarian and knows no caste, allows various levels of society to take part in literacy activities—reading and writing—without being separated by social status; (iv) Its deployment tends to be adaptive, flexible, and does not completely eliminate socio-cultural roots and belief systems that are still inherent as community traditions—especially in Java, does not create conflict and hostility, and (v) the strong influence of local clerics and their approaches which is socio-cultural and non-confrontational in introducing Islam, causing Islam to be accepted without resistance, without hard opposition. Everything seems to have been taken for granted; there were no issues.

If we trace the manuscripts stored in the sultanates and Islamic boarding schools in the archipelago, we can be certain that we will find thousands of intellectual works written by past poets and scholars, both written in Arabic, Jawi, or Pegon letters. Initially, all the written works were referred to in the literature. Subsequently, the researchers sorted them according to variety, content, types, and themes contained in the texts.

The wealth of literary products produced by Indonesian scholars, poets, and intellectuals emphasizes that the people in the archipelago, for more than ten centuries since the arrival of the Indians who introduced Hinduism to the establishment of Islamic sultanates in various regions of the archipelago before the arrival of the Europeans, were already familiar with the world of literacy. Just look at the writing of poems, saga, and rhymes, which are still being written by people today.

Thus, reading and writing activities are not foreign to the people of the archipelago. The world of literacy has grown and developed in the palace and empire environments. In addition, in several areas, we can find ethnic languages and writings (: regional scripts) live and grow within local communities. Some of these, among others, are the Balinese script, Batak, Bima, Bugis, Cirebon, Javanese, Kerinci, Lampung, Rejang, and Sundanese. It does not include writing in Pegon letters (the local language uses Arabic). Why does it seem as if the tradition of intellectual civilization is no longer recognized by the current generation? Why is the legacy of rich literacy not introduced into the school education system?

The third wave of social change in the archipelago was marked by the entry of Europeans who came in two phases. The first phase occurred in the early 15th century—perhaps before that—by Portuguese and Spanish sailors. Pioneering was done by Vasco da Gama in his search for black gold (spice) that opened shipping-travel routes to India and continued to the "Spice Islands," a source of black gold that can be obtained easily and cheaply! These two islands provide abundant black gold: Ternate and Tidore!

This voyage route was continued by Ferdinand Magellan. The 16th-century voyages of Magellan and his successor, Juan Sebastian de Elcano, were the first and most important recorded European maritime expeditions to circumnavigate the world. The voyage then placed it as Magellan Circumnavigation, which proved that the shape of the Earth is round. Ternate and Tidore then became the epicenters that determined the formation of global geopolitics, because they played the role of the world's center for spices. From there, the hunt for spices and the struggle for power in the seas pushed the European shipping world to the archipelago, creating competition, conflict, and war. This was the second phase of the arrival of the Europeans to the archipelago.

The domination of the shipping route of the spices and the struggle for Portuguese and Spanish influence over several sultanates adjacent to the "Spice Islands" essentially had an economic origin and aim: to open the Nusantara-Europe trade route. The Portuguese succeeded in controlling shipping lanes, even in the sea area of Java Island. From there, the most influential European trading company at that time, the Vereenigne Oostindische Compagnie (VOC), which also had an interest in controlling economic resources in the eastern region (Nusantara), did not remain silent. History then records: The VOC succeeded in eliminating Portuguese influence in the archipelago. As a result of the massive corruption within the trading company, the VOC failed to maintain its reputation and slowly collapsed. In 1799, the Dutch government took over VOC leadership. The Dutch government plays the role of colonization in the archipelago. The

Dutch then called the territory they controlled the Dutch East Indies!

***

When Europeans came to the archipelago, residents in various regions, especially in kingdoms, sultanates, and Islamic boarding schools, were already undergoing literacy activities as part of their daily lives. Correspondence written in Jawi or Latin letters between the sultanates of Aceh, Banten, Makassar, Palembang, and Ternate with Portuguese, Spanish, or Dutch envoys since the early 17th century, for example, emphasized that world literacy matters (read–write) is very common. So no wonder that we can find treatises on the results of negotiations or agreements with foreign parties in the texts stored in the sultanates.

Tracing the path of the development of Malay literature written in the Jawi script, we can see that its distribution was so wide that it reached almost the entire archipelago. Moreover, the Malay language roadmap even breaks through the Malay Peninsula from Pattani to Mindanao. Likewise, cultural products, especially Javanese and Sundanese art and literature, which are written in the Pegon letter, continue to grow and develop not only in the palace environment but also within the common people circle. Everything grew and developed firmly, although recently, a dichotomy between the noble palace culture and populist folk culture emerged. However, this distinction does not give the impression that one cultural product degrades another because the world of creation and the goals of its people are different.

In fact, the Dutch East Indies government, geopolitically, succeeded in securing its position of power in the Dutch East Indies. The Portuguese, for example, no longer have an influence in the Eastern Region of the archipelago. The same happened in England. Through the signing of the London Treaty on March 17, 1824, which divided the Malay world into two parts, the British were comfortable occupying the Malay Peninsula. Incidental conflict events, such as rebellions perpetrated by several sultanates, did not have a broad impact and were resolved relatively quickly, either through negotiations, pitting against one another, or crushing with weapons. What problems did the Netherlands face?

The main problem faced by the Dutch Government compared to the British, for example, was the lack of confidence in exercising its power over such a large area and the diverse socio-cultural backgrounds of its inhabitants. This is where the Malay language as a lingua franca played an important role for the Dutch in exercising their power. Even so, not many Dutch people mastered the Malay language. As was also faced by missionaries in their efforts to translate the Bible, the choice of using low Malay was easier for the natives to understand than court Malay—which referred to classical texts. At that time, in the Eastern Region, especially Minahasa, the Dutch sent missionaries to set aside the Portuguese footprint and remove Catholic influence and replace it with Protestantism.

The tug-of-war between market Malay (low) and court Malay (high) became more complicated because the Dutch themselves had difficulty in learning Malay. The main problem lies in the use of Jawi letters. If they want to learn Malay, they must first know the Arabic-Malay alphabet. As van Ronkel put it: "Speaking in Malay was normal for us. ... unfortunately Dutch people who can "read" (understand Arabic letters) are still very rare."

Facing this reality, Governor General JJ Rochussen (1850) proposed that Malay be the language of instruction in the Archipelago. This proposal was followed by enforcing the use of Latin letters in Malay to replace the use of Arabic-Malay letters in the Dutch East Indies. This is language politics which not only marginalizes the writing of the Jawi script in Malay, but at the same time drowns it. The widespread domino effect has resulted in the further exclusion of the use of Pegon letters and regional scripts.

In terms of Latinization of the Malay language, the Dutch government ignored William Marsden's spelling (1812) or referred to writing Jawi letters and chose to incorporate Dutch spelling elements. However, Marsden's latinization adheres to the Jawi spelling. So, there is a kind of uniformity in writing Malay with Latin letters. That's what the Netherlands didn't do. As a result, the vowels / oe / for / u /, consonants / dj /, / tj /, and / nj / for / j /, / c /, and / ny / are entered, which in Jawi writing, /u/ uses the letter /wau —w/

and /j/ use the letter / jim— j/, while /tj/ and /nj/ use one sign.

The absence of spelling of the Malay language with Latin letters as a reference, coupled with the tendency to write certain words based on the sound of speech or utterances, causes one particular word to be written differently. For example, the word / woman / which is written in Jawi letters: pa-ro - mim - pa - wau - nun . Because you don't pay attention to the form of writing in Jawi and tend to rely on spoken or spoken sounds, you can write in Latin letters / prampoean /, / prampoewan /, / prempoewan /, / prempoean / / parempoean /, /perampoean/ or / perempoean /.

The chaos was getting out of control, because the early newspapers, such as Soerat Kabar Bahasa Melaijoe (4 January 1856), Bintang Oetara: Soerat Chabar Bharoe (5 February 1856), Bintang Betawi (1956), Soerat Chabar Batawie (3 April 1958), and other newspapers managed by Dutch businessmen used Malay spellings which underlie word forms based on speech sounds or utterances. The Bintang Oetara newspaper (published in Rotterdam, February 5, 1856) managed by Philippus Pieter Roorda van Eysinga, a philologist and linguist who has explored Sumatra and Java for many years, emphasized that this newspaper used the Inner Malay (High Malay) language. However, in practice, there is no consistency in the use of spelling and writing of certain words.

After van Eysinga died in Utrecht, October 14, 1856, his son WAP Roorda van Eysinga replaced his father's position as administrator and also chief author. The newspaper then used the outer Malay language, even though the spelling was almost the same as before. Pay attention to the excerpt of the text of the announcement which show this matter: : "Deri sebab kapala mengarang soerat chabar ini, toean hakim Dr. P.P. Roorda van Eysinga, itoe soedah meninggal doenia ini, djadi sekarang pengarang itoe djatoh atas kita s'orangan sadja. Maka bapa kita soedah memang soeka sekali toelis Malajoe dalam basa tinggi sabagimana itoe Malajoe deri Padang, deri Palembang dan lain-lain negri, tetapi sebab soerat ini paling lakoe di tanah Djawa djadi kita maoe toeroet adatnja orangnja itoe jang pake basa Malajoe loear." (Bintang Oetara, 8 Djanoeari 1857).

The same thing happened to Soerat Chabar Batawie. This newspaper intentionally includes its text in two forms of writing: the column on the left uses Latin letters and the column on the right uses Jawi letters. Even so, the text using Latin letters still shows its confusion, as can be seen from the following quote: “Ieni soerat chabar depane di tjitaq saparo with hoeroef Walanda, saparo with hoeroef Malaijoe.” (Soerat Chabar Batawie, Nommer 1, Saptoe, harie 3 boelan April 1858).

According to the classification carried out by Francois Valentijn (1713) and William Marsden (1812) the Malay language as used by the newspapers included colloquial Malay, outer Malay, low Malay or kacukan Malay. Later, the Chinese people also realized the importance of mastering the Malay language compared to their ancestral language, for various matters of communication with the Dutch and the native population, in addition to obtaining information related to their business. Right after, several Chinese entered the business of printing and publishing newspapers. The Malay language used in the newspapers also uses the model of the previous newspapers. It can be said that all newspapers published in the 19th and early 20th centuries used colloquial Malay. From there, a variety of newspaper Malay languages were formed, the spelling and writing methods of which were different from the Malay language found in classical Malay texts.

In its development, the business of printing and publishing newspapers began to be dominated by Chinese entrepreneurs. They also began to publish well-known literary works and translations of Chinese literature. The Malay language used, of course, refers to the previous newspapers. It was from there that the term Chinese (Malay) Peranakan language and literature emerged.

It may be because of the chaos, Lie Kim Hok wrote a spelling book (which he called Betawi Malay spelling, and not Chinese Malay), entitled: Melajoe Betawi, Kitab deri hal perkataan-perkataan Melajoe, hal memetjah oedjar-oedjar Melajoe dan hal pernahkan tanda-tanda batja dan hoeroef-hoeroef besar (Betawi: Albrecht & Rusche, 1891, 116 pages). If we look at the date on the Preface of the book, October 1883, it can be confirmed that the error is very common for publishers. Even so, Lie Kim Hok's own book is not organized systematically, so the description is not so clear. It also does not refer to the Jawi spelling and writing system, but focuses more on spelling and punctuation matters that are often ignored by (almost) all newspapers published at the time. So, the problem of writing words that correspond to the writing of Jawi letters, is not touched upon at all.

At that time, if you look at a number of newspapers and magazines, as well as literary works in the form of rhymes, poems and saga published in the mass media, it seems that each publisher and printing company had their own conventions or rules in terms of writing words and spelling application. For the Dutch government, this chaos naturally made it difficult to carry out government administration, even though since 1850 Governor General Rochussen had decreed the use of Malay—with Latin letters—as the language of instruction in government schools for native children.

This decision was strengthened by AA Fokker. In 1897, he proposed uniforming the Malay language with Latin letters. This was also one of the reasons Charles Adrian van Ophuijsen was assisted by Moehammad Ta'ib Soetan Ibrahim – a teacher at Kawedanan Oud Agam, from Kota Gadang – and Engkoe Nawawi Degree Soetan Ma'moer – an assistant teacher at the Rajo School – in 1896 to compile the spelling of the language Standard Malay and sourced from classical Malay. Thanks to that effort, the Melajoe Dialect Book was composed; Woordenlijst voor de spelling der Maleische taal (Batavia, 1901) which later became better known as van Ophuijsen Spelling. A year after that (1902), the Director of Education Abendanon, made it mandatory for all schools in the Dutch East Indies to use this book as a spelling guide for Malay with Latin letters. Apart from making it mandatory for all schools, the Dutch Government also urged private publishers, especially newspapers, to use this spelling.

The enactment of the obligation to use the van Ophuijsen spelling in all schools in the Dutch East Indies and private publishers, followed by language politics by building a noble image of Malay in schools and government and a bad stigma of Malay in newspapers and private publishers. In this way, a dichotomy was created for the Malay language, namely school Malay, high school Malay, and aristocratic Malay using the van Ophuijsen spelling - and colloquial Malay, lower Malay, commercial Malay, and kacukan Malay, on the other hand. That is the politics of (Malay) language marginalization.

Image building and creating stigma then became an important part of Dutch colonial politics when private publishers who issued newspapers, magazines or books whose contents often portrayed the negative side of Dutch people, not infrequently also attacked government policies. The bi-weekly newspaper Bientang Timoor (published in Surabaya, 1 July 1862—since 5 January 1870, the orthography of the heading changed to Bintang Timor), for example, apart from containing advertisements, auction news, commodity prices, and transfers or replacements of Dutch officials, it also contained news social problems, poverty, and criminal events. A publisher in Semarang published novels by movement figures, such as Soemantri (Rasa Merdika: Hikajat Soedjanm), Mas Marco Kartodikromo (Studen Hijo), Semaoen (Hikajat Kadiroen) whose contents depict bad Dutch figures. The novels were originally published as newspaper serial stories, not to mention the short stories or serial stories of Tirto Adhi Soerjo.

The existence of social and national awareness exhaled by a number of mass media and publishers certainly made the Dutch government worried. The movement was seen as dangerous for the continuity of his power in the Dutch East Indies. The Dutch government unilaterally said that the movement was carried out by: "Book merchants who are less pure in heart, irresponsible publishers, agitators and their works as wild reading!" In order to stem the influence of such readings, the Dutch Government felt the need to establish a publishing institution which would publish works in accordance with the spirit of building the image of the Netherlands as the messiah and creating the stigma of the natives being ignorant, backward, and other negative characters. That was the background for the establishment of the Commission for Indigenous School Reading and Folk Reading (Commissie voor de Inlandsche School en Volkslectuur) in 1908, as well as the realization of Dutch ethical politics. After the institution progressed, on September 22, 1917 the institution changed its name to the People's Reading Office (Kantoor voor de volkslectuur), which is better known as Balai Pustaka.

If in terms of the Malay language, the Dutch made a dichotomy: high Malay—Balai Pustaka Malay, school Malay, Riau Malay, Church Malay—and low Malay, then in literature, the Dutch made a dichotomy: Balai Pustaka literature and wild readings, including in it, the works of Chinese descent. That is the political root of the marginalization of Indonesian literature. Stamps for wild reading, Chinese peranakan literature, Medan literature, and dime romance—the terms used by Roolvink, are stigmatizations to place literary works outside Balai Pustaka publications as cheap, lowly, and wild literature. Cheap because the quality of the paper, print, and packaging is poor; low because the contents tend to be just cheap entertainment, sometimes also porn, and wild because the language is full of immodesty and contains political propaganda. Such is the stigma applied to privately published works. However, in reality, it's not like that. In fact, there are not a few works published by the private sector, the quality of which exceeds the works published by Balai Pustaka.

It was as if this marginalization gained socio-cultural legitimacy and spread to traditional literature when the magazine Poedjangga Baroe (July 1933)—through the view of Sutan Takdir Alisjahbana (STA) created another dichotomy, namely pre-Indonesian culture and Indonesian culture. Traditional literature as old literature born from pre-Indonesian society (before 1900) is seen as static, frozen, palace centric, and full of all evils. Meanwhile, modern literature, as new literature, was produced by Indonesian society which received Western influence. This view has persisted to this day, because literature textbooks in schools follow A. Teeuw's view of making Indonesian literature canonical. The impact is amazing! Balai Pustaka's works became important milestones in the journey of Indonesian literature, while works beyond that simply sank into oblivion, including literary treasures originating from oral traditions and ethnic literature which are actually an inseparable part of the mosaic of Indonesian literature and culture.

***

This book contains a number of research results on (ethnic) language and literature that are not recorded in the canonization of Indonesian language and literature. These research works are important, because they reveal local wisdom values, cultural pearls, and unique ethnic languages which are actually an inseparable part of Indonesian culture. Won't Indonesia be incomplete as a nation, if their presence is eliminated or is deemed non-existent? Doesn't Indonesia exist because Aceh, Bali, Batak, Bugis, Dayak, Javanese, Minangkabau, and so on, exist within it? Isn't literature originating from oral traditions and ethnic languages spread across various regions a cultural product of the Indonesian nation itself?

Thus, if we wish to see a portrait of Indonesian culture as a whole and as a whole, then we cannot rely only on canon literature or a number of works which are used as study material in schools. Excluding canon literature or not being subject matter at school doesn't mean the work doesn't exist! We don't necessarily judge it a priori as a lowly work with poor quality. It is time for hegemonic perspectives and contempt for literary and linguistic treasures that are outside the mainstream, to be stored in a vault. How is it possible for people to know the philosophical spiritualism, strengths, human values, and aesthetic models of these works, if academics and researchers always close their eyes and ignore their existence? Don't these works also have the right to exist and the right to grow in their society? However, these works are an integral part of the large cultural landscape of Indonesia.

Compared to the canonical works which are later often designated as important milestones in the journey of Indonesian literature, the treasures of literature and the wealth of languages beyond that are often considered insignificant or do not contribute anything to the culture, to the people. Therefore, these works should have a place in various studies carried out by the nation itself, and not consider them non-existent, unimportant, and of low quality. It is possible that from the results of this research, it is found that not only local wisdom, but also knowledge that is unique and only applies to that area. This is where courage is needed to determine a socio-cultural approach or another approach that is more appropriate, and not dwell on theories that come not from one's own cultural tradition.

Based on the descriptions above, we can conclude at least three things.

(1) The replacement of Jawi letters with Latin letters has had a very wide impact. The literacy tradition of our scholars, poets and intellectuals seems to have sunk and the world of literacy in the archipelago seems to have started from writing Latin letters.
(2) Long before Westerners came to the archipelago, we were already living in a literacy civilization. However, as a result of the politics of marginalization, the Jawi script and other regional scripts are considered meaningless in the past. It is time for the wealth of world literacy to be introduced at all levels of education with a more positive image to foster pride in one's own cultural wealth.
(3) The politics of Dutch colonial marginalization and stigmatization of literary treasures originating from oral traditions, were unknowingly being reproduced in literature lessons at school. As a result, a bad image is created for the product of the nation's own past literacy. The dichotomy of old-new, traditional-modern, national-regional literature emerged as a result of the continuation of the politics of marginalization and stigmatization. Thus, a shared awareness is needed to build a more just and holistic literacy movement. A number of research results contained in this book is one effort to raise that awareness.

Bojonggede, 20 May 2023

The Babanada Spells in the Performance of Lengger Wanasabaan Mask Dance

A Representation of the Religiosity of the Social Community of its Owners

Ery Agus Kurnianto(erya002@brin.go.id) | **Derri Ris Riana**(derri.ris.riana@brin.go.id) |
Rissari Yayuk(yayuk.yrissariyayuk@yahoo.co.id) | **Jahdiah**(diah.banjar@yahoo.co.id) |
Resti Nurfaidah(resti013@brin.go.id)
National Research and Innovation Agency, Archaeological, Language and Literature Research Organization

INTRODUCTION

Spells are also known as oral literature. Spells are spoken orally by a shaman or handler (Andalas, E.F., 2017). Pitriani stated that spells are utterances used to remember and control thoughts (Elika & Nurhayati, 2022:1). Spells are part of an oral tradition that places a mystical element as a dominating force in the form of symbols as a request to those in power (Supriyanto, 2023:1). A Spell is an act of communication to the rulers of nature which contains requests, wishes, and prayers (Hasisah & Chandra, 2021:3).

The Babadana Spell is a type of oral literature in Central Java, Wonosobo, used to accompany the Lengger Mask Dance performance. Etymologically, babadana comes from babad, which gets the ending ana which means 'cut', 'open', and 'clean it up'. Grammatically, this word can be interpreted as a step to clean oneself or purify oneself, leaving behind things that are not good when the Topeng Lengger Dance performance is to be held (Interview with Agus Wuryanto was held on 26 February 2020).

The spell is recited by singing, accompanied by traditional musical instruments. In the order of the Lengger Mask Dance performance, the

Babadana spell is recited in pre-action, when the elders prepare everything needed for the performance, for example, preparing offerings. By connoisseurs of the Lengger Mask Dance, this spell is a sign that the show will be held soon. In addition, this mantra is considered a media of communication between elders and ancestors in negotiating so that the performance can run smoothly and successfully. The elements that make up the Babadana spell consist of two parts: literary art (the poetry spoken) and musical art (accompanying the utterance of the spell to create a sacred atmosphere or situation).

Oral literature is not born from a void of meaning. There is something that the creator wants to convey through the sentences he says. Therefore, Horatius stated that literature has two uses for its owners and connoisseurs: dulce (used as a medium to obtain entertainment) and utile (used to obtain benefits). When we enjoy the babadana spell, we will get entertainment through the aesthetics of rhyme and rhythm, the choice of words used, and the creation of the nuances that emerge. These aesthetic elements will make the connoisseur unconsciously dissolve and be actively involved in every moment that appears. Literature connoisseurs also benefit from the literary work they enjoy. This is because every part of oral literature represents the meaning of noble values , which contains moral teachings in living life as individuals and as social beings. This is because oral literature originates from values or norms of life which are believed to be accurate and applied and are passed down from one generation to the next. (Ocampo Alvarez, 2021); (Tang, 2022); (Gordanpour & Rezaei, 2021); (Lüleci, 2022); (Gombozhapov & Zhalsanova, 2022); (Kunkel, 2021); and (Lyutskanov, 2021) state that literature has educational and intellectual value for its owners. Literature also talks about human connectedness with socio-cultural life and the natural environment. Literature has a function for the community and can be studied in various studies. (Suyitno, 1986) states that oral literature is influenced by the values of the life of the social community of its owners in the form of social rules, noble values, and teachings about goodness. Related to this, Danandjaja (Danandjaja, 2002); (Sedyawati, 1984); (Hutomo, 1991) state that oral literature has a significant role or function in the social and personal life of its social community. Social functions are related to human relationships with individuals, society, and nature, while personal functions are related to human relationships with God and himself.

(Teeuw, 1969); (Mangunwijaya, 1988); (Atmosuwito, 1989); (Frye, 2000); (Damono, 2011) state that literature is religious. This is because, in literary works, the values, attitudes, and religious behaviour are represented by the creators of literary works in offering alternative solutions or choices about life, believing in the prima causa, which is used as the basis for facing and living life in their social community. (Hastuti et al., 2019:1); (Alnizar, 2019, p. 4188) state that religion can protect against behaviour. (Indriyani, 2022:1) states that in art, religious aspects can be instilled in the people who own them. (Ahmadi et al., 2019:1123); (Kretzler et al., 2022:45); (Norenzayan et al., 2014:1); (Pasek, 2021:68); (Amin Abdullah, 2014:175) state that religion will affect one's way of life and social culture.

(Mangunwijaya, 1988); Glock and Stark (Dister, 1988); Suhardiyanto (Adhim, 2009); and Suhardiyanto (Mahyudin, 2018) state that religiosity places more emphasis on a person's religious attitude in carrying out what is recommended and prohibited by God in daily life. (Darmayenti et al., 2021:169) states that religion is related to prayer and ethics by religious guidelines. (Hynson, 2021:1) state that religion contains aspects of prayer based on the beliefs held. (Abas & Kaur, 2019:162); (Alcorta & Sosis, 2017:323) state that religion is related to supernatural elements.

According to Glock & Stark (Ancok, 2001), there are five dimensions of religiosity. The five dimensions are

1. the dimension of religious belief (the ideological dimension) focuses on the issue of belief in something one believes in;
2. the ritual dimension of religious practice (the ritual dimension) focuses on the issue of a person's obedience in carrying out rituals that must be carried out according to what he believes, indications that can be used to carry out prayers, zakat, fasting, going to the mosque to worship, go to church to worship;
3. the dimension of the experience of religious feeling (the experiential

dimension) focuses attention on what humans feel and do in interacting with other humans according to what their beliefs teach;

4. the dimension of experiencing the religious effect (the consequential dimension) focuses attention on how a person should behave towards others as a form of application to the teachings of the beliefs he believes in;
5. the intellectual dimension of religious knowledge (the intellectual dimension) focuses on knowledge about the beliefs one believes in. Several indicators can be used to identify them, attending Islamic lectures and attending Sunday school for those with Christian beliefs.

Research on literary works, whatever the genre and form, will produce an interpretation of a social community's attitudes, behaviour, and beliefs related to the problem of people's belief in their God contained and represented in work. Related to this, the issue that will be examined in this paper is how the babadana spell represents the religious values of the social community that owns it. This study aims to describe how the babadana spell represents the religious values of the owner's social community.

The spell is an oral literature that is often found in social communities in Indonesia. Spells were originally part of a ritual performed by the community for a specific purpose. Spells are spoken to heal sick people, protect themselves, get ease and smoothness of activity, and so on. Not everyone can cast spells with the desired effect. Only certain people who have done 'practice' can recite and produce something as intended when the spell is recited.

(Soekmono, 1982); (Djamaris, 2002); (Kertanegara, 2011); (Amir, 2013); (Maryam, Siti, Sulaiman, Munawar, 2013); (Royani, Kiki Indah, Syaiful Arifin, 2020) spell is the oldest oral literature in the form of poetry. Spells are created by their creators to get or obtain supernatural powers, which are believed to have extraordinary powers so that they can grant the wishes of the spell caster. The recitation of the spell will result in something real from the magical power implicit in the words used. The appearance of the spell represents the belief of a social community which is animism and dynamism. They believe that everything in nature, mountains, seas, big trees, big rocks, and so on, has a spirit and power that can be used as a medium by humans to bring disaster or grace. (A. Ahmadi, 1986); (Amir, 2013); (Bahardur, Iswahdi & Ediyono, 2017) state that spells are spoken to bring or have a purpose.

Previous research examining traditional dance performances has been carried out by (Jain et al., 2021) with the title An Enhanced Deep Convolutional Neural Network for Classifying Indian Classical Dance Forms. The following researchers (Van Huis, 2019) with the title Cultural Significance of Lepidoptera in sub-Saharan Africa. Meanwhile, (Krisnawati et al., 2019) the title Original Research Identity Exhibition in Batik Motifs of Ebeg and Pataruman. These three studies examine the traditions of traditional dance oral performances in each country. These three studies have differences and similarities with what the researchers are doing. The difference is in terms of the regional origin of the dances and the findings. (Jain et al., 2021) explores Indian classical dance, which can support the learning of mathematics and geometry. (Van Huis, 2019) examines African dances to provide information about sources of inspiration for traditional African dances. Meanwhile, (Krisnawati et al., 2019) discuss classical dances from West Java, Indonesia, which are part of traditional batik motifs in West Java. As for what the researchers did, there was a difference in that the research object was the Lengger Mask Dance performance in Wonosobo, Central Java, focusing on findings on aspects of religious meaning in the spells recited before the event.

However, there are similarities between the three previous studies; both reveal the community identity of a local community from a traditional dance with religious aspects in local socio-cultural life. For example, one of the traditional Indian dances studied by (Jain et al., 2021) is Bharatanatyam. Behind the usefulness found by Jain et al., this dance is full of religious symbols of worship of Gods. Likewise, (Van Huis, 2019) finds a religious aspect behind the butterfly-inspired dance. Butterflies are associated with symbols of belief in something sacred, such as religious leaders or Gods in Africa. (Krisnawati et al., 2019) found that aspects of the traditional ebeg dance, part of West Javanese batik motifs, are related to transcendental values with certain rituals before performances.

Thus, this strengthens the fact that there is always a religious aspect in every oral performance art in traditional dance in communities from various countries. This can be seen in various forms of expression, such as body gestures, symbols, dance patterns, or utterances before performances or spells. It is this religious element contained in the spell recited before the performance that the researchers explored, particularly in the performing art of the Lengger Mask Dance Wonosobo, Central Java, Indonesia.

The previous research that examined the Lengger mask dance was carried out by (Layly et al., 2020) with the title The dynamics of the Lengger art in Prapah village, Panti, Jember 1900-2017. He explained the origin of the Lengger mask dance in Prapah Hamlet, Panti District, Jember Regency, from before and after Dutch colonialism until now. Lengger's art has developed a lot in terms of nails, clothing, appearance, and attributes used to function. This research does not explore religious elements in the spells contained in the arts. Meanwhile, this art cannot be separated from the elements of the spell.

Meanwhile, another study examining spells was conducted (Karasinski-Sroka & Sharman, 2022) under The Young Goddess Who Dances through the Ordinariness of Life—A Study on the Tantric Traditions of Kerala. The findings revealed that spells were recited in a ritual in essential rites of passage for various Indian Tantric communities with a sacred religious aspect. The spell contains self-identity, character and desire. (Hasisah & Chandra, 2021) with the title The Relation of Human Beings and Environment in the Cultural Event of Laesan Performance. He discovered that the Laesan dance from Java has a spirit of spell through the accompanying songs. This song can influence the audience's or dancers' minds to make specific movements. Next, (Supriyanto, 2023) researched Cowongan in Javanese Islamic mysticism: A study of Islamic philosophy in Penginyongan society. The results of the study found that there was a Cowongan ritual in Plana Village, Somagede District and Banyumas Regency. This ritual has the goal of asking the Almighty for rain to fall. The puppeteer or rain charmer follows the event by dancing and spell recitation. Javanese culture in this tradition is a syncretic result between Islamic mysticism and the local culture of the local community so that it becomes supernatural mystical for the social life of Panginyongan. Another researcher (Elika & Nurhayati, 2022) with the title The Communication Pattern of Wahyu Turonggo Aji Reog Dance in Merti Dusun Kemawi Sumowono as a Means of Preserving Environment. These two researchers found a form of communication with the Above through a spell in a Merti hamlet village ritual. This ritual is intended to signify gratitude: Merti, Kemawi Hamlet featuring Reog Wahyu Turonggo Aji. The spell used has the function of summoning and returning spirits.

These four studies emphasise the vital role of spells in a ritual ceremony with various accompaniments, such as dance, rites, songs, and attractions. Through this spell, the cultural and religious values of the local community are represented, which combine to become a unified whole to achieve the desired goals. This becomes part of the foundation of how important it is to research spells in the Lengger Mask Dance in Wonosobo, Central Java, which other researchers have not done so far. (Caesar & Sanasam, 2018:29) states in his research findings, namely, the importance of protecting the diversity of traditional music from the influence of gravity through a variety of meanings in a broad socio-cultural context to maintain the wisdom of the lyrics of the community that owns the arts as well as for national identity based on moral values traditional.

This study's results will reveal the dimensions of religiosity related to the ideological, ritual, experiential, consequential, and intellectual of the social community that owns the art of the Lengger mask dance. It is hoped that in the future, it will add to the treasures of documentation of oral traditions which are studied in a directed and systematic manner, as well as being part of the information that supports the teaching of regional local content.

A descriptive method using a pragmatic approach is applied in this study. Pragmatics is a branch of linguistics which is the object of language in its use, such as spoken or written communication; according to (Leech

(1993); (Wijaya, 1996), pragmatics is a branch of linguistics that examines the use of language with integrity with grammar consisting of phonology, morphology, and syntax. Yule (2006) also defines pragmatics as the study of the meaning conveyed by speakers (writers) and interpreted by listeners (readers). Understanding of meaning from a pragmatic perspective is influenced by expressions of relative distance which causes speakers to consider what is said and not said. A pragmatic assessment of language can provide benefits Jahdiah (2019). Listeners try to interpret speech speakers so that the speaker's meaning, intent and purpose will be obtained. Meanwhile, Jumanto (2017) defines pragmatics as studying the simplest to the most complex language or verbal utterances based on the context involving the text itself and the situations and conditions that exist outside the text, including who (speaker or reader) we communicate with. Pragmatics is the study of the speaker's meaning adapted to the context so that it is possible to know more about what is communicated than what is said. Jahdiah (2019) pragmatics is an approach that can accurately assess the intended problem regarding all aspects of speech, both verbally and sincerely. Pragmatics understands meaning contextually (Yayuk, 2018).

The Babadana spell is analysed using Glock and Stark's theory of the religiosity dimension. This classification of the religiosity dimension is used as the basis for identifying and inventorying the elements of religiosity represented in the babadana spell.

This research data is the Babadana spell—the spell spoken at the opening of the Lengger Wanasabaan Mask Dance show. The Babadana spell is obtained by using the observation method. A data collection method is carried out by coming to the research location and meeting several people to be used as informants related to the Babadana spell. The observation method was done with interview techniques, notes, and records. All information obtained from informants was noted and recorded. The observation method is also used to get an overview of society's political, economic, social and cultural conditions. In addition, data collecting was also carried out using the library method. This method is carried out by reading writings, textbooks, papers, and the results of previous research related to the Babadana spell problem.

The method used to inventory data is the method of observation and literature. The library method obtains information about the Wanasabaan Lengger parikan from books or previous research results. The observation method was carried out by meeting several informants, actors, practitioners, cultural observers, and the Tourism and Culture Office of the Wonosobo Regency, who had information about the Wanasabaan Lengger parikan. In addition to obtaining parikan information, the observation method is also used to obtain an overview of the physical and social environmental conditions of the Wonosobo people.

The steps taken to identify and inventory the dimensions of religiosity in the Babadana spell include several stages,

1. transcribing the Babadana spell data in the form of recorded notes;
2. transliterating data from the local language, Javanese, into Indonesian;
3. identifying and classifying the religiosity values represented in the Babadana spell; and
4. using a pragmatic approach to interpret, examine, and describe the religiosity values of the Babadana spell.

DISCUSSION

Overview of the Babadana Spell

The Babadana spell is an oral literature that is used as a medium for the spread of Islam. This spell is the result of acculturation between Hinduism, Buddhism and Islam. This can be seen by the words ya Allah Allah hu Allah at the end of each sentence and the end of each line of the spell. In practice, the spell chanting is complemented by the presentation of offerings and the burning of incense as a supporting medium for communicating and negotiating with the spirits of the ancestors. Before the influence of Islam entered, some of the diction or choice of words that appeared had elements of eroticism. It was inappropriate (Results of an interview with Agus Wuryanto, a Wonosobo humanist, held on March 14, 2020).

The Babadana spell is spoken as the opening act of the Lengger Wanasabaan Mask Dance. This spell is recited to accompany a traditional Javanese musical instrument, the gamelan. Gamelan accompaniment has the function of creating conditions or situations that are wise. Not infrequently, when this spell is uttered, some audience members are in a trance. Those in a trance will usually behave according to the behaviour of the spirit that enters them, some crawling, shouting angrily, behaving like a tiger, and some dancing according to gamelan accompaniment. According to Agus Wuryanto (based on an interview conducted on March 14 2020), those in a trance are generally spectators who are too carried away by the chanting of spells and gamelan accompaniment. Speeches and gamelan chants sweep away their souls and minds. At this moment of blank mind, they were electrocuted by magical power.

In the Lengger Wanasabaan Mask Dance performance, the Babadana spells have a function.

1. as a sign that the Lengger Wanasabaan Mask Dance performance will soon begin when this spell is chanted;
2. as a medium for communication and negotiation with ancestral spirits. Through the process of communication and negotiation, it is hoped that the show will run smoothly and without any obstacles that will hinder it; and
3. as an element of religion or the beliefs of the people who own oral literature. By chanting the Babadana spell, it is hoped that God will bestow safety, protection and guidance during the performance.

Religious Values in the Babadana Spell

Babadana

Para dulur jeneng sira dha elinga, marang Gusti Kang Kuwasa

Para dulur jeneng sira dha elinga, marang Gusti Kang Kuwasa

Mumpung sira isih ana ngalam Donya, ngudiya laku utama

Babadana pangeran sung tilaksana Allah hu Allah
Babadana Pangeran sung tilaksana Allah hu Allah
Babadana Pangeran sung tilaksana, Pangeran sung tilaksana

Pada lingsa rambut dadi surenana ya Allah Allah hu Allah
Pada lingsa rambut dadi surenana ya Allah Allah hu Allah
Pada lingsa rambut dadi surenana, rambut dadi surenana

Simak-ramak palilahe sun suwune ya Allah Allah hu Allah
Simak-ramak palilahe sun suwune ya Allah Allah hu Allah
Simak-ramak palilahe sun suwune, palilahe sun suwune

Satuhune Pangeran kang paring sandhang ya Allah Allah hu Allah
Satuhune Pangeran kang paring sandhang ya Allah Allah hu Allah
Satuhune Pangeran kang paring sandhang, Pangeran kang paring sandhang

Sekar Gadhung-gadhunge kang maya-maya ya Allah Allah hu Allah
Sekar Gadhung-gadhunge kang maya-maya ya Allah Allah hu Allah
Sekar Gadhung-gadhunge kang maya-maya, gadhunge kang maya-maya

Iman slamet tak suwun baliya slamet ya Allah Allah hu Allah
Iman slamet tak suwun baliya slamet ya Allah Allah hu Allah
Iman slamet tak suwun baliya slamet, tak suwun baliya slamet.

Bilahi kulon tinolak baliyo ngulon ya Allah Allah hu Allah
Bilahi kulon tinolak baliyo ngulon ya Allah Allah hu Allah
Bilahi kulon tinolak baliyo ngulon ya, tinolak baliyo ngulon

Wong ginau mah omah nang pinggir kali ya Allah Allah hu Allh
Wong ginau mah omah nang pinggir kali ya Allah Allah hu Allh
Wong ginau mah omah nang pinggir kali, mah omah nang pinggir kali
Sung ginau ing tembe amrih tentreme ya Allah Allah hu Allah
Sung ginau ing tembe amrih mulyane ya Allah Allah hu Allah

Sung ginau ing tembe amrih tentreme ya, ing te,be amrih tentreme

The spell represents several things related to the community's belief that it owns it. The essence of every animate or inanimate life is God. Each level or cycle of life is centred on God's power and power over his creatures. Humans live in the womb, are born as babies, grow into children, mature, age, and die because of God's will and power. Therefore, man must present God in every activity of his life as proof of his piety. The sentence ya Allah Allah hu Allah that appears at the end of each line of the spell represents that God has the power to make everything that does not exist come into being, everything that has not yet happened to happen. This illustrates the belief of the community that owns this spell that everything will happen if Allah permits and wills it. This belief reflects the piety of the Wonosobo people to Allah, who created the earth and everything in it.

From the results of the identification and classification of the Babadana spell, there are several dimensions of religiosity presented by Glock & Stark. This can be seen in the following table.

No.	Types of Religiosity Dimensions	Quote in the Babadana Spell
1.	The Ideological Dimension	*Para dulur jeneng sira dha elinga, marang Gusti Kang Kuwasa* *Para dulur jeneng sira dha elinga, marang Gusti Kang Kuwasa* *Mumpung sira isih ana ngalam Donya, ngudiya laku utama* *Babadana pangeran sung tilaksana Allah hu Allah* *Babadana Pangeran sung tilaksana Allah hu Allah* *Babadana Pangeran sung tilaksana, Pangeran sung tilaksana* *Satuhune Pangeran kang paring sandhang ya Allah Allah hu Allah* *Satuhune Pangeran kang paring sandhang ya Allah Allah hu Allah* *Satuhune Pangeran kang paring sandhang, Pangeran kang paring sandhang*
2.	The Ritual Dimension	*Pada lingsa rambut dadi surenana ya Allah Allah hu Allah* *Pada lingsa rambut dadi surenana ya Allah Allah hu Allah*

No.	Types of Religiosity Dimensions	Quote in the Babadana Spell
		Pada lingsa rambut dadi surenana, rambut dadi surenana *Iman slamet tak suwun baliya slamet ya Allah Allah hu Allah* *Iman slamet tak suwun baliya slamet ya Allah Allah hu Allah* *Iman slamet tak suwun baliya slamet, tak suwun baliya slamet.*
3.	The Experiential Dimension	*Sekar Gadhung-gadhunge kang maya-maya ya Allah Allah hu Allah* *Sekar Gadhung-gadhunge kang maya-maya ya Allah Allah hu Allah* *Sekar Gadhung-gadhunge kang maya-maya, gad-hunge kang maya-maya*
4.	The Consequential Dimension	Pada lingsa (telur kutu) rambut dadi surenana (sisir untuk mencari telur kutu dan kutu) ya Allah Allah hu Allah Pada lingsa (telur kutu) rambut dadi surenana (sisir untuk mencari telur kutu dan kutu) ya Allah Allah hu Allah Pada lingsa (telur kutu) rambut dadi surenana (sisir untuk mencari telur kutu dan kutu), Pada lingsa (telur kutu) rambut dadi surenana (sisir untuk mencari telur kutu dan kutu)
5.	The Intellectual Dimension	*Sung ginau ing tembe amrih tentreme ya Allah Allah hu Allah* *Sung ginau ing tembe amrih mulyane ya Allah Allah hu Allah* *Sung ginau ing tembe amrih tentreme ya, ing te,be am-rih tentreme*

1. The Ideological Dimension

All rituals and techniques of worship and worship to God as a form of piety and human devotion are the essential elements in one's life, one's belief in the existence of an almighty power beyond their control and power. This causes the emergence of different ritual forms as the application of attitudes of belief and worship by beliefs. In everyday life, people cannot be separated from these rituals.

The Babadana spell is a ritual performed by the Wonosobo social community as a medium to pray and ask God so that the show will run smoothly and not be constrained by anything.

Belief in God is a form of genuine appreciation and acknowledgement that truth is conveyed and must be applied daily. This belief is manifested in obedience to God Almighty in the form of faith, namely acknowledging that God exists and that all forms of content and the course of one's life are arranged and outlined by God.

The belief in God's power and love represented in the Babadana spell is a step or effort from the ancestors to pass on and preserve noble cultural values that form the basis and role models in interacting with other humans in their social environment. This is one of the social capitals that must be possessed by every human being in developing attitudes and behaviour based on the noble values that emerged, grew, and developed and were applied since the days of ancestral civilisations. It cannot be denied that these values are an integral part that cannot be separated from the Indonesian nation.

Para dulur jeneng sira dha elinga, marang Gusti Kang Kuwasa
Para dulur jeneng sira dha elinga, marang Gusti Kang Kuwasa
Mumpung sira isih ana ngalam Donya, ngudiya laku utama
Babadana pangeran sung tilaksana Allah hu Allah
Babadana Pangeran sung tilaksana Allah hu Allah
Babadana Pangeran sung tilaksana, Pangeran sung tilaksana

Satuhune Pangeran kang paring sandhang ya Allah Allah hu Allah
Satuhune Pangeran kang paring sandhang ya Allah Allah hu Allah
Satuhune Pangeran kang paring sandhang, Pangeran kang paring sandhang

In this quote, the ideological dimension is represented in the belief of the people who own the spell in Islamic religious doctrine or theology. The words *Alla hu Allah* and *Pangeran Sung Tilaksana* contain cultural meanings related to religious meanings or are commonly referred to as doctrinal terms for a belief, namely Islam. The word *Allah hu Allah* in the teachings of Islam is a sentence of remembrance which represents the meaning of glorifying the greatness of Allah. These words represent respect for Allah

SWT as the creator of nature and everything in it. The word Allah, repeated in a dhikr, reminds people, especially adherents of Islam, that all majesty and greatness belong to Allah. *Pangeran Sung Tilaksana*, in the teachings of Islam, refers to the Prophet Muhammad. The word *Pangeran* is aimed at a figure that has the meaning of noble and commendable character. In Muslim beliefs, the Prophet Muhammad is considered the first and foremost example of a prophet with noble and commendable morals in all aspects of life. Therefore, the word *Pangeran Sung Tilaksana* represents a belief that Muslims must follow and emulate the morals and behaviour of the Prophet Muhammad SAW.

The two choices of diction contain Muslim doctrines. The doctrines are in the form of 1) tauhid, the repetition of the diction of *Allah hu Allah* represents a belief that is certain that Allah SWT is the only God that Muslims worship. The concept of belief like this in Islamic teachings is called tauhid, namely belief in the oneness of (Allah SWT; 2) cultivating confidence in the exaltation of God. Zikr *Allah hu Allah* represents the belief that Allah is the only God with dominion over all things; and 3) fostering belief in the exemplary moral teachings and behaviour of the Prophet Muhammad, referred to as the sunnah in Islamic teachings. These diction choices have the power of belief in the power of God which will constantly be reminded and strengthened in the daily lives of the Wonosobo people.

2. The Ritual Dimension

The ritual dimension refers to human experiences and activities in religious practices that they must do according to their beliefs. These religious practices usually have patterns and rules that humans must obey. As an activity in religion, this ritual dimension is considered to have a very significant role in the stability and sustainability of humans in living their religious life. This is because this dimension has a powerful effect on God, who is believed in and with fellow human beings with the same belief. Through this dimension, a belief will emerge that humans will have a good and harmonious relationship with the God they believe in. In the Babadana spell, this dimension is reflected in the following quote.

Pada lingsa rambut dadi surenana ya Allah Allah hu Allah
Pada lingsa rambut dadi surenana ya Allah Allah hu Allah
Pada lingsa rambut dadi surenana, rambut dadi surenana
...
Iman slamet tak suwun baliya slamet ya Allah Allah hu Allah
Iman slamet tak suwun baliya slamet ya Allah Allah hu Allah
Iman slamet tak suwun baliya slamet, tak suwun baliya slamet.

The babadana spell quote reflects several vital aspects of the religious ritual dimension. The aspects represented are the practice of prayer in daily life, the Arabic language used, and the repetition of a word or phrase as a form of religious ritual.

The phrase *rambut dadi surenana* means that hair can be used as a symbol. The symbol represented is cleanliness, purity, and respect for Allah SAW. In this case, in the Islamic religion, keeping the body clean is the most crucial part of carrying out religious rituals. Before carrying out religious rituals, and prayers, a Muslim is expected to clean himself of dirt and odour. This is a form of respect for Muslims addressed to Allah before interacting in religious rituals.

Reduplication in the sentence *Iman slamet tak suwun baliya slamet*, tak suwun baliya slamet represented a ritual dimension in the form of a prayer uttered by humans addressed to God. This prayer asks for protection and blessings from Allah SWT, which Muslims chant or recite when performing religious rituals according to their beliefs. The words ya Allah and Allah hu Allah are in Arabic, used as a medium to communicate with Allah in Islamic religious beliefs, which means Allah, He is Allah. Muslims often use this sentence when carrying out religious rituals of remembrance or praying. This religious ritual has the meaning of remembering and praising the greatness and glory of Allah SWT. The addition of the word hu in the sentence reinforces the meaning that there is only one prima causa substance that is obligatory and worthy of worship, namely Allah. The repetition of the word Allah in the babadana spell represents ritual practices in Islam and the repetition of the holy verses of the Al-Qur'an and dhikr.

These ritual practices can strengthen one's faith and grow and create inner peace in living everyday life.

3. The Experiential Dimension

The experiential dimension becomes a dimension that has a significant role in one's religious life. This is because this dimension can present and grow a powerful influence on religious life beliefs. In addition, the experiential dimension will have a powerful impact on strengthening one's religious identity. Through this dimension, a person will experience a relationship with his God with greatness in religious rituals and his relationship with fellow members of a religious community. This is represented in the following babadana spell quote.

Sekar Gadhung-gadhunge kang maya-maya ya Allah Allah hu Allah
Sekar Gadhung-gadhunge kang maya-maya ya Allah Allah hu Allah
Sekar Gadhung-gadhunge kang maya-maya, gadhunge kang maya-maya

Iman slamet tak suwun baliya slamet ya Allah Allah hu Allah
Iman slamet tak suwun baliya slamet ya Allah Allah hu Allah
Iman slamet tak suwun baliya slamet, tak suwun baliya slamet.

The two stanzas in the babadana spell describe the dimensions of a person's religious practice, which include understanding God's will, awareness and belief in destiny, the importance of maintaining faith, and efforts to obtain salvation in life.

The quote Sekar *Gadhung-Gadhunge kang maya-maya ya Allah hu Allah* represents meaning in religious life. This means acknowledging and believing in God's will that comes suddenly or unexpectedly in human life. Through this meaning, a form of religiosity is represented in the belief that everything that happens, both blessings and calamities, that befall humans in their daily lives are the will of Allah SWT.

The quote *gadhunge kang maya-maya* (vague) represents a meaning that is human awareness and sincerity about destiny that must be accepted.

Accepting blessings and misfortunes as a form of destiny from God means that God is the ruler and giver of all things. Therefore, humans must eliminate dishonesty and reject the destiny God has determined for them. This will grow and develop the nature of gratitude in humans for all events and incidents that befall them. Besides that, humans must keep trying to get the best in their daily lives. This shows that awareness of destiny and remaining trusting in Allah is a form of practising the teachings of Islam.

The quote *Iman slamet tak suwun baliya slamet ya Allah Allah hu Allah* implies acknowledging the importance of maintaining faith in everyday life. This represents that the effort to maintain faith is a form of practising religious teachings that Muslims must carry out in Islam. The phrase *suwun baliya slamet* conveys meaning as a form of human efforts to obtain salvation from God in carrying out daily activities. This salvation includes the life of this world and the life hereafter.

4. The Consequential Dimension

The consequential of religious life cannot be separated from the concept of noble morality, the life of the world, and the life hereafter. A person's understanding of the religion he believes in will make that person transform into a person with good character. Therefore, humans will not carry out an activity or activity that is contrary to the religion they believe in. In addition, noble morals will make humans become figures who will always consider the life of the world and the hereafter.

The consequential dimension gives humans the competence to understand the religion they believe in. This will result in humans carrying out religious teachings, obedience in worship, and avoiding behaviour contrary to their religion. The following quotations represent these things.

Pada lingsa (telur kutu) rambut dadi surenana (sisir untuk mencari telur kutu dan kutu) ya Allah Allah hu Allah

Pada lingsa (telur kutu) rambut dadi surenana (sisir untuk mencari telur kutu dan kutu) ya Allah Allah hu Allah

The stanza in the quote represents the practice of keeping body parts clean, which correlates with consequential dimension values, especially values in the Islamic religion. The activity that represents this hygiene practice describes how a person looks for nits by combing his hair and throwing away the nits he finds. These activities will cause body parts, especially hair, to be kept clean. Maintaining the cleanliness and purity of the body is a form of appreciation for religious values because it is an obligation that humans must carry out. For example, in Islam, there is a teaching called *taharah. Taharah* is a form of human activity in the form of preparations that must be made before performing religious rituals. *Taharah* is done to make the body pure and clean. Cleanliness of the body is believed to be a sign of purity of heart and a form of respect for life that God has bestowed on humans.

The repetition of the phrase *Allah Allah hu Allah* can be interpreted as a form of appreciation for religious values in Islam. The thing that is represented from the dimension of this appreciation is human obedience to God. The repetition of the phrase *Allah Allah hu Allah* is an expression that reminds people and strengthens their belief in Allah's existence, majesty and power. In the babadana spell, the phrase is repeated to indicate how important the phrase is. The repetition that occurs in this phrase can be interpreted as a human effort to strengthen faith, strengthen human relationships with God, and gain peace and peace of mind. The effect that arises is a belief that the activity will produce something expected by the desired hope. In addition, the phrase *Allah Allah hu Allah*, which is repeated repeatedly, represents a belief that expresses human obedience to *Allah* as God Almighty. Muslims believe that by saying *Allah Allah hu Allah* in any problematic situation, humans will get calm and peace of mind so that Allah will bring miracles in the form of solutions or ways out of the problems they face.

Besides representing obedience, the repetition of *Allah Allah hu Allah* also represents human self-awareness. A form of self-awareness that humans are weak servants of God, so they need help and assistance from God. This phrase represents a meaning to invite people to be more aware of the existence of Allah and the power of Allah. Therefore, humans should strengthen their faith and piety, practice His teachings, and create healthy interactions with their Lord.

5. The Intellectual Dimension

The intellectual dimension is related to the understanding and knowledge humans possess about the religion they believe in. Understanding and knowledge of religion give humans the power to defend their faith in their chosen God. In addition, humans will also have a basis of belief to carry out and practice their religious doctrines and beliefs through religious ritual practices. This is represented in the following babadana spell quote.

Sung ginau ing tembe amrih tentreme ya Allah Allah hu Allah
Sung ginau ing tembe amrih mulyane ya Allah Allah hu Allah
Sung ginau ing tembe amrih tentreme ya, ing te, be amrih tentreme

This quote can be interpreted as "a person who has a calm, peaceful state of mind and heart will be able to understand and feel more deeply about the concept of heart and feeling." In this quote, there is a statement that refers to learning to get peace of mind. In this case, learning is interpreted by learning about the religion that is believed and leads to a deepening understanding and knowledge of religion.

Learning about religion is believed to be a mandatory activity. This is because studying religion will give moral, ethical, and life values guidelines that can be used as a basis for everyday behaviour. Through deepening religion, a person will also get a clear direction and purpose through the guidance of the religion he believes in. In addition, learning about religion also opens human insight to understand better and respect the diversity of cultures and beliefs that exist so that peace and harmony between humans can be created. By studying religion, humans will gain the competence to manage their own emotions well. For example, through reciting prayers that are mastered, a person will gain strong confidence to overcome the anxiety and stress he is experiencing.

The diction *amrih* in the quote also represents an intellectual dimension. *Amrih* in Indonesian means 'heart'. *Amrih* can be interpreted as something that implies that there is an understanding and appreciation of the concept of the heart or feeling in a religion or belief that is believed. In religious life, *amrih* or rasa is believed to be the centre of spirituality in humans. The heart is believed to be the source of the emergence of wisdom, understanding, and appreciation of religious teaching. In Islam, the heart is called the *qalb*, which is believed to be the source of faith. In Catholic and Protestant Christianity, the heart is believed to be the centre of spiritual life and where the holy spirit resides. Hinduism terms the heart with the word *chitta*, believed to be the centre of human consciousness. Buddhism refers to the heart as the *citta*, believed to be the centre of human experience.

In addition, the diction *mulyane* in Indonesian can be interpreted as 'blessing' or 'grace'. The intellectual dimension that emerges from this diction is an understanding of the concept of grace from God in the religion one believes in. Grace can be understood using rational thoughts and abstract concepts related to God. Grace is a concept that correlates with forgiveness, compassion, and nobility. The diction of *amrih* in the babadana spell can be interpreted as a concept about the nature of God, who is Forgiving and Merciful to His people.

CONCLUSION

The babadana spell is one of the oral traditions owned by the Wonosobo people. This spell is being recited to pray for the safety and smoothness of the Lengger Mask Dance performance. In the babadana spell, elements of religiosity represent the faith of the owner's social community. The five dimensions of religiosity are 1) the ideological dimension, manifested in people's obedience to God through faith. Glorifying Allah and emulating the behaviour of the Prophet Muhammad SAW is represented in the diction of *Allah Allah hu Allah* and *Pangeran Sung Tilaksana*; 2) the ritual dimension, which is manifested through prayers chanted in daily life, strengthening faith through the repetition of the diction of *Allah Allah hu Allah*; 3) the experiential dimension which is manifested in the form of acknowledging God's will, believing in destiny, keeping the faith and trying to get salvation; 4) the consequential dimension is manifested in the form of keeping the body clean, obedience to God, and self-awareness that God is omnipotent; and 5) the intellectual dimension is manifested in the form of learning activities and deepening religious knowledge. Through this activity, humans will get moral, ethical, and life directions from religious guidance.

The five dimensions of religiosity contained in the babadana spell have significant benefits or functions for human success in establishing relationships with God and other humans in the surrounding environment. The five dimensions of religiosity significantly increase the faith and belief in God one chooses to believe in.

References

Abas, N., & Kaur, S. (2019). Theologising the discourse of representation through 'faith' and religion in football news. *3L: Language, Linguistics, Literature*, 25(3), 150–162. https://doi.org/10.17576/3L-2019-2503-12

Adhim, F. (2009). Pengaruh Religiusitas Terhadap Prestasi Kerja Pegawai Alumni dan Bukan Alumni Pesantren (Studi Pada Kantor Depag Kabupaten Bangkalan). *Ekonomi Modrnisasi*, 5(2), 127—154.

Ahmadi, A. (1986). *Antropologi Budaya*. Pelagi.

Ahmadi, F., Erbil, P., Ahmadi, N., & Cetrez, Ö. A. (2019). Religion, Culture and Meaning-Making Coping: A Study Among Cancer Patients in Turkey. *Journal of Religion and Health*, 58(4), 1115–1124. https://doi.org/10.1007/s10943-018-0646-7

Alcorta, C. S., & Sosis, R. (2017). Ritual, emotion, and sacred symbols: The evolution of religion as an adaptive complex. *Intelligent Design and Religion as a Natural Phenomenon*, 5(4), 321–357.

Alnizar, F. (2019). Pretext for religious violence in Indonesia: An anthropolinguistic analysis of fatwas on Ahmadiyya. *Studia Islamika*, 26(3), 417–444. https://doi.org/10.36712/sdi.v26i3.8719

Amin Abdullah, M. (2014). Religion, science and culture: An integrated, interconnected paradigm of science. *Al-Jami'ah*, 52(1), 175–203. https://doi.org/10.14421/ajis.2014.521.175-203

Amir, A. (2013). *Sastra Lisan Indonesia*. ANDI.

Ancok, D. dan F. N. S. (2001). *Psikologi Islami: Solusi Islam atas Problem-problem Psikologi*. Pustaka Pelajar.

Andalas, E.F., dan S. (2017). *Sastra Lisan*. Madani.

Atmosuwito, S. (1989). *Perihal Sastra dan Religiusitas dalam Sastra*. Sinar Baru.

Bahardur, Iswahdi & Ediyono, S. (2017). Unsur Ekologi dalam Sastra Lisan Mantra Pengobatan Sakit Gigi Masyarakat Kelurahan Kuranji. Basindo Jurnal Kajian Bahasa, Sastra Indonesia, dan Pembelajarannya. *BASINDO: Jurnal Kajian Bahasa, Sastra Indonesia, Dan Pembelajarannya*, 1(2). https://doi.org/http://dx.doi.org/10.17977/um007v1i22017p024

Caesar, T., & Sanasam, R. (2018). The Oral Folk Literature of the ancient meiteis of Manipur: An Analysis of its cultural significance. *Space and Culture, India*, 6(1), 29–37. https://doi.org/10.20896/saci.v6i1.307

Damono, S. D. (2011). *Esai-Esai Java*. Gramedia Pustaka.

Danandjaja, J. (2002). *Folklor Indonesia, ilmu gosip, dongeng, dan lain-lain*. Pustaka Utama Grafiti.

Darmayenti, Besral, & Yustina, L. S. (2021). Developing efl religious characters and local wisdom-based efl textbooks for Islamic higher education. *Studies in English Language and Education,* 8(1), 157–180. https://doi.org/10.24815/siele.v8i1.18263

Dewa Putu Wijaya. (1996). *Dasar-Dasar Pragmatik.* ANDI.

Dister, N. S. (1988). *Psikologi Agama.* Kanisius.

Djamaris, E. (2002). *Pengantar sastra Rakyat Minangkabu.* Obor Indonesia.

Elika, N., & Nurhayati, N. (2022). The Communication Pattern of Wahyu Turonggo Aji Reog Dance in Merti Dusun Kemawi Sumowono as a means of Preserving Environment. *E3S Web of Conferences, 359.* https://doi.org/10.1051/e3sconf/202235903029

Frye, N. (2000). *Anatomy of Criticism: Four Essays.* Princeton University Press.

Gombozhapov, A. D., & Zhalsanova, V. G. (2022). Transformation of Mongolia's Traditional Nomadic Society: *The Modernization Trend Analyzed. Mongolian Studies,* 14(3), 566–577. https://doi.org/10.22162/2500-1523-2022-3-566-577

Gooerge, Y. (2006). *Pragmatik.* Pustaka Pelajar.

Gordanpour, Y., & Rezaei, T. (2021). Form and Perception of Nature in Elizabeth Bishop's "Questions of Travel." *Revista de Estudios Norteamericanos, 25,* 281–296. https://doi.org/10.12795/REN.2021.I25.14

Hasisah, S. N., & Chandra, O. H. (2021). The Relation of Human Being and Environment in the Cultural Event of Laesan Performance. *E3S Web of Conferences, 317.* https://doi.org/10.1051/e3sconf/202131701032

Hastuti, L., Lestari, L., Wuriani, Makmuriana, L., Pratama, K., & Gusmiah, T. (2019). Multivariate Analysis of the Effectiveness of School-Base Reproductive Health Promotion Programs for Early Adolescents. *Journal of Physics: Conference Series, 1179*(1). https://doi.org/10.1088/1742-6596/1179/1/012153

Hutomo, S. H. (1991). *Mutiara yang Terlupakan.* HISKI.

Hynson, M. (2021). A Balinese 'Call to Prayer': Sounding religious nationalism and local identity in the Puja Tri Sandhya. *Religions, 12*(8). https://doi.org/10.3390/rel12080668

Indriyani, P. D. (2022). Nilai-Nilai Religius Dalam Kesenian Tradisional Masyarakat Banjar. *Indonesian Journal of Performing Arts Education, 1*(1), 33–41.

Jahdiah, J. (2019). Kesantunan Berbahasa Tuturan Suami Istri Keluarga Banjar: Tinjauan Sosiopragmatik. Madah: *Jurnal Bahasa Dan Sastra, 10*(2), 161. https://doi.org/10.31503/madah.v10i2.914

Jahdiah, N. (2019). Penanda Kesantunan Imperatif dalam Bahasa Banjar : Tinjauan Pragmatik. *Telaga Bahasa,* 7(1), 45–54.

Jain, N., Bansal, V., Virmani, D., Gupta, V., Salas-Morera, L., & Garcia-Hernandez, L. (2021). An enhanced deep convolutional neural network for classifying Indian classical dance forms. *Applied Sciences (Switzerland),* 11(14). https://doi.org/10.3390/app11146253

Jumanto. (2017). *Pragmatik:Dunia Lingusitik Tak Selebar Daun Kelor.* Morfolingua.

Karasinski-Sroka, M., & Sharman, G. S. K. (2022). The Young Goddess Who Dances through the Ordinariness of Life—A Study on the Tantric Traditions of Kerala. *Religions, 13*(7). https://doi.org/10.3390/rel13070667

Kertanegara, M. (2011). *Kebudayaan Jawa dan Kearifan Lokal: Sebuah Pengantar Etnosains.* Pustaka Pelajar.

Kretzler, B., König, H. H., Brandt, L., Weiss, H. R., & Hajek, A. (2022). Religious Denomination, Religiosity, Religious Attendance, and Cancer Prevention. A Systematic Review. *Risk Management and Healthcare Policy, 15*, 45–58. https://doi.org/10.2147/RMHP.S341085

Krisnawati, E., Sunarni, N., Indrayani, L. M., Sofyan, A. N., & Nur, T. (2019). Identity Exhibition in Batik Motifs of Ebeg and Pataruman. *SAGE Open, 9*(2). https://doi.org/10.1177/2158244019846686

Kunkel, N. (2021). Understanding, Interpretation, Modeling: Does Digital Literary Studies Need a Digital Hemeneutics? *Lili - Zeitschrift Fur Literaturwissenschaft Und Linguistik, 51*(4), 813–819. https://doi.org/10.1007/s41244-021-00233-z

Layly, S. N., Sumarno, & Soepeno, B. (2020). The dynamics of the Lengger art in Prapah village, Panti, Jember 1900-2017. *IOP Conference Series: Earth and Environmental Science, 485*(1). https://doi.org/10.1088/1755-1315/485/1/012135

Leech, G. . (1993). *Principles of Pragmatic*. Longman.

Lüleci, Ü. M. (2022). Romantic Bandits: A Devaluation Attempt on the Literary Representations of Zeibek/Efe Tradition in Turkish Culture. *Milli Folklor, 2022*(136), 140–153. https://doi.org/10.58242/millifolklor.974111

Lyutskanov, Y. (2021). The verbal-visual architecture and symbols of sacred history in Russian emigre newspapers of Bulgaria. *Quaestio Rossica, 9*(2), 547–561. https://doi.org/10.15826/qr.2021.2.595

Mahyudin. (2018). Dimensi Religiusitas dan Pengaruhnya Terhadap Organizational Citizenship Behaviour (Studi pada Universitas Jenderal Soedirman Purwokerto). *Jurnal Ekonomi, Bisnis, Dan Akuntansi* (JEBA), 20(3).

Mangunwijaya, Y. B. (1988). *Sastra dan Religiusitas.* Kanisius.

Maryam, Siti, Sulaiman, Munawar, dan A. S. (2013). *Aksara Bima.* Alam Tara Institut.

Norenzayan, A., Shariff, A. F., Gervais, W. M., Willard, A. K., McNamara, R. A., Slingerland, E., & Henrich, J. (2014). The cultural evolution of prosocial religions. *Behavioral and Brain Sciences, 39*, 1–19. https://doi.org/10.1017/S0140525X14001356

Ocampo Alvarez, D. (2021). Literatura infantil y juvenil antiautoritaria en América Latina. Contrastes entre la literatura y la escuela al representar la realidad. *Literatura: Teoría, Historia, Crítica, 23*(2), 167–191. https://doi.org/10.15446/lthc.v23n2.94886

Pasek, Z. (2021). *CZY MIESIĘCZNICE SMOLEŃSKIE BYŁY UROCZYSTOŚCIAMI RELIGIJNYMI ? PRAWO A POLSKA KULTURA RELIGIJNA Miesięcznice Smoleńskie można uznać za uroczystości religijne 1 . Wiąza - uczestnicy byli oskarżani o zakłócanie aktu religijnego . Emocjonalny ton tej debaty* . 0–3.

Royani, Kiki Indah, Syaiful Arifin, dan N. Q. H. P. (2020). Analisis Ciri dan Fungsi Mantra Pengobatan pada Tuturan Belian Bawo di Barong Tongkok. *Jurnal GENRE. Vol.2 No. 1. Hlm. 46—51.*, 2(1), 46–51.

Sedyawati, E. (1984). *Press Tari, Tinjauan dari Berbagai Segi.* Dunia Pustaka Jaya.

Soekmono. (1982). *Mantra Jawa: Metrik dan Intepretasi.* Kanisius.

Supriyanto, S. (2023). Cowongan in Javanese Islamic mysticism: A study of Islamic philosophy in Penginyongan society. *HTS Teologiese Studies / Theological Studies, 79*(1), 1–6. https://doi.org/10.4102/hts.v79i1.8234

Suyitno. (1986). *Sastra Tata Nilai, dan Eksegesis.* PT Hanindita.

Tang, X. (2022). Creation of Drama Art Based on Deep Learning and Evolution Strategy. *Scientific Programming, 2022.* https://doi.org/10.1155/2022/6217325

Teeuw, A. (1969). *Sastra dan Religiositas*. Djambatan.

Van Huis, A. (2019). Cultural significance of Lepidoptera in sub-Saharan Africa. *Journal of Ethnobiology and Ethnomedicine, 15*(1), 1–13. https://doi.org/10.1186/s13002-019-0306-3

Yayuk Rissari. (2018). PRAGMATIC IMPERATIVE FORMS OF BANJAR. *International Journal of Malay-Nusantara Studies*, 1(2), 1–11.

Structure Analysis of Syllables and Hyphenations in Pattage Language

Herianah(heri031@brin.go.id) | **Jerniati I.**(jern001@brin.go.id) | **Abdul Asis**(abdu077@brin.go.id)
Besse Darmawati(bess001@brin.go.id) | **Abd. Rasyid**(abdr002@brin.go.id)
National Research and Innovation Agency, Archaeological, Language and Literature Research Organization

INTRODUCTION

The regional language condition nowadays, which is spread throughout Indonesia, is highly worrying. It is due to the decreasing quantity of spoken regional languages. Regional languages that should be proud of are no longer a concern for the community about their identity. It is due to increasingly sophisticated technological developments eroding these regional languages' speakers. (Erniati & Sanjoko, 2020). It is known that the language used as the first language in communication is the mother tongue or regional language. Different languages are also used by various ethnic groups spread throughout the archipelago (Erniati, 2018). Among the many languages spoken in West Sulawesi is the Pattae language. The Pattae language is one of the regional languages used by the community as the mother tongue for the Pattae people who live in Polman Regency, West Sulawesi.

The Pattae language's existence is essential in Mandarese life. Information about the existence of the Pattae language in the Polewali Mandar area was written by Str MMe. She wrote extensively on the PUS language or

Pitu Ulunna Salu (Friberg, 1987) PUS is interpreted as pitu 'seven,' ulunna 'upstream,' and salu 'river.' The native speaker of this language located in Tabulahan, Aralle, Mambi, Bambang, Rantebulahan, Matanga, and Tabang. Subsequent research by the Summer Institute of Linguistics stated that in Pitu Ulunna Salu (PUS) are Bumal, Bambam, Mehala'an-Eastern, Rantebulahan, Pattae, Matangnga, Issilita', Salu Mukanan, and Pakkau languages (Grimes. BF, 1992). Research on the vitality of the Pattae language has been conducted by (Ratnawati. Et.al., 2019) The results showed that the vitality of the Pattae language was 0.63. According to the language vitality criteria measured based on the mean value of the Patta language including (0.61-0.80). It means that Pattae is in a stable position but has the potential to experience a setback.

The vitality of the Pattae language, which is reclining, is seen as a marginal or isolated language. According to (Badan Pengembangan dan Pembinaan Bahasa, 2016) in KBBI, the meaning of marginal relates to boundaries (edges), being on the sidelines, and not being very profitable. Pattae language is considered a language that is not significantly profitable for its speakers because it does not positively impact their lives. As a result of this view, the position of this language is that language is rarely used, only among the elderly who are still active in this Pattae. It means that the Pattae language is in a marginal position today. Therefore, conservation efforts are urgently needed to prevent this language from going extinct. Efforts can be made to conserve language from its structural aspects, namely the structure of syllables and hyphenations in the Pattae language.

Language is formed by rules or rules and patterns that cannot be violated so as not to disrupt the communication that occurs. The rules and patterns formed include sound, form, and sentence. (Pt. Gita Mertasih, I Gede Nurjaya, 2015). In this case, including the rules of sectioning and decapitation of words. The hyphenation in writing must be well managed. A hyphen is the small horizontal mark that separates two or more elements of a split word or separator at the end of a line of printed output. Word separation is the separation of letters/groups of letters from words. (Yuyun Pertiwi et al., 2019). The pronunciation of syllables consists of several phonemes and is pronounced in exhalation. In a row of common consonants, also called a series of consonants, there are rows of consonants that are more than two or even more and are included in different syllables. Likewise, there is the term vowel cluster; there is a row of vowels in a syllable.

According to Alwi, syllables mean that when an utterance is uttered in exhalation accompanied by several phonemes, it will form a syllable. In addition, there are consonant cluster terms, namely sequential consonants or two consonants or more. In contrast, the term consonant series is understood as sequential consonants in one syllable. The term diphthong in the form of a vowel sequence and two or more sequential consonants found in one syllable of the same type are termed consonant clusters. Meanwhile, a series of two or more consonants belonging to different syllables contain one syllable Alwi in (Erniati & Sanjoko, 2020).

In addition, there is another opinion about syllables, parts of words that consist of several phonemes spoken in one breath. For example, the word table is written me- and -ja when spoken in one breath. If the syllables are broken down, they will become [ma] and [ja]. In this case, a vowel sound is called a diphthong sound if similar sounds exist. To mark the syllable form in a consonant that is denoted by the letter (K), while the vowel form is denoted by the letter (V) and the consonant that comes before the vowel is written with the letter (KV). At the same time, syllables consisting of two or more consonants are termed onset; if rhymes are pronounced, follow them for syllables with vowels and are formed as rhymes if any consonants accompany them. (Yuli, 2015). Syllables or syllables at the phonological level refer to rows of vowels and consonants marked with term markers, stress for both vowel and consonant sounds. In addition, the term syllable phonetically refers to a series of sounds that have a loudness rating. However, it is unrelated to the stress and pitch levels in this case. The vowel in a sound is identified by a loud sound, while the consonant sound is not. (Robins. R. H., 1992).

The rules for the formation of each language are different. It is due to differences in terms of syllables and structure. According to phonological studies, in a language, the formation of different syllables is influenced by the existence of phonotactic rules. The definition of phonotactic (Kentjono. Ed, 2003). is the existence of a series of phonemes that are sequentially in one unit and in which there are speakers according to social rules approved by the users of the language. It can affect a pattern of appreciation in the language concerned. For example, in Indonesian, no syllables end in phonemes /c/ and /j/, while in foreign languages, such as coach and jump are found in English. Meanwhile, phonemes that start with phonemes /ŋ/ have not been found in English. Meanwhile, it is the beginning of a word that starts with that phoneme, like the words [nga] and [ngilu] found in Indonesian.

Syllabification is closely related to terrific unity, while word fragmentation is related to words in a series of writings. A word hyphen has a small horizontal dash as a separator for two or three elements of a split word or a separator at the end of a line in a printed output. The name of the hyphenation terms this decapitation. Thus, this word split can make the quality of a printed text more aesthetically pleasing and neater.

The term phrenologist is an organization that has developed hyphenation algorithms in more than fifty languages since 1985. At this time, the ability to hyphenate systems is developing very rapidly. There are various algorithm technologies developed to create neat cutting positions. In this case, the principle is to recognize all lists of characters contained in a word and match them with the criteria for placement of hyphens (this depends on the language rules). In addition, specific language units have several possible combinations of characters (*Bahasa.daerah.akan.punah.H,* 2020)

In this study, the autography principle is still used in Indonesian beheading. The principle of autography is as follows:

1) In splitting a word, it is done if there are sequential vowels and splitting is done between the vowels;
2) Beheading is done on the part of the word which consists of one vowel;
3) Words in Indonesian that contain consonant clusters, such as au, oi, ae, ei, and ui, are classified as one-syllable and loan words that con-

tain these consonant clusters.

4) In a word split, it is done if there is a consonant letter and the beheading occurs before the consonant letter;
5) If a consonant consists of two consecutive letters but does not represent one phoneme, then the two consonant letters will be separated.
6) Beheading a word is done if, in the middle, there is a unitary letter (digraph) in the form of a single phoneme so that it is maintained in the state.

According to Sunendar, word splitting can use derivative words with the condition that the derived word can be done between the basic form and its constituent elements. Apart from that, the derivation of derived words whose basic form has changed, as well as the inserted words (Sunendar, 2016).

The syllable pattern varies depending on the language used. Several previous studies regarding sizing and scaping words, including "Decapitation of Basic Indonesian Words using the Syllabification Algorithm" by (Novi Yusliani, Rezi Apriliansyah, 2016), discuss the structure of Indonesian syllables and algorithms for identifying syllables in Indonesian words. The algorithm implements a set of syllable division rules based on General Indonesian Spelling Guidelines. Experiments on random samples show that the syllable division algorithm achieves 100% word accuracy. The random sample contains 300 Indonesian words. The weakness of this algorithm is that it cannot handle Indonesian words containing 'ng,' 'ny,' 'kh,' 'sy,' and 'ks,' and words containing three consecutive consonants. Another study entitled Description of the Wemale Language Syllable Patterns ((Erniati & Sanjoko, 2020) shows that the Wemale syllable pattern consists of V, KV, VKV, KVV, and ½ KV.

Furthermore, foreign research entitled Analysis of Punjabi Syllable Structure (Habib & Khan, 2021) focuses on analyzing the structure of Punjabi syllables in terms of Generative Phonology Theory. The study results show that Punjabi speakers use four main patterns for syllable construction: CV, CVC, V and V.C. Another research is entitled An analysis of the

Syllable Structure of Kikamba Nouns (Kimongo & Ong'onda, 2020). This study found that the syllable structure of Kikamba nouns has four syllable structures: CV, V, CV and CCV. This study contributes significantly to the theoretical study of phonetics and phonology by exploring how phonotactic constraints in Kikamba lead to word organization. Furthermore, research on Some Characteristics of Syllable Structure in Qassimi Arabic (Q.A.): An Optimality Theoretic Framework was done by Alhoody & Aljutaily (2020). the results show that Q.A. has seven basic syllable structures, and it groups into three categories, i.e., light syllables (CV), heavy syllables (CVV and CVC), and super heavy syllables (CVVC, CVCC, CCVVC and CVVCC). The study entitled The Syllable Structure of Tiv (U. & I.A., 2021) found several syllable structures that are permitted in Tiv, including vowels and consonants such as v, cv, ccv, cccv, cvc and Tiv have various phonotactic constraints which if studied can contribute to the development of the Tiv language.

Based on the results of these previous studies contributes to the current research. However, each differs in the focus of its research. The syllables are immensely meaningful in Pattae to know. Consistent with the above arguments, the formulation of the problem in this research is how to divide and decapitate Pattae words. This research aims to discover the linguistic system, namely the suffixation and decapitation of Pattae words. The study results can contribute to the linguistic theory itself, while the practical benefit is providing an overview of the language's sound system concerning the phonology of the Pattae language.

The research data was collected using the conversant method, followed by the conversant technique. In face-to-face conversation, researchers directly go to the field to meet respondents to obtain information (Sudaryanto., 2015). In order to obtain accurate data in a study, informants who are truly native speakers of the Pattae language who live in that location are required. The instrument in this qualitative study was the researcher himself, or inter-researcher triangulation. The researchers are not in an "empty" state but already have knowledge and theories related to the topics studied in this study (Garing et al., 2021).

This Pattae language conservation research was carried out in Polewali Mandar District, Binuang District, and Anreapi Village, Anreapi District, concentrating on three villages as observation areas Batetangnga Village, Kuajang Village and Anreapi Village. The instruments used in the research are arranged based on the needs of the research focus data. The focus of this research is the sound system of language. Therefore, the instrument used is vocabulary registered in the Swadesh vocabulary of 200 basic cultural vocabularies. Research data was collected using an instrument of 200 basic Swadesh vocabularies and 200 basic cultural vocabularies involving 40 informants and three sources. There were 40 informants divided into three observation points: Binuang District, Batetangga Village; 16 informants, Kuajang Village; 13 informants, and Anreapi Village, 11 informants. While the procedure for collecting data uses elicitation, recording, and recording techniques, the data analysis procedure is by the structural analysis model, namely the data that has been collected is transcribed phonetically according to the IPA (The International Phonetic Alphabet) version, classifies vowel-consonant sounds and describes them in a vowel-consonant plan, determines Pattae language phonemes using pairs at a minimum, both KLS and KLM sound suspicious, determine the pattern of syllables and their phoneme distribution, describe the structure of word fragments and describe the pattern of sentence fragments.

RESULTS AND DISCUSSION

1. Syllable patterns and distribution

A word can consist of one or more syllables as a phonological unit. They are, likewise, forming syllables following patterns that are arranged and structured. It applies to every language, which of course, has different characteristics and patterns of syllables. In the study of phonology, the sounds of language in an utterance can be said to be the minor units, and these sound units will form units called syllables or syllables. Phonological studies also study another element, namely suprasegmental. It concerns the pressure, tone, stop, and duration. However, it can be seen that there are differences between syllables and morphemes if morphemes are included in morphological studies and have meaning, while syllables do not (Chaer, 2012).

2. Syllable Pattern

The structure of syllables and appreciation can show two aspects: obedience and the onset of denial. Zahrani also talked about the phonological behavior of compliance and onset denial in BM. The presence of adherence onset can lead to the implementation of glottic insertion. He also said that the presence of glottic stops could be through an insertion process driven by the necessity and constraint of onset, where it is said that each syllable must have an onset, Zaharani in Hasan & Syed Jaafar (2017). In the Pattae language, syllable patterns can be identified. Likewise, in the formation of syllables, find out where a word's loudness peak or sonority is located. The peak of loudness is usually a vowel sound commonly referred to as a syllable. Usually, in one syllable, loudness is found in one or more. Thus in the Pattae language, the word saŋa 'name,' is pronounced as [saŋa]. The loud sound is between two consonants in the letter [a]. [s] and [ŋ]. Meanwhile, the word [saŋa] has a row of syllables: [sa-ŋa]. As for another word, namely the word [mapondi'] 'short,' there are three-syllable peaks, namely the vowels /a/, /o/, and /i/, which have three syllables, namely [ma-pon-di']. Likewise, his vocabulary can be seen at the height of his loudness.

The language rules known as phonetics are word formation that begins with a high-loudness sound in the word and the sequential order of vowels and consonants. Likewise, the phonetic rules govern the limitation of consonant and vowel rows in finding the peak loudness or syllable. Syllable patterns have characteristics: the sound (V) indicates a vowel, and (K) indicates a consonant sound. In the following description, there is a gloss that originates from the basic vocabulary and culture of the Pattae language.

Table 1. The Two-Syllable Pattern

Gloss	Syllables	Syllable Pattern	Meaning
ulu	*[u-lu]*	V-KV	Head
ula	*[u-la]*	V-KVK	Snake
buku	*[bu-ku]*	KV-KV	Book
matua	*[ma-tua]*	KV-KVV	Old
tallu	*[tal-lu]*	KVK-KV	three
litak	*[li-tak]*	KV-KVK	Land

Table 2. The Three-Syllable Pattern

Gloss	Syllables	Syllable Pattern	Meaning
manipi	*[ma-ni-pi]*	KV-KV-KV	Thin
Makundu	*[ma-kun-du]*	KV-KVK-KV	Blunt
digajaŋ	*[di-ga-jaŋ]*	KV-KV-KVK	Stab
manipi	*[ma-ni-pi]*	KV-KV-KV	Thin
maborruŋ	*[ma-bor-ruŋ]*	KV-KVK-KVK	Blow

Table 3. The Four-Syllable Pattern

Gloss	Syllables	Syllable Pattern	Meaning
makaruen	*[ma-ka-ru-en]*	KV-KV-KV-VK	Afternoon
limappulo	*[li-map-pu-lo]*	KV-KVK-KV-KV	Fifty
lajang-lajang	*[la-jaŋ-la-jaŋ]*	KV-KVK-KV-KVK	Kite

Table 4. The Five-Syllable Pattern

Gloss	Syllables	Syllable Pattern	Meaning
tambuk barannik	*[tam-buk ba-ran-nik]*	KVK-KVK KV-KVK-KVK	Epigastrium

Based on the vocabulary of Pattae on the above table, the Pattae syllables consist of two, three, four, and five syllables.

3. Distribution of Pattae Language Syllables

Based on the above data, the syllable patterns of the Pattae language can be seen in the syllable distribution in the following table.

Table 5. Distribution of Syllables

Pattern	Syllabing	Meaning
V	*i-ko*	You
	ɛ-lo?	Saliva
	u-la?	Snake
	a-to?	Base
	a-la	Take
VK	*in-de*	Here
	ɛk-ko?	Tail
	um-bo	Where
	an-na	Save
	on-do	Swing
KV	*ba-le*	Fish
	so-la	Friend
	li-ma	Hand
	ta-li-nga	Ear
	pa-sa-nang	Parents in law
KVK	*lus-suq*	Free
	lem-baq	Bear
	jil-loq	Show
	sem-pak	Kick
	kap-piq	Deflated

4. Word Hyphenations Structure

In this study, apart from syllables, is also discussed about decapitation. These two things are almost identical because both use the same sign. The sign is a small horizontal line as a sign of the dividing element of a word. Therefore, the separation of words with syllables needs to be clearly distinguished. These characteristics are signs of a pattern of syllables closely related to the word as a unit of sound, while word fragmentation is related to the word in writing. An example of its use can be seen in the following table.

Table 6. Syllables and Hyphenations

Gloss	Syllables	Syllable Pattern	Meaning
manipi	*deng-an-ni*	*de-ngan-ni*	Pernah
Makundu	*Bua*	*bu-a*	Buah
digajaŋ	*Dio*	*di-o*	Disitu
manipi	*ka-li*	ka-li	Gali
maborruŋ	*ba-le*	*ba-le*	Ikan

The pattern of syllables and hyphenations has its own rules or rules. Likewise, sizing and splitting words can produce a different pattern as in words (*denganni, bua, dio*), while they can also produce the same pattern as words (*kali, bale*). It also occurs; in other words.

5. Hyphenations Word Pattern

In the Pattae language, word hyphenation follows six conditions, as follows.

1) There is a word split which contains vowel letters successively in the middle, and a split is done between the two letters.

Example 1

di-ong 'below;
ja-iq 'sewing'
ta-εq 'no'
pu-aq 'father'

The above example, the hyphenations pattern are KV-VK.

2) Hyphenations of a part of a word consisting of one vowel in front or behind.

Example 2

i-ko 'you'
u-ma 'field'
a-ka 'what'
a-su 'dog'

Example 3

tu-o 'life'
ta-u 'people'
la-o 'go'
sa-ɛ 'come'

In example 2, the hyphenation pattern consists of one vowel letter in front of the V-KV pattern and the one letter hyphenation behind in Example 3, which has the KV-V pattern.

3) Syllables containing vowel groups or diphthongs ai and au are treated as one syllable.

Example 4

u-^{w}ai 'water'
a-^{w}u 'dust'

Based on example 4, the hyphenation pattern can be identified as V-V.

4) The hyphenation pattern is made if there is a consonant letter in the middle of the base word and it is located between two vowels; the hyphenation pattern is made before the consonant letter.

Example 5

te-keq 'packhorse'
ta-sik 'sea'
la-buq 'sink'
bɛ-sɛk 'ordinal'

Example 6

ba-le 'fish'
tu-nu 'burn'
ko:-na 'due to'
be-ni 'seed'

Based on example 5, it can be seen that the hyphenation pattern is KV-

KVK, and in Example 6, the hyphenation pattern shows the KV-KV.

5) If two consecutive consonants do not represent phonemes, the hyphenation is done between the two consonants.

Example 7

sur-ru	'breath'
tin-do	'sleep'
lin-do	'forehead'
par-ra	'squeeze'

Example 8

il-long	'nose'
an-ning	'eyebrows'

Based on Example 7 above, the hyphenation pattern can be identified, namely KVK-KV, and Example 8 shows the pattern VK-KVK.

6) If there is a combination of consonants (digraphs) that represent a single phoneme, then the hyphenation pattern is made while maintaining the unity of the digraph.

Example 9

pang-geq	'thigh'
bony-nyoq	'cook once about fruit'
jang-guq	'boxing'
lang-goq	'tall'

The above Example 9 shows a hyphenation pattern with a KVK-KVK pattern.

Nine hyphenation patterns were found based on the six hyphenation terms above in the Pattae language. The nine patterns are a hyphenation structure. The nine-hyphenation structures are described in the following table for more details.

Table 7. Hyphenation Structure

Hyphenation Structure	Base Words	Meaning
KV-VK	*di-ong*	Under
V-V	*u-ai*	Water
V-KV	*u-lu*	Head
KV-V	*ta-u*	Person
KV-KV	*ba-le*	Fish
KV-KVK	*pi-ran*	When
KVK-KV	*gut-tu*	Knee
VK-KVK	*il-long*	Nose
KVK-KVK	*dɛq-dɛq*	Hit

6. Basic Hyphenation

Based on the nine structures of the Pattae language, the distribution of the root hyphenation is described into three types according to the data corpus, namely a) hyphenation-two, b) hyphenation-three, and c) hyphenation-four. The three distributions of hyphenation follow the autography of the Pattae language.

6.1. Distribution of Base Word Hyphenation

Table 8. Distribution of Two-Hyphenation Base Words

Structure	Two-Hyphenation	Meaning
V-KV	*a-la* *a-re* *i-si* *a-su*	'take' 'chin' 'meat' 'dog'
KV-V	*ta-u* *sa-ɛ* *si:a* *pa-o*	'person' 'come' 'salt' 'mango'
VK-KV	*al-lo* *ap-po* *an-na* *in-de*	'afternoon' 'grandchild' 'save' 'this'
KV-KV	*bu-da* *tu-nu* *ra-ra* *bu-lo*	'lots' 'burn' 'blood' 'bamboo'

Structure	Two-Hyphenation	Meaning
VK-KVK	*an-ning* *il-long* *is-song*	'eyebrow' 'nose' 'rub'
KVK-KVK	*ros-soq* *dɛq-dɛq* *ron-noq*	'smash' 'fall'

Table 9. Distribution of Three-Hyphenation Base Words

Structure	Three-Hyphenation	Meaning
KV-KV-KV	*ma-si:-gi* *ka-de-ra* *ba-ra-ni* *ma-ta-ri* *ka-mu-ku*	'mosque' 'chair' 'brave' 'cramps' 'nail'
KV-KVK-KV	*sa-baq-na* *pa-liq-pi* *ma-kan-ja* *ka-sal-le*	'because' 'temple' 'good' 'big'
KV-KV-KVK	*bu-ri-rang* *bu-la-wang* *ka-lo-long*	'star fruit' 'gold' 'eggplant'
KAK-KVK-KVK	*kam-bun-duq* *kan-doc-coq*	'swallow' 'jitak'

Table 10. Distribution of Four-Hyphenation Base Words

Structure	Four-Hyphenation	Meaning
KV-KV-KV-VK	*ka-la-pu-ang* *ma-ka-ru-en*	'turtle' 'afternoon'
KV-KVK-KV-KVK	*ja-ngang-ja-ngang'* *la-jang-la-jang*	'dove' 'kite'
KV-KVK-KV-KV	*ka-lin-jo-ro* *pi-tup-pu-lo* *li-map-pu-lo*	'worm' 'seventy' 'fifty'

6.2. Hyphenation of Derivative Words

Hyphenation of derived words is usually done between the base form and its constituent elements unless the base form changes. Derivative word-forming elements can be in the form of prefixes, suffixes, and confixes. The following describes the distribution of the Pattae language hyphenation.

Table 10. Distribution of Four-Hyphenation Base Words

Base Words	Affixes	Derivative Words	Hyphenations
kelong	*ma-*	*makkelong* 'sing'	*ma(k)-kelong* KVK-KD
sempa?	*ma-*	*massempaq* 'kick'	*ma(s)-sempaq* KVK-KD
angka?	*ma-*	*maqangkaq* 'lift'	*ma(q)-angkaq* KVK-KD
rekeng	*ma-*	*marrekeng* 'count'	*ma(r)-rekeng* KVK-KD
burrung	*ma-*	*maqburrung* 'blow'	*ma(q)-burrung* KVK-KD
banua	*-na*	*banuanna* 'his/her home'	*ba-nu-an-na* KV-KV-VK-KV
lima	*-na*	*limanna* 'his/her hands'	*li-man-na* KV-KVK-KV
jama	*-na*	*jamanna* 'his/her work'	*ja-man-na* KV-KVK-KV
siri	*pa--ang*	*passiriang* 'shy'	*pa(s)-siri-ang* KVK-KD-VK
cai	*pa--ang*	*paccaiyang* 'grumpy'	*pa(c)-ca-i-yang* KVK-KD-VK
cabolo	*pa-*	*paccabolo* 'sulk'	*pa(c)-cabolo* KVK-KD
tasik	*pa-*	*pattasik* 'fisherman'	*pa(t)-tasik* KVK-KD
bijaga	*pa-*	*paqbijaga* 'animal handler'	*pa(q)-bijaga* KVK-KD
Bulu	*ki-*	*kibulu* 'hairy'	*ki-bulu* KV-KD
wai	*ki-*	*kiwai* 'watery'	*ki-wai* KV-KD
watang	*ki-*	*watang* 'pregnant'	*ki-watang* KV-KD

Hyphenation, which is done for derived words as in the table, is generally done by cutting off the affixes of the base word. However, there is one example where the beheading is done the same way as the base word beheading. It is done because the primary forms of the word /banua/, /lima/, and /jama/

change when affixation with the suffix /-na/. The change is the appearance of /n/ in the formation. So banua + -na becomes banuanna. If the derived word is cut off, it will become /ba-nu-an-na/ with the pattern KV-KV-VK-KV.

CONCLUSION

Regional languages are spread throughout this archipelago and are a symbol of the identity of each supporting area. The existence of these regional languages has different structures, including one of the rules for word formation. Likewise, the Pattae language in West Sulawesi has a pattern of syllables and word fragments. There is a difference between syllables and word fragments. The syllable is related to the unity of sound, while the separation of words is related to the words in a text. The instruments used in the research are arranged based on the needs of the research focus data. The focus of this research is the sound system of language. Therefore, the instrument used is vocabulary, namely a list of 200 Swadesh vocabularies and 200 basic cultural vocabulary.

Based on the results of this study, there are several conclusions as follows: 1) The pattern of Pattae language syllables are found in two, three, four and five syllables. The syllable patterns are V, VK, KV, and KVK. 2) There are two-word division structures in the Pattae language: the base word separation and the derivative word structure. Hyphenation s done for derivative words, generally by hyphenation affixes from the base word. 3). There are nine Pattae language hyphenation patterns, namely V-V, V-KV, KV-V, KV-KV, KV-KVK, KVK-KV, VK-KVK and KVK-KVK.

Preserving the Pattae language in the form of phonological studies, especially regarding the phonology of syllables and word fragments in marginalized languages such as Pattae, can be one of the efforts to preserve regional languages, especially regional languages in West Sulawesi, the extinction of local languages can be avoided. Hopefully, the results of this research can be helpful and increase public knowledge, mainly regarding the Pattae language in West Sulawesi.

References

Alhoody, M., & Aljutaily, M. (2020). Some Characteristics of Syllable Structure in Qassimi Arabic (QA): An Optimality Theoretic Framework. *International Journal of English Linguistics*. https://doi.org/10.5539/ijel.v10n4p193

Badan Pengembangan dan Pembinaan Bahasa. (2016). *KBBI Daring*. Kementerian Pendidikan Dan Kebudayaan Indonesia.

Bahasa.daerah.akan.punah.H. (2020). Liputan6. Com/Cek-Fakta-Separu.-. (n.D.).

Chaer, A. (2012). *Pengantar Lingustik Umum*. Rineka Cipta.

Erniati, E. (2018). POLA SUKU KATA BAHASA LISABATA [Lisabata Syllabe Pattern Language]. *TOTOBUANG*. https://doi.org/10.26499/ttbng.v5i2.44

Erniati, E., & Sanjoko, Y. (2020). DESKRIPSI POLA SUKU KATA BAHASA WEMALE A Description of Syllabic Patterns of Wemale Language. *Jurnal Lingko : Jurnal Kebahasaan Dan Kesastraan*. https://doi.org/10.26499/jl.v2i1.48

Friberg, T. (1987). South Sulawesi Sosiolinguistic Surveys. Work Papers in *Indonsian Language and Cultures*, 5.

Garing, J., Agus, N., Arisnawati, N., & Mappau, R. (2021). SISTEM FONOLOGI BAHASA LIMOLA/PHONOLOGY SYSTEM IN LIMOLA LANGUAGE. *Aksara*. https://doi.org/10.29255/aksara.v33i1.671.153-168

Grimes. BF. (1992). *Etnologue: Language of the Words.* SILL.

Habib, M. A., & Khan, A. A. (2021). Analysis of Punjabi Syllable Structure. *Global Social Sciences Review.* https://doi.org/10.31703/gssr.2021(vi-iv).05

Hasan, N. A., & Syed Jaafar, S. R. (2017). Struktur Suku Kata Terbitan Dialek Terengganu. Akademika. https://doi.org/10.17576/akad-2017-8701-12

Kentjono. Ed. (2003). *Dasar-Dasar Linguistik Umum*. FSUI.

Kimongo, D. M., & Ong'onda, A. N. (2020). An analysis of the Syllable Structure of Kikamba Nouns. *International Journal of English Literature and Social Sciences.* https://doi.org/10.22161/ijels.55.64

Novi Yusliani, Rezi Apriliansyah, T. W. A. (2016). Pemenggalan Kata Dasar Bahasa Indonesia menggunakan Syllabification Algorithm. *Konferensi Nasional Teknologi Informatika Dan Aplikasinya.*

Pt. Gita Mertasih, I Gede Nurjaya, S. A. P. S. (2015). ANALISIS FONOTAKTIK POLA PENYUKUAN KATA TUTURAN GURU BAHASA INDONESIA DAN SISWA KELAS XI IPB DALAM DISKUSI ANTARKELOMPOK DI SMA NEGERI 1 NUSA PENIDA. *Jurusan Pendidikan Bahasa Dan Sastra Indonesia Undiksha, 3*(1).

Ratnawati. Et.al. (2019). *Vitalitas Bahasa Pattae. Naskah Hasil Penelitian Bahasa Daerah Ham-*

pir Punah.

Robins. R. H. (1992). *Linguistik Umum Sebuah Pengantar. Kanisius.*

Sudaryanto. (2015). *Metode dan Aneka Teknik Analisis Bahasa Pengantar Penelitian Wahana Kebudayaan secara Linguistis.* Sanata Dharma University Press.

Sunendar, D. (2016). *Pedoman Umum Ejaan Bahasa Indonesia.* Badan Pengembangan dan Pembinaan Bahasa.

U., E., & I.A., F. (2021). The Syllable Structure of Tiv. *International Journal of Literature, Language and Linguistics.* https://doi.org/10.52589/ijlll-p2unambu

Yuli, G. (2015). *The Study Of Language (Diterjemahkan Oleh Astry Fajria).* Erlangga.

Yuyun Pertiwi, Y. P., Otang kurniaman, O. kurniaman, & Gustimal witri, G. witri. (2019). *ANALISIS KEMAMPUAN PEMENGGALAN KATA SISWA KELAS III SD NEGERI 37 PEKANBARU. JURNAL PAJAR (Pendidikan Dan Pengajaran).* https://doi.org/10.33578/pjr.v3i1.6322

Vocabulary Sustainability of Traditional Medicine Plants in the Indonesian Ex-timor Leste Community in Malaka Regency, East Nusa Tenggara Province

Hestiyana[1](hestiyana@brin.go.id) | **Maximus M Taek**[2](maximusmt2012@gmail.com)
Riani[3](riani017@brin.go.id) | **Dede Hidayatullah**[4](dede032@brin.go.id)
Amran Purba[5](amra001@brin.go.id)
National Research and Innovation Agency, Archaeological, Language and Literature Research Organization [1, 3, 4]
Department of Chemistry, Faculty of Mathematics and Natural Sciences, Universitas Katolik Widya Mandira, Kupang [2]

INTRODUCTION

Indonesia is bordered by many other countries, both land and sea. Indonesia's land areas are directly bordered by other countries. Provinces of West Kalimantan and East Kalimantan are bordered by Malaysia, Papua is bordered by Papua New Guinea, and East Nusa Tenggara by Timor Leste. Meanwhile, Indonesia's maritime territory is bordered by Malaysia, Papua New Guinea, Timor Leste, Singapore, India, Australia, Vietnam, Thailand, the Philippines and Palau. An understanding of the border area creates a process of adaptation in society. This adaptation is not only related to aspects of the state's territorial boundaries, but in the views of the people towards cultural patterns and local wisdom. One of them is the culture of traditional medicine as ancestral heritage.

In 1999, through a UN-supported referendum, the majority of the people of Timor Leste, known as East Timor Province at that time, voted to separate from the Republic of Indonesia. Then, through the referendum, the Indonesian National Armed Forces (TNI) together with the anti-independence militias of Timor Leste organized and encouraged more than 300,000

East Timorese to flee to West Timor (East Nusa Tenggara Province). Then, the people of East Timor occupied some areas in the East Nusa Tenggara, including Belu Regency, Malaka Regency, South Central Timor Regency (TTS), North Middle East Regency (TTU), and Kupang Regency.

Although Timor Leste is now independent and separate from Indonesia, this separation of the governments does not seem to separate Indonesia and Timor Leste's relations in terms of (1) the land and sea territories of the two countries remain connected and this situation is eternal and (2) the people in the border areas of the two countries, who are mostly made up of several ethnic groups, have a historical background, maintain and develop relatively the same culture ((Patji, 1994). This shows that the cultural relations of the two countries are inseparable, such as the existence of similarities in cultural practices in one ethnic community who happen to live in the border areas of the two countries.

The ex-Timor Leste people who live in Malaka Regency use the Timor Leste Tetun language to communicate with fellow residents in the villages that were once the basis of their refugee camps. They also try to adapt to the life of the local community, including understanding the local wisdom of the indigenous people. It can be said that the lives of the Indonesian ex-Timor Leste communities belong to the marginal group. Their economic level can be said to be apprehensive. Lewis (in Patji, 2014: 355) explains that the culture of poverty is defined as a way of life that is inherited from generation to generation through the family line, which is an adaptation or adjustment as well as a reaction of the poor to their marginal position in a class stratified society, highly individualistic, and capitalistic.

The culture of poverty is caused by internal environmental factors, occurs as a result of cultural values shared by a group of people and comes from the unique characteristics of the poor themselves. People become poor because they do not want to work hard, are wasteful, do not have a plan, lack an entrepreneurial spirit, are fatalistic, and have no desire to achieve (Suparlan, 1993: 3). Starting from this statement, the poverty experienced by some of the ex-Timor Leste people is not a culture of poverty. They don't make their poverty a way of life. They were hard workers, farming the barren land, and raising livestock.

Sayogyo (1994: 128) identifies poverty in East Nusa Tenggara as low levels of livestock or rice field ownership, inadequate housing conditions, food patterns dominated by certain types of food cassava and corn, and the inability to send children to school. All of that shows poverty economically, a problem of ownership, production, consumption, and distribution, not indicating a culture of poverty. Land ownership is also a crucial issue, in addition to the topography of the land which generally consists of rocky and barren land which is difficult to cultivate.

Since fleeing, the people of ex-Timor Leste have made a living by being agricultural labourers, but the land they work on is only limited to borrowed land. They use traditional patterns in agricultiral works. Septia (2014: 220) says that the reality of the ability of human resources, especially farmers in general, in managing the agricultural sector is still relatively underdeveloped. Most of them still use the traditional system in running their farming business.

Such a life, forcing them to adapt to the natural environment. They make use of what is available in the forest and its surroundings, such as building houses with large wooden pillars and roofs made of palm leaves. In fact, they also use plant species as traditional medicine. This is what is interesting to study in depth regarding the survival of the vocabulary of traditional medicinal plants in the Indonesian ex-Timor Leste community in Malaka Regency. Because the mingling of culture with technological advances and environmental changes has resulted in reduction of local knowledge of the younger generation about traditional medicine.

This has also resulted in the fading of local knowledge of the vocabulary of medicinal plants used by their ancestors. If this is allowed to continue, it can result in the cultural richness associated with traditional medicine being slowly lost. In addition, the influence of the economic aspect on inter-ethnic relations or local residents with the ex-Timor Leste people influences each other, such as in terms of the economic sector, scarce resources, and exploration of border areas. Of course, an in-depth study is needed regarding the lives of the ex-Timor Leste community on cultural patterns and local knowledge of medicinal ingredients and traditional medicinal practices.

Traditional medicine or what is known as ethnomedicine is at least related to two things, namely ethnicity and medicine. Ethnomedicine are beliefs and practices related to disease that are the result of indigenous cultural developments and are not derived from the conceptual framework of modern medicine (Foster, M.G & Barbara, 2015: 6). Traditional medicine is a cultural phenomenon of a society related to the disease and treatment (Hestiyana, 2022: 56).

Ethnomedicine is a local knowledge about developing medicine based on local cultural meanings with integration strategies between beliefs and treatment practices for certain diseases. Ethnomedicine is not influenced by knowledge of modern medicine, so that ethnomedicine knowledge for each ethnicity is unique Sumawardani (in Wulandari, 2018: 1). In the field of medical anthropology, ethnomedicine raises various terminologies. This field is often called traditional medicine or primitive medicine, but the term ethnomedicine feels more neutral (Foster, M.G & Barbara, 2015: 62).

Ethnomedicine is a cultural product, as a result of the thinking of ancient people to care for health and protect life. Studies on ethnomedicin are not only limited to studies on methods of treatment and medicinal ingredients containing pharmacologically active chemical substances, but also on culture and life in general. Therefore, research that uses ethnomedicine as study material is very diverse, not only carried out by researchers in the fields of science, pharmacy and medicine, but also by researchers in the fields of social sciences and culture. An ethnomedicine research is not only useful for the discovery of new drugs and new strategies that support disease control programs, it is also important as an effort to preserve ancestral cultural heritage. More than that, a comprehensive ethnomedicine research can lead us to retrace the historical traces of our ancestors, which is useful for maintaining and strengthening national identity and unity (Taek, 2020: 21).

A research related to traditional medicine that is focused on a particular isolated ethnic community or community, makes it possible to rediscover traces of local knowledge that are still preserved. In addition, it can be linked to biological diversity and cultural practices. Traditional medicine is an effort to heal in a traditional way, rooted in traditions, beliefs, and treatment practices for certain diseases.

Several studies similar to this study have been carried out by other researchers, including by Widiantana (2022) and Ilviyanti, et al. (2020). Widiantana's research entitled "Survival of Vocabulary of Traditional Medicinal Plants in the Lontar Taru Pramana in Padangaji Village, Selat District, Karangasem" found 156 vocabularies of traditional medicinal plant species written in the Lontar Taru Pramana manuscript. Only 40 of 156 plant species are known to be used by the people of Padangaji. The survival of the medicinal plant vocabulary is not closely related to the persistence of the use of traditional medicinal plants in the village. Even though its use has not survived, the vocabulary of medicinal plants is still known and survives in the life of the people in Pangaaji Village. Research of Ilviyanti, et al. (2020) entitled "The Survival of the Kulisusu Language Vocabulary in the Field of Agriculture in Wamoule Village, North Kulisusu District, North Buton Regency" found that the Kulisusu language vocabulary in the agricultural field in Wambule Village survives with an overall survival rate of 75.8%.

This research is different from some of the previous ones that have been carried out. This research focuses on the survival of the vocabulary of traditional medicinal plants in the Indonesian ex-Timor Leste community in Malaka Regency, East Nusa Tenggara Province. The results of a literature search show that this topic has relatively not been studied much. In fact, the vocabulary of medicinal plants is important because apart from their function of being able to prevent and treat disease, they are also a manifestation of the local knowledge of the community.

Traditional medicine using medicinal plants is considered cheaper and safer. This is because traditional medicine does not have many side effects for human health. Traditional medicine that uses medicinal plants is also a form of preserving the environment and maintaining the existence of plant ecosystems. From a linguistic perspective, the existence of medicinal plants greatly influences the persistence of the vocabulary of these medicinal plants which are increasingly unknown to the Indonesian ex-Timor Leste community, especially the younger generation. If this is allowed to continue, it can cause the loss of local knowledge related to the vocabulary of medicinal plants, even experiencing extinction due to modern civilization. Therefore, it is very necessary to study the resilience of medicinal plant vocabulary, especially in the ex-Timor Leste community.

Based on the explanation above, the problem of this research is how the survival profile of traditional medicinal plant vocabulary among ex-Timor Leste community in Malaka Regency. Thus, this study aims to describe the persistence of the vocabulary of traditional medicinal plants in this community in this place. In addition to preserving the vocabulary or terms of medicinal plants, this research is present as a form of effort to preserve cultural aspects related to local knowledge in traditional medicine and its practices.

Language is a cultural product that is inseparable from culture. Language can change and shift due to the development of a particular culture. Wardhaugh (2006: 109) mentions that language shifts and changes continuously over time. This is emphasized by Goddard, Cliff & Wierzbicka (2014: 3) that a change and shift in the number of lexicons of a language can occur due to additions or subtractions, even omissions due to an elimination process. This is as stated by Fatehah (2007: 339) that the development of a culture can also affect the development of the lexicon or terms related to a particular culture.

According to Poedjosoedarmo (in (Widiantana, 2022 105), there are many kinds of language change processes, and at least two kinds of changes identified, (1) internal changes that occur in the grammatical system and (2) external changes caused by the influence of other languages. Usually, internal changes occur gradually and slowly, while external changes are the opposite, that is, they occur quickly. These changes usually start from changes in vocabulary or lexicon. Fadli (2021) adds that changes externally are not only limited to the richness of the lexicon, but can spread to other language elements. Broadly speaking, external factors that drive language change include migration of speakers, attitudes of speakers, discovery and spread of technology, and the political situation in society (Jendra, 2012a: 151).

The existence of a naming language or a term used by a group by its members relatively shows the existence of a language. Sumarsono (in Al-Pansori, M.J. & Ediyono, 2017: 657) says that in language maintenance, the people collectively decide to continue using the language they are used to. Language maintenance itself is related to language contact, bilingualism and multilingualism, code mixing, code switching, language shifting, and language maintenance.

The survival of a language occurs due to language shift factors. This shift in language is influenced by economic, social, political, demographic, behavioral, and value factors in a community (Holmes, 2021). Migration is the strongest factor in language shifts because speakers of that language have to adapt to the language of a new community. This is as stated by Mardikantoro (2007: 43) that language shift involves the use of language by a speaker or a group of speakers that occurs as a result of moving from one speech community to another speech community. Sailan (2014: 196) adds that generally the symptoms of a language shift start from bilingual and multilingual people because when faced with a choice of language, they prefer to use big language rather than small language.

With regard to language maintenance, Jendra (2012b: 2) says that language maintenance is a situation where a community can maintain or continue using their language from generation to generation even though there are conditions that can influence them to switch to using another language. Furthermore, Fishman (in Syahriyani, 2017: 255) explains that language maintenance occurs not solely because of high loyalty or strong feelings towards nationalism within a group. Thus, it can be said that language maintenance is the attitude of speakers of a language to continue using the language they are used to. The essence of language resilience is the condition of how certain speech communities maintain their language in the midst of language shifts due to the mingling of collectivist cultures and social behavior. This also happens to the existence of the vocabulary of a language in certain communities, if it is rarely used it will cause it to disappear or become extinct.

Vocabulary is a wealth of words contained in a language Soedjito & Saryono (2011: 3). Keraf (2009: 80) says that vocabulary is all the words that are in someone's memory which will immediately cause a reaction when they hear reading material. Soedjito (in Muttaqien, 2014: 13) suggests that vocabulary can be interpreted as: (1) all the words contained in a language, (2) the wealth of words that a speaker/writer has, (3) words used in a field of knowledge, and (4) a list of words arranged like a dictionary accompanied by a brief and practical explanation. Vocabulary can also be said as: (1) all the words contained in the language; (2) words mastered by a person or words used by a group of people in the same environment; (3) a list of a number of words or phrases from a language arranged alphabetically along with the language and description Adwinata (in Munirah & Hardian, 2016: 82).

Vocabulary is a glossary or lexicon (Tim Editor, 2009: 315). The same opinion was also expressed by Kridalaksana (2011: 137) who stated that vocabulary is a collection of words, treasures of words, or lexicon. So, vocabulary can be referred to as a glossary, lexicon, or a collection of words in a language.

Elson and Picket (in Suktiningsih., 2016: 139) state that the lexicon is the vocabulary of a language, or vocabulary owned by a speaker of a language, or the entire number of morphemes or words of a language. Wierzbicka (1997: 4) explains that words can reflect and tell the characteristics of the speaker's way of life and way of thinking, and can also provide valuable clues in efforts to understand the speaker's culture. Foucault (2007: 101) explains that the vocabulary owned by speakers is an authoritative recording of the speaking community. All existing knowledge can be compared if circumstances are different or change at different times because everything that is known in nature is marked and coded lingually, especially in the form of lexicon units. So, vocabulary is a wealth of words or components of words that are owned by a language that is used to convey thoughts and express people's perspectives on life.

Wierzbicka (1997: 11) states that there is a close relationship between the life of a society and its lexicon or language vocabulary. In this case, research on the persistence of medicinal plant vocabulary is not only seen from a linguistic aspect, but also includes cultural practices that are still used by the Indonesian citizens of ex-Timor Leste.

This study uses a qualitative descriptive method with an ethnographic approach. Spradley (2007: 13) says that ethnography is a building of knowledge which includes research techniques, ethnographic theory, and various kinds of cultural descriptions. Ethnography means to build a systemic understanding of all human culture from the perspective of people who have studied that culture. Ethnography is based on the assumption that knowledge from all cultures is highly valued. Mahsun (2013: 233) states that descriptive research focuses on indicating meaning, description, clarification, and placement of data in their respective contexts and the data is in the form of words. Furthermore, Moleong (2011: 4) suggests that the qualitative method is a procedure that produces descriptive data in the form of written or spoken words from people and observable behavior.

A qualitative-ethnographic data collection was carried out in the field (field study) in October 2022 by means of interviews, observation, and documentation. To support the results of this qualitative research, library research was also carried out, which at the same time was a triangulation step towards field research.

This study uses two types of data, primary and secondary data. Primary data is data obtained directly from the results of interviews with informants at the research location and data from observations in the field, namely Indonesian ex-Timor Leste citizens in Malaka Regency. Meanwhile, secondary data comes from a literature study on documents and results of previous research related to the vocabulary of traditional medicinal plants and traditional medicinal culture which is used as a complement and comparison to data obtained directly in the field.

Participant observation, listening, and recording techniques were used to collect data from the informants. Observations were also carried out in the field by direct observation of research objects, such as traditional medicinal culture with the aid of a notebook. The technique of listening is done by listening to the use of language (Sudaryanto, 2015: 203). In that case, listening is done by paying attention to the use of the language spoken by the ex-Timor Leste people. Then, in the recording technique a recording device is used to facilitate data collection.

After data collection, the next step is to perform data analysis. Bogdan & Biklen (in Moleong, 2011: 248) explain that data analysis is an effort made to organize data, sort data into manageable units, synthesize data, search and find data patterns, discover what is important and what is learned of the data, and to decide what to tell others about the data. Data analysis was carried out with the following steps: (1) transcribing the data obtained through the results of notes and recordings; (2) identify the vocabulary data of medicinal plants; (3) classifying the vocabulary data of medicinal plants according to their persistence; (4) analyze and conclude as a whole.

DISCUSSION

Plants have various benefits and one of them is as a medicinal ingredient. Each region has its characteristics and uses of plants as medicines, including the ex-Timor Lest community in Malaka Regency. Based on findings in the field, there are medicinal plants that are still used as traditional medicinal ingredients. However, people are more familiar with this plant as a seasoning ingredient. Only a few use the plant as a traditional medicine. This is influenced by the development of increasingly modern medical treatment.

Based on the results of interviews with several informants in the field, there were several perceptions or views conveyed by informants regarding medicinal plants. There are informants who have heard the name of medicinal plants, but do not know the shape of the plant. Then there are those who know the types of medicinal plants, but do not know the benefits of these medicinal plants. This will have an impact on reducing local knowledge related to traditional medicine.

The knowledge of the ex-Timor Leste people in Malaka regarding the vocabulary of medicinal plants is a type of family medicinal plants (Tanaman Obat Keluarga, TOGA). TOGA are medicinal plants that are cultivated on a plot of land, either in yards or yards, gardens, or fields that are used for medicinal needs for the family. Apart from being easy to find, they are more familiar with the names of plants that have actually been encountered and cultivated in their yards. In general, the types of medicinal plants that are known are plants that are often used to treat and prevent diseases that have been or are often experienced. The following are the names of medicinal plants whose functions have been found to still survive as medicinal plants.

Table 1. Plants that are still in use

No.	Plant name in Indonesian	Scientific name
1	Asam	*Tamarindus indica L*
2	Cabai merah	*Capsicum frutescens*
3	Genoak	*Acorus calamus*
4	Jahe	*Zingiber offcinale*
5	Jambu biji	*Psidium quajawa L*
6	Jarak pagar	*Jatropha curcus L*
7	Jinten	*Coleus amboinicus L*
8	Kelor	*Moringa oleifera*
9	Kemangi	*Ocimum basilicum L*
10	Kunyit	*Curcuma domestica*
11	Mengkudu	*Morinda citrifolia L*
12	Minjangan	*Eupatorium odoratum*
13	Pinang	*Areca catechu*
14	Pisang	*Musa*
15	Pohon afrika	*Vernonia amygdalina*
16	Reo	*Lannea coromandelica*
17	Secang	*Biancaea sappan*
18	Sirih	*Piper bettle L*
19	Srikaya	*Annona squamosa*
20	Temulawak	*Curcuma zantorrhiza*

Based on the interviewes data from field study, the forms of medicinal plant vocabulary can be classified in two: (1) vocabulary in the form of basic words (monomorphemic) and (2) vocabulary in the form of phrases. From the overall results of the study (Table 1), 16 medicinal plant vocabularies are in the basic words or monomorphems, and 4 are in the phrase forms.

The lexicons or vocabularies in the form of basic words are: (1) asam, (2) genoak, (3) jahe, (4) jinten, (5) kelor, (6) kemangi, (7) kunyit, (8) mengkudu, (9) minjangan, (10) pinang, (11) pisang, (12) reo, (13) secang, (14) sirih, (15) srikaya, and (16) temulawak. Then, the vocabularies of medicinal plants in phrases are (1) cabai merah, (2) jambu biji, (3) jarak pagar, and (4) pohon Afrika. From the limited vocabularies of medicinal plants known by the ex-Timor Leste community in Malaka, it can be concluded that the use of traditional medicinal plants among this community is not sustainable. Knowledge of the vocabulary of traditional medicinal plants is more due to their function as food plants and complementary to traditional ceremonies, not as medicinal plants. Although, there are some medicinal plants that are still used as traditional medicine.

Referring to Poedjosoedarmo's opinion (in Widiantana, 2022: 105), the finding of this field indicates that the survival of the vocabulary of traditional medicinal plants among ex-Timor Leste people in Malaka is mainly influenced by external factors. This happens because there is language contact that affects the existence of the vocabulary, as well as the function of medicinal plants which are increasingly being abandoned and replaced by medical treatment. In addition, medicinal plants are more functioned as food plants by the community.

In connection with the theory of language change expressed by Jendra (2012a: 151) that, in general, external factors that drive language change include migration of speakers, attitudes of speakers, invention and spread of technology, and the political situation in society, it can be said that change almost entirely due to external factors, namely the migration of speakers, the invention and spread of technology that affected the community, as well as the political situation that occurred after the separation of East Timor from the Republic of Indonesia.

CONCLUSION

Based on the results of the analysis, the survival of the vocabulary of traditional medicinal plants in the Indonesian ex-Timor Leste community in Malaka Regency shows signs of being less resilient. People are more familiar with this plant as a seasoning or food ingredient. Only a few use the plant as a traditional medicine. This is influenced by the development of increasingly modern medical treatment.

The vocabulary of the medicinal plants known by the people of ex-Timor Leste can be classified into vocabulary in the form of basic words and in the form of phrases. There are 20 medicinal plant vocabularies found in field study, including 16 vocabularies in the category of basic words, and 4 vocabularies in the form of phrases.

The survival of the vocabulary of traditional medicinal plants in ex-Timor Leste community in Malaka is more influenced by external factors. This happens because of the language contact that affects the existence of the vocabulary and the utilization of the functions of medicinal plants. The language changes found in the ex-Timor Leste community were almost entirely due to external factors including the migration of speakers, the invention and spread of technology that affected their society, and the political situation that occurred after the separation of East Timor from the Republic of Indonesia.

References

Al-Pansori, M.J. & Ediyono, S. (2017). "Pemertahanan Bahasa Sasak di Kecamatan Utan Sumbawa (Perpektif Bodily Hexis Sosiokultural)." In *Proceeding of International Conference on Art, Language, and Culture*, pp. 656–665.

Fadli, M. R. (2021). "Memahami Desain Metode Penelitian Kualitatif". *Humanika, 21*(1), 33–54.

Fatehah, N. (2007). *Wanita Pengrajin Batik Pekalongan: Kajian Eksistensi dan Faktor Penghambatnya (Penelitian Studi Kajian Wacana).* Semarang: Lembaga Penelitian Universitas Negeri Semarang.

Foster, M.G & Barbara, G. (2015). *Antropologi Kesehatan.* Jakarta: Universitas Indonesia.

Foucault, M. (2007). Order of Thing. *Arkeologi Ilmu-Ilmu Kemanusiaan. The Order of Things, An Archaelogy of Human Sciences.* (B Priambodo & Pradana Boy, penerjemah). Yogyakarta: Pustaka Pelajar.

Goddard, Cliff & Wierzbicka, A. (2014). *Words & Meanings: Lexical Semantics Across Domains, Languages, and Cultures.* Oxford: Oxford University Press.

Hestiyana. (2022). "Bentuk Kosakata Flora Fauna dan Praktik Budaya Pengobatan Tradisional Masyarakat Banjar". *Genta Bahtera,* 8(1), 52–68.

Holmes, J. (2021). *Learning about Language: An Introduction to Sociolinguistics.* England: Edinburgh Gate.

Ilviyanti, Wa Ode Fitri dan Halfian, W. A. (2020). "Kebertahanan Kosakata Bahasa Kulisusu di Bidang Pertanian di Desa Wamoule Kecamatan Kulisusu Utara Kabupaten Buton Utara". *Cakrawala Listra*, 3(2), 190–205.

Jendra, M. I. I. (2012a). *Sociolinguistics the Study of Societies Language.* Yogyakarta: Graha Ilmu.

Jendra, M. I. I. (2012b). *Sosiologi Bahasa Bali Pengantar bagi Pemahaman Konsep-Konsep dan Teori-Teori Sosiolinguistik untuk Kajian Pemakaian dan Pendidikan Bahasa Bali.* Vidia.

Keraf, G. (2009). *Tata Bahasa Indonesia.* Ende: Nusa Indah.

Kridalaksana, H. (2011). *Kamus Linguistik.* Jakarta: Gramedia Pustaka Utama.

Mahsun, M. S. (2013). *Metode Penelitian Bahasa: Tahapan Strategi, Metode, dan Tekniknya.* Jakarta: RajaGrafindo Persada.

Mardikantoro, H. B. (2007). "Pergeseran Bahasa Jawa dalam Ranah Keluarga pada Masyarakat Multibahasa di Wilayah Kabupaten Brebes". *Humaniora, 19*(1), 43–51.

Moleong, L. J. (2011). Metode Penelitian Kualitatif. Bandung: Remaja Rosdakarya.

Munirah & Hardian.(2016). "Pengaruh Kemampuan Kosakata dan Struktur Kalimat terhadap Kemampuan Menulis Paragraf Deskripsi Siswa SMA". J*urnal Pendidikan Bahasa Dan*

Sastra, 16(1), 78–87.

Muttaqien, R. N. (2014). *"Kemampuan Pemahaman Kosakata Pada Siswa Tunarungu Kelas D2 di SLB Wiyata Dharma 1 Tempel". Skripsi*. FIP. Universitas Negeri Yogyakarta.

Patji, A. R. (1994). "Pengembangan Wilayah Nusa Tenggara Timur: Perpektif Kebudayaan". In Wuryandari (Ed.), *Pengembangan Wilayah Nusa Tenggara Timur dari Perspektif Sosial: Permasalahan dan Kebijakan* (pp. 323–366). Jakarta: LIPI Press.

Sailan, Z. (2014). "Pemertahanan Bahasa Muna di Kabupaten Muna Sulawesi Tenggara". *Litera, 13*(1), 191–200.

Sayogyo. (1994). *Kemiskinan dan Pembangunan di Provinsi Nusa Tenggara Timur.* Jakarta: Yayasan Obor Indonesia.

Septia, Y. (2014). "Pengembangan Wilayah Nusa Tenggara Timur dari Perspektif Ekonomi". In Wuryandari (Ed.), *Pengembangan Wilayah Nusa Tenggara Timur dari Perspektif Sosial: Permasalahan dan Kebijakan* (pp. 213–276). Jakarta: LIPI Press.

Soedjito & Saryono, D. (2011). *Kosakata Bahasa Indonesia.* Malang: Aditya Media Publishing.

Spradley, J. P. (2007). *Metode Etnografi.* Yogyakarta: Tiara Kencana.

Sudaryanto. (2015). *Metode dan Aneka Teknik Analisis Bahasa Pengantar Penelitian Wahana Kebudayaan secara Linguistis.* Yogyakarta: Sanata Dharma University Press.

Suktiningsih. (2016). "Leksikon Fauna Masyarakat Sunda: Kajian Ekolinguistik". *Retorika, 2*(1), 142–160.

Syahriyani, A. (2017). "Pemertahanan Bahasa Jawa Dialek Banten pada Guyup Tutur di Kelurahan Sumur Pecung Serang". *Buletin Al-Turas*, 23(2), 251–266.

Taek, M. M. (2020). Etnomedisin Pengobatan Tradisional Penyakit Malaria Masyarakat Tetun di Timor Barat. Yogyakarta: Pohon Cahaya.

Tim Editor. (2009). *Tesaurus Alfabetis Bahasa Indonesia.* Jakarta: Pusat Bahasa.

Wardhaugh, R. (2006). *An Introduction to Sociolinguistics 5th ed.* Oxford: Blackwell.

Widiantana, I. K. (2022). "Kebertahanan Kosakata Tanaman Obat Tradisional dalam Lontar Taru Pramana di Desa Padangaji, Kecamatan Selat, Karangasem". *Dharma Sastra: Jurnal Penelitian Bahasa dan Sastra Daerah, 2*(2), 103–111.

Wierzbicka, A. (1997). *Understanding Cultures Through Their Key Words: English, Russian, Polish, German, and Japanese.* New York: Oxford University Press.

Wulandari, A. (2018). "Eksplorasi Pengetahuan Lokal Etnomedisin dan Tumbuhan Obat di Desa Pagar Dalam, Pelita Jaya, Tanjung Raya dan Ulok Manek Kecamatan Pesisir Selatan Kabupaten Pesisir Barat". *Thesis.* Fakultas Tarbiyah dan Keguruan Universitas Islam Negeri Raden Intan Lampung.

Propositional Meaning and Non-Propositional Meaning in Minangkabau Song Lyrics

Ermitati(ermi002@brin.go.id) | **Tri Saptarini**(tris017@brin.go.id) | **Sri Winarti**(sriw015@brin.go.id)
Menuk Hardaniwati(menu001@brin.go.id) | **Yulino Indra**(yuli051@brin.go.id)
National Research and Innovation Agency, Archaeological, Language and Literature Research Organization

INTRODUCTION

The fact shows that Indonesia is ethnically diverse, with most people identifying with their ethnic identity. This causes the meaning of ethnicity from a single aspect, for example, Minangkabau ethnic, is interpreted as a designation or identity of ethnic groups living in West Sumatra. As stated by (Humaedi, 2020, p. 3--4) that when we mention one ethnicity, such as Dayak ethnic, it seems to be understood only as one definition, namely one ethnic group. All domains related to that identity are also revealed in it. Likewise, Minangkabau ethnic that inhabits the western region of Sumatra is not merely interpreted by the definition of one ethnic group in Indonesia. In the identity of Minangkabau ethnic, there is also a linguistic identity, namely Minangkabau language, Minangkabau ethos, and there is a unique kinship system, namely matrilineal, even there is also a philosophy of life that is agreed upon, *adat bersandi syarak, syarak bersandi kitabullah* (all actions should always follow customary and religious rules and not conflict with one another). Minangkabau customary philosophy is interpreted as a philosophy of life held by the people as a guide to life. The matrilineal

Minangkabau community has a life philosophy known as *adat bersandi syarak, syarak bersandi kitabullah*. It is accustomed to using proverbs and adages in their lives to apply the philosophy of life in real life (Zahari, 2021, p. 5).

Because it has a matrilineal system and inherits certain elements differently than other ethnic groups in Indonesia, Minangkabau is frequently considered a distinct and unique ethnic group. This system was formerly well-governed by Minangkabau people in accordance with their customary and cultural norms. All these things must be subject to the agreed philosophy of life, namely, "*adat basandi syarak, syarak basandi kitabullah, syarak mangato adat mamakai, alam takambang jadi guru*" (Zahari, 2021, p.13).

Minangkabau language documents the culture of Minangkabau people. Minangkabau song lyrics, for instance, as part of Minangkabau language's linguistic data, encapsulate the diverse cultures of Minangkabau people. According to (Ermitati, 2014), language and culture are inseparable parts of human life because language is utilized by its speakers to convey their culture (Minangkabau people).

As a product of Minangkabau language, Minangkabau song lyrics encode numerous cultural messages and details about Minangkabau people. The information conveyed in the lyrics of Minangkabau songs may not be perfectly understood by the listeners due to the extensive use of pantuns and parables in the lyrics. These expressions have non-propositional meanings that the music enthusiasts must comprehend. To decipher the non-propositional meaning in the lyrics of Minangkabau song, music enthusiasts must comprehend the cultural context that influences the composition of music. (Meigalia, 2019, p. 9) notes that, in accordance with the proverb "*alam takambang jadi guru*" (Everything in this universe is a gift from God that can be used as a guide in the order of social life) and the lyrics of Minangkabau songs are constantly inspired by it.

Minangkabau songs are interesting to study due to their distinctive lyrics. The distinctiveness of Minangkabau song lyrics rests in their rhythmic structure and terminology. The lyrics of Minangkabau songs are presented in the form of Minangkabau pantun with several terms in the form of idioms and parables. According to (Zahari, 2021), comprehending Minangkabau pantun is one approach to comprehending the personality, work ethic, and lifestyle philosophy of the Minangkabau people. As (Sapir, 1949: 162) observed, a society's actual reality is constructed according to its language patterns. This suggests a reciprocal relationship exists between an ethnic group's way of speech, thinking, and behaviour. According to (Ristianti, 2018), psychologists believe that the culture in which humans live and develop significantly impacts human behaviour and mindset. Hence, the capacity to comprehend pantun and produce pantun is directly tied to the capacity to comprehend and employ language, such as employing *kieh* (figurative) language in Minangkabau society. This is conceivable due to the frequent occurrence of figurative language in the text of Minangkabau pantun and its prefatory statement. Also, the ability to comprehend pantun and produce it is significantly tied to the capacity to comprehend societal difficulties. Because the Minangkabau way of thinking is generally metaphorical (Anwar, 1992, p. 25, in (Gani, 2012) and tends not to be plain, especially for very sensitive things, and affects self-esteem, the capacity to comprehend both is essential.

This research reveals the non-propositional meaning encoded in Minangkabau pantun in Minangkabau song lyrics. The data of this research is limited to song lyrics in Minang Pop Album sung by Elly Kasim and Tiar Ramon. This research discusses two problems related to the non-propositional meaning encoded in Minangkabau pantun in the lyrics of Minangkabau songs produced by Tanama Record. The first problem is, what are the non-propositional meanings encoded in Minangkabau pantun contained in the lyrics of Minangkabau songs in the Minang Pop Album? The second problem is, what word choices are used by the lyricist to encode the non-propositional meaning in Minangkabau *pantun* in the song lyrics?

This study uses a qualitative research method to reveal the meaning encoded in Minang pantun in the lyrics of Minangkabau songs in the Minang Pop Album, sung by Elly Kasim and Tiar Ramon. This method is elaborated in techniques that are in accordance with the nature of this research. This research data was collected by using the listening method with note-taking techniques. The listening method was used to obtain data by listening to spoken language, in this case, in the form of Minangkabau song lyrics sung by Elly Kasim and Tiar Ramon. Furthermore, the note-taking technique is used to transcribe the lyrics of Minangkabau songs in the Pop Minang Album in written data. In addition, the recording technique was used to note additional information needed by the researcher in identifying the data, especially to check the validity of the data obtained. The note-taking technique was also used to record this researcher's data, which was done if the required data was not found in the primary source.

The data was analyzed using a descriptive method with its translation techniques: defining, analogizing, and contextualizing. The definitional technique is used to define each lexeme that encodes non-propositional meaning. Then, this researcher determines the intrinsic characteristics of a lexeme. The intrinsic feature of the lexeme can be a revealer of the non-propositional meaning encoded in it. The analogy technique is used to analogize the intrinsic features of a lexeme with a person's behaviour, state, action, or nature. This technique determines the non-propositional meaning encoded in the propositions in the song lyrics. Meanwhile, the contextualization technique is used to place an expression in the context of its use.

The non-propositional meaning in Minangkabau pantun on Minangkabau song lyrics is analyzed with the theory of sentence meaning proposed by (Lyons, 1996, p. 201) states that the definition of sentence meaning that only depends on the content of the proposition and the truth condition has a weakness because the various types of meaning encoded in the lexical elements and grammatical structure of a sentence cannot be explained only based on the content of the proposition. Therefore, (Lyons, 1996, p. 44--45) states that sentences and speech meanings have propositional and non-propositional meanings. Propositional meaning is the meaning encoded in natural language expressions, which can be true or untrue depending on the truth or untruth of a proposition. In contrast, non-propositional meaning relates to subjective meaning and social meaning. Lyons formulates subjective meaning as a type of sentence meaning characterized by expressing the speaker's attitude or illocutionary power. In contrast, social meaning is related to the possibility of a language speaker expressing his feelings or attitudes with different forms encoded in the language system.

Language as a human communication tool encodes various meanings related to the speakers' sociocultural society. According to the cognitive approach, human communication relies on two components in cognition: the meaning construction system and the meaning expression system. According to this cognitive approach, every linguistic form expresses the construction of meaning. This cognitive view raises problems because the grammar of a language cannot describe the various types of situations we face in communication (Fauconnier, 1997). The various language combinations speakers can create will result in many meaningful situations. Fauconnier and Turner in (Ghani, 2021) state that the speaker's general view of the conceptual structure is encoded by the linguistic structure, which the interlocutor in the conceptual structure then re-encodes. Furthermore, Fauconnier and Turner in (Ghani, 2021) mention that conceptual systems are broad, numerous, and open, while linguistic systems are narrow and limited. How could the linguistic system express the product of the conceptual system? In line with this statement, (Evans, 2006, p. 492) states that the vocabulary of a language tends to be in a constant state, while the meaning value of words and expressions continues to change based on their use. Furthermore, (Evans, 2006, hal. 496) mentions that, in essence, meaning does not belong to language, but the meaning is a function of language use. Thus, the characteristics of the meaning construction process are not related to the unloading of information stores, as assumed in the traditional view. However, meaning construction is a constructive process that involves lexical units in differential access to conceptual knowledge. Such conceptual knowledge only presents the possible meanings of words realized in language use. The process of revealing the meaning of words is part of our knowledge of the world that is enabled by using words in context (Evans, 2006, p. 493).

(Kecskes, 2008) refutes Evans' statement, claiming that Evans ignores words that reveal essential features of their use in previous contexts. So, when Evan says "context," he only means the actual context. According to Kecskes (Kecskes, 2008, p. 388) , the dynamic behaviour of human speech implies a reciprocal process between language (message) and the actual situation's context. Messages are encoded in previous contexts and used to create meaning in the current situation. As a result, messages are never context-free. Because every lexical unit is a repository of past context, no meaning is context-free. It is registered implicitly in the repeated past context references.

To analyze the data of this paper, in addition to using the theory of sentence meaning (Lyons, 1996), it also uses the theory of the dynamic meaning model. The dynamic meaning model combines the external contextual approach and the internal contextual approach to context. This approach considers the communication process as a structured process. It can be related to Sciabarra's (2002:381) in (Kecskes, 2008) understanding of the dialectic of context. According to Sciabarra, dialectics is the art of maintaining context because we must understand the context of each object through abstraction and integration techniques. By understanding objects from different perspectives, we will have a more comprehensive understanding of an object.

Contextual rules in meaning construction are the focus of dynamic meaning theory. According to (Kecskes, 2008, p. 385), the value of a word's meaning encodes the context of prior experience, acting as a rule in the situational context in which meaning construction rules are used—dialectical and relational encoding and updating of knowledge of the world. The historical context is used to view the current situational context. This method holds that meaning emerges as a natural community culture when combining past and present experiences. Current experience is formally revealed in the linguistic interactional context that is created spontaneously and is the result of the influence of reciprocal interaction between the speaker's context description and the interlocutor's interpretation of the actual situational context. Experience is revealed in the meaning value of lexical items, which causes the use of speech by speech participants (Kecskes & Kecskes, 2014, p. 2005).

DISCUSSION AND RESULTS

The lyrics of Minangkabau songs in Pop Minang Albums are delivered as pantun, which is one form of indirect speech. Besides using pantun, the lyrics of Minangkabau songs in this Minang Pop Album also use indirect speech in the form of figurative expressions and parables. Therefore, people who like and enjoy Minangkabau songs need help understanding the meaning of the lyrics.

The use of indirect speech is one of the strategies of Minangkabau people to keep the language they use more subtle. Leech (1983) states that pragmatics can be classified into two components: pragmalinguistic and sociopragmatic. Pragmalinguistics refers to the resources for conveying communicative acts and relational or interpersonal meanings. These resources include pragmatic strategies, such as continuity and non-continuity. Both forms of language are related to politeness and continuity, and continuity can intensify or soften communicative acts. So, language speakers use indirect forms to maintain politeness in speech acts. The statement is also supported by (Wulansari, 2016) that expressing things indirectly so that the meaning to be conveyed remains polite and polite is part of the use of pantun in everyday life as applied by the Bangka Malay community for generations.

The use of language in the form of indirect speech encodes various non-propositional meanings. Concerning that, this paper discusses the non-propositional meaning encoded in Minangkabau pantun in the lyrics of Minangkabau songs in Minang Pop Albums. Non-propositional meaning is related to subjective meaning and social meaning. Subjective meaning is formulated by Lyons as a type of sentence meaning characterized by the expression of the speaker's attitude or illocutionary power, while social meaning is a type of meaning related to the possibility for a speaker to express his feelings or attitudes with different forms encoded in the language system.

1. Non-Propositional Meaning in *Ayam Den Lapeh* Lyric

Ayam Den Lapeh is one of the old songs. This song is still often sung and rearranged by Minang musicians. The lyrics were created by Abdul Hamid and first sung by a Minang singer named Nurseha or better known as Elly Kasim. The lyrics of this song are made in the form of pantun consisting of four stanzas. Each stanza is composed of four lines. Between the stanzas, there are additional lines, namely ai ... ai ... *ayam den lapeh.* The lyrics of this song have an a-b-a-b rhyme, as in (1a) below.

(1a)	*Luruihlah jalan payakumbuah*	'Straight road to Payakumbuh'
	Babelok jalan ka andaleh	'The road turns to Andaleh'
	Dima hati indak karusuah	'How this heart will not be restless'
	Ayam Den Lapeh,	'My hen has escaped'
	ai ai ... Ayam Den Lapeh	'Ai... ai... My hen has escaped'

In the first stanza of the song *Ayam Den Lapeh,* the lyrics describe Minangkabau landscape in Payakumbuh. It is expressed by the lyricist based on his past experiences and world knowledge. The proposition *Luruihlah jalan payakumbuah* and the proposition *Babelok jalan ka Andaleh* contain propositional meaning according to what is stated in the two propositions. Both propositions are true because they express his world knowledge about the landscape of Payakumbuh. In the content of the pantun in the fourth line, the lyricist uses the word *ayam* (hen) as a simile. The word *ayam* in the proposition *Ayam Den Lapeh* is understood based on the context of the lyrics. Therefore, the proposition *Ayam Den Lapeh* encodes a non-propositional meaning due to using the lexeme *ayam* in figurative meaning.

Ayam lexeme has the intrinsic characteristics of a domesticated animal and is commonly kept by humans. The intrinsic feature of tame means 'conquerable or manageable', and the intrinsic feature of keepable has the concept of 'guarding and protecting.' The intrinsic characteristics of ayam can be analogized to the intrinsic characteristics of a lover. So, the meaning encoded in the content of pantun *Dima ati indak karusuah* and *Ayam* den *lapeh* is 'how the heart is not restless, the loved one is taken away.' In the content proposition of the *pantun*, the lyricist uses an expression in the form of an analogy, namely *ayam den lapeh.* This proposition is a proposition that contains non-propositional meaning, and it is encoded in the word ayam.

This word in the proposition is used as a simile that refers to 'a lover or life partner'. As stated by (Astuti, 2020, p. 45--46) that the use of the word *ayam* in the pantun is used as a metaphorical icon, which is a relationship based on similarity even though only partially, such as roses and girls who are considered to have similarities in terms of beauty and freshness.

In the second stanza of *ayam den lapeh*, the *sampiran* (prefatory statement) describes Minang landscape in Bukittinggi—the lyrics of the second stanza rhyme a-b-a-b, as in (1b) below.

(1b)	*Mendaki jalan Pandaisikek*	'The road climbs to Pandaisikek'
	Manurun jalan ka palupuah	'The road goes down to Palupuah'
	Dima hati indak kamaupek	'How the heart does not hurt'
	Awak takicuah,	'I have been fooled'
	ai ai ... Ayam den lapeh	'Ai ... ai ... my hen is ecaped'

The proposition *Mendaki jalan Pandaisikek* and the proposition *Manurun jalan ka Palupuah* are true propositions because both contain propositional meanings about Minang nature. Pandaisikek is one of the villages in Sepuluh Koto District, Tanah Datar Regency, West Sumatra Province. It is located near Batusangkar, the capital of Tanah Datar Regency. Pandaisikek Village is located in the valley of Mount Singgalang. To get there, we have to climb the foot of Mount Singgalang, then walk down the valley with views of rice fields and vegetable fields. Meanwhile, Palupuah is one of the districts in Agam Regency, West Sumatra Province. We will take a downhill road from Bukittinggi to Palupuh.

The contents of the *pantun Di ma hati indak kamaupek* and *Awak takicuah* are also true propositions because they do not encode non-propositional meaning. *Di ma hati indak kamaupek* and *Awak takicuah* tell about past experiences of 'the sadness due to infidelity.'

The song Ayam Den Lapeh is not only about the sadness of losing a lover or partner, but it contains advice for caring for loved ones. If infidelity occurs, a person may lose their partner and their mistress. This is illustrated in the following rhyme (1c).

(1c)	*Sikucapang sikucapeh*	'One flies, and one escapes'
	Saikua tabang saikua lapeh	'One flies, and one escapes'
	Tabanglah juo nan karimbo	'Flying into the jungle'
	Oilah malang juo	'Oh, what a misfortune this fate is'

The advice in the pantun *Sikucapang sikucapeh* and *Saikua tabang saikua lapeh* is that having an affair is unacceptable. Infidelity is wrong because it hurts the cheated-upon party, and she/he will also leave.

The proposition *Tabanglah juo nan karimbo* encodes a non-propositional meaning because the word *rimbo* 'jungle' in the proposition is used as a simile. The word *rimbo* 'jungle' has the intrinsic feature of wilderness. Based on world knowledge, the wilderness is a vast forest inhabited by various wild animals. Therefore, if someone goes into the wilderness, it is almost impossible for that person to return because they are preyed upon by wild animals. Thus, the proposition *Tabanglah juo nan karimbo* encodes the non-propositional meaning of 'someone who has gone and will never return.'

The fourth lyric *Ayam Den Lapeh* depicts the feeling of a woman who always daydreams of thinking her lover. It can be shown in the following pantun (1d)

(1d)	*Pagaruyuang batusangka*	'Pagaruyung Batusangkar'
	Tampek bajalan urang baso	'The areas where Baso people pass by'
	Duduak tamanuang tiok sabanta	'Often sits pensively'
	Oi takana juo	'Oi... always remembered'
	ai ai ... Ayam den lapeh	'Ai ... ai ... my hen has escaped'

Ayam Den Lapeh's song lyrics in the fourth stanza are pantun that rhyme a-b-a-b. It uses the proposition *Pagaruyuang batusangka* and the proposition *Tampek bajalan urang baso*. Both propositions are true because they reveal the lyricist's past experiences about the state of the region in West Sumatra. This is in accordance with the lyricist's world knowledge and experiences. The cover of the pantun is used as an introduction to the content of the pantun, namely the proposition *Duduak tamanuang tiok sabanta* and the proposition *Oi takana juo.* The content of pantun tells the story of a person's sadness at losing his lover. The deep sadness causes him always to sit pensively thinking about his beloved.

Ayam Den Lapeh's lyrics are written in the form of pantun, and each *sampiran* (prefatory statement) contains descriptions of natural forms and life stories. This is based on Minangkabau people's traditional ideology. There is always something to be learned from the natural surroundings. Nature has a significant philosophical importance for Minangkabau people, for whom it is not only a place to be born, live, and grow. Hence, every Minangkabau *sampiran* (prefatory statement) expresses the form, character, and natural life (Navis, 1984, p. 59).

2. Non-proporsitional Meaning in the Lyric of *Usah Diratoki Song*

The parable using *ayam* also can be found in the song of *Usah Diratoki* created by Yusah Rahman, and Sayang *Tak Sudah* by Anas Yusuf. Tiar Ramon was the first singer who sang and popularized both songs. The song's lyrics contain some animals' names like *alang* (eagle), *cikok*, and *ayam putiah*. The lyrics used not only the animals but also the name of plants, such as *daun sirih* and *pinang jo tampuaknyo*. The use of parable diction in the lyrics makes the non-propositional meaning uneasy to understand. Take a look at the lyrics of *Usah Diratoki* (2a) below.

(2a)	*Anak urang si Kubang Putiah*	'There was a boy named Kubang Putih'
	Pai ka balai, hari sanjo	'Going to the market in the dusk'
	Mamakai baju guntiang cino	'Wearing a Chinese-shape shirt'
	Ulah rayu si daun siriah	'Because of the persuasion of the betel leaf'
	Bacarai pinang jo tampuaknyo	'Separating the reins of an areca nut'
	Apo katenggang si carano, si carano	'There is nothing cerana (betel box) can do'

The first stanza (2a) of the song *Usah Diratoki* is a *pantun* consisting of six lines and rhymes a-b-c-a-b-c. This *pantun* is beautiful because it uses words in the form of similes. The cover consists of three lines that contain propositional meaning as stated in the proposition. The propositions contained in the cover are the lyricist's world knowledge and past experiences. Meanwhile, the propositions contained in the content of the *pantun* contain non-propositional meaning because they use similes, such as *daun siriah* (betel leaf), *pinang jo tampuaknya* (areca nut with its rind), and *carano* (betel box). The phrase *daun siriah* in the proposition *Ulah rayu si daun siriah* refers to 'a person (usually called a third person) having a romantic relationship with someone else's partner'. The expression *Bacarai pinang jo tampuaknyo* encodes the non-propositional meaning of 'the breakup of a romantic relationship between lovers or husband and wife'. The meaning of *carano* in the proposition *apo katenggang si carano* refers to 'the person whose feelings are hurt'. So, pantun (2a) tells the story of a third person who ruins the romantic relationship between a married couple or lovers resulting in someone being hurt. Therefore, we should not do things that hurt other people's feelings.

The second stanza of the song *Usah diratoki* is a pantun consisting of four lines and rhymes a-b-a-b. *Sampiran pantun* (prefatory statement) (2b), as an introduction to the contents of the pantun, tells the story of the lyricist's experience regarding the activities of the Kapau people in the morning and the clothes that they usually wear, namely *kodek*. *Kodek* is a batik sarong usually worn by Minangkabau women in their daily activities. Kapau is one of the sub-districts in Tilatang Kamang District, Agam Regency, West Sumatra Province. The proposition *sarupo codek jo bajunyo in pantun* (2a) encodes the culture of Minangkabau women's dress in the past. This is revealed in the following poem (2b).

(2b)	*Urang Kapau pai ka lading*	'Kapau people go to the fields'
	Sarupo kodek jo bajunyo	'Wearing the same sarongs and dresses'
	Iyo buruak lakunyo alang	'How horrible the behaviour of the eagle is'
	Ayam tapauik disembanyo	'It snatched the tied hens'

The content of *pantun* (2b) reveals the behaviour of a third person who likes to snatch someone's husband or wife. The behaviour of the third person is analogous to the behaviour of an eagle, which usually snatches its prey and does not care whether the prey is a pet or not. This is encoded in the proposition *Iyo buruak lakunyo alang* and the proposition *Ayam tapauik disembanyo*. The lyricist analogizes the *alang* 'eagle' behaviour that snatches its prey with the behaviour of someone who likes to snatch someone's husband or wife. Meanwhile, the lyricist also uses the idiom *ayam tapauik* to refer to 'someone already married or engaged.' The non-propositional meaning encoded in the proposition *Ayam tapauik disembanyo* is 'someone's wife/husband or fiancé is snatched by someone else.'

The cover of *pantun* (2c) contains the proposition *Urang Sariak babaju ganiah* and the proposition *Pai manggaleh ka Padang Lua*. Sariak or Sariak River is a sub-district in Padang Pariaman Regency, West Sumatra Province. Meanwhile, *Baju ganiah* is an old Minangkabau men's clothing made of cotton like a Chinese shirt but has no collar and no pockets. Both propositions contain propositional meaning and are true propositions because they express the lyricist's experience and world knowledge. In addition, the proposition *Urang Sariak babaju ganiah* encodes the culture of how Minangkabau men dressed in the past. The proposition *Pai manggaleh ka Padang Lua* encodes a culture related to the profession of Minangkabau men who are good at trading in the market.

(2c)	*Urang Sariak babaju ganiah*	'Sariak people wear cotton clothes.'
	Pai manggaleh ka Padang Lua	'Going trading to Padang Luar'
	Iyo sarik ba ayam putiah	'It's hard to have a white-feathered hen.
	Kok indak cikok alang manyemba	'If it's not an eagle, the hawk will grab it'

In the third stanza, the lyrics of the song *Usah Diratoki*, the lyricist uses the idiom *ayam putih* (white-feathered hen) and the names of the animal *cikok* and *elang* (eagle). The use of *ayam putih* idiom in the contents of the pantun (2c), namely the proposition *Iyo sarik ba ayam putih* encodes a non-propositional meaning of 'a young girl who is very beautiful, very good, very smart or a girl who is respected'. The word *cikok*, in Minangkabau language, is a type of eagle that preys on mammals with small bodies, such as mice, fish, chicks, and several other small animals because of their smaller body shape than eagles. The intrinsic feature of the *cikok*, which is that it is smaller than an eagle, is analogous to 'an ordinary man who has the behaviour of snatches other people's girlfriends/wives'. Eagle in Indonesia Dictionary (KBBI) is defined as a bird of prey with sharp eyesight, a hooked beak, and a firm grip, which catches its prey by grabbing. The intrinsic characteristics of the eagle are analogous to the behaviour of a rich man who likes to snatch other people's lovers/wives.

In this proposition, the lyricist deliberately contrasts the *cikok* and *alang* (eagle), focusing on their ability to snatch larger prey. The intrinsic feature is used to analogize one's ability which is associated with one's power or wealth. Using the words *cikok* and eagle in the proposition *Kok indak cikok alang manyemba* encodes non-propositional meaning. The word *cikok* in the proposition encodes the non-propositional meaning of 'an ordinary man who likes to take other people's lovers/wives.' In contrast, the word elang encodes the non-propositional meaning of 'a rich man or a man with power who likes to take other people's lovers/wives'.

The behaviour of a third person who likes to snatch someone's husband/ wife or fiancé results in someone else being hurt. This is revealed in the fourth stanza of the song *Usah Diratoki* (2d). The song lyrics in the fourth stanza are written in the form of a *pantun*, which consists of six lines rhyming a-b-c-a-b-c. *Pantun* (2d) tells the story of the sadness experienced by someone because his lover had an affair with a third person.

(2d)	*Jikok mandi denai di hulu*	'If I bathe upstream'
	Aia nan usah adiak sauak,	'You do not need to draw water'
	Disauak usah dikaruahi, dikaruahi	'If you draw it, do not make it murky, do not make it murky'
	Jikok mati denai dahulu	If I die first
	Mati nan usah adiak janguak,	'If I die, you do not have to come'
	Dijanguak usah diratoki, diratoki	'No need to come, no need to mourn'

The pantun (2d) reveals a person's suffering because of being left by a lover who is having an affair with a third person. In addition, the proposition contained in the *sampiran* (prefatory statement) (2d) also encodes the culture of Minangkabau people in the past regarding the culture of bathing in the river. This is revealed in the proposition that *Jikok mandi denai di hulu*. The word *hulu* (upstream) contained in the proposition relates to the river, namely the upper part of the river.

3. Non-propositional meaning in the lyrics of the song *Sayang Tak Sudah*

The song *Sayang Tak Sudah* composed by Anas Yusuf also uses the word *ayam* as a parable which refers to 'a girl who is loved', and the word *musang* (weasel) as a parable which refers to 'a man who is not married or single', as in pantun (3a) following.

(3a) *Iyo iyo, Taluak Bayua ikannyo jinak*
Baok mamapeh, baok mamapeh, hai dari sampan
Ayam sikua, ayam sikua, musang kok banyak
Raso ka lapeh, raso ka lapeh hai dari tangan
'In Teluk Bayur the fish are tame'
'Fish are caught from the boat'
'There is only one hen, but there are many weasels'
"As if the hen will disappear"

The lyrics of *Sayang Tak Sudah* in the first stanza (3a) are a pantun consisting of four lines and rhymes a-b-a-b. The proposition in the content of the pantun has words used as similes, namely *ayam,* and *musang*. The use of the words *ayam* and *musang* in the proposition *Ayam sikua, ayam sikua, musang kok banyak* contains non-propositional meaning. The word *ayam* in the proposition encodes the non-propositional meaning 'a girl who is someone's fiancée or lover,' and the word musang encodes the non-propositional meaning 'an unmarried man.' Thus, the proposition *Ayam sikua, ayam sikua, musang kok banyak,* and the proposition *Raso ka lapeh, raso ka lapeh hai dari tangan* tell a story about the fear of losing a lover because many people like her/him.

Furthermore, the song Sayang *Tak Sudah* lyrics in the second stanza (3b) is written as pantun consisting of four lines and rhymes a-b-a-b. The *sampiran* (prefatory statement) as an introduction to the content of *pantun* (3b) are not related to the content of the pantun itself. In the body of the pantun, the lyricist uses the expression *laut dalam* (deep sea), which encodes a non-propositional meaning of 'a hard life due to mental and emotional turmoil due to deep grief'.

(3b) *iyo iyo, rang Parik Putih balapauu ranadah*
Mambaok balam, mambaok balam dalam sarangnyo
Kasih putuih, kasih putuih sayang tak sudah
Lauik nan dalam, lauik nan dalam nan dihadangnyo
'Orang Parit Putus has a small shop'
'Carrying a turtledove in its nest'
'Love is broken, but affection remains'
'The deep ocean to be faced'

So, the propositions *Kasih putuih, kasih putuih sayang tak sudah* and *Lauik nan dalam, lauik nan dalam nan dihadangnyo* tell the story of someone who experienced a breakup with his girlfriend because of a third person. The incident caused his life to become miserable because of the pain he felt.

4. Non-Propositional Meaning in the Song *Indak Ka Barulang*

The story of the sadness of having one's heart broken by someone is narrated in the song *Indak Ka Barulang*, sung and popularized by Elly Kasim in 1972. Yusaf Rahman created the song. The lyrics (4a) describe the nature and life of humans. Pantun in the lyrics (4a) has the rhymes a-b-a-b and a-a-b-b. In the first stanza, the lyricist used a prefatory statement to depict the heavy life of someone who does not have a wife or husband. It can be seen in the proposition *Nan bak mano ribuk di nan tido* as having a non-propositional meaning. Using *ribuk* 'wind' in the proposition encodes the non-propositional meaning 'suffering.' The prefatory statement of pantun (4a) in the second stanza, *Kayu gadang banyak badahan,* describes nature with propositional meaning.

(4a)	*Nan bak mano ribuik di nan tido (ondeh sayang)*	'What is the power of the wind that has nothing'
	Kayu gadang banyak badahan	'A big wood has many branches'
	Nan bak mano hati ndak kan ibo (ondeh sayang)	'How the heart will not be sad'
	Kasiah nan surang yo lapeh dari tangan	'Lovers escape from the embrace'

The content of *pantun* (4a) tells about the suffering experienced by someone because of the loss of a lover. This is expressed in the proposition *Nan bak mano hati ndak kan ibo* and the proposition *Kasiah nan surang yo lapeh dari tangan.* Both propositions contain the propositional meaning of 'the suffering experienced by someone who experienced a breakup with his lover.'

In the lyrics of *Indak Ka Barulang,* the second stanza (4b) is written as a pantun with a-a-b-b rhyme. All the propositions contained in the pantun (4a) contain propositional meaning because every word used in the proposition is not in the form of a simile.

(4b)	*Baitu bana kasiah ka nan surang*	'Too in love with someone'
	Jadi panyakik malam jo siang	'Will be a burden on your mind night and day'
	Baitu bana kasiah ka nan hilang	'Too in love with a former lover'
	Kasiah lamo indak ka barulang	'Past love will never happen again'

The second stanza of *Indak Ka Barulang* tells about someone who loves his ex-lovers so that he always remembers her day and night. Somehow, the romantic story will not happen again.

In the third stanza (4c), the lyricist used idioms for nature, such as plants in the proposition *Batang kapeh tumbuahnyo condong* and *Tumbuh luruih dakek tapian.* Both propositions consist of propositional meaning, as mentioned in that preposition. The meaning of those propositions is 'the cotton plant grows slanted' and 'it grows straight near the pond.'

In the content part of *pantun*, the lyricist says that if we feel hot, we can take shelter, but a restless heart cannot be hidden.

(4c)	*Batang kapeh tumbuahnyo condong (ondeh sayang)*	'Cotton stalks grow crookedly'
	Tumbuah luruih dakek tapian	'It grows straight near the pond'
	Jikok paneh yo dapek balinduang (ondeh sayang)	'When it's hot, you can take shelter'
	Hati nan rusuah kamano disuruakkan	'The restless heart where to hide'

5. Non-proporsitional Meaning in Kelok-44 Lyrics

Apart from telling love stories, many Minangkabau song lyrics also tell stories about 'merantau' (journeying in search of success). As we know, *merantau* is a tradition passed down from generation to generation in Minangkabau society. *Merantau* is one of the local wisdom of the Minangkabau people. *Merantau*, for Minangkabau people, is a place to learn to live independently and make a living so as not to depend on parents. In addition, *merantau* can also shape a person's personality so that they dare to make decisions and can determine what can and should not be done. *Merantau* for Minangkabau people is an effort to maintain the izah of the family, the community, and Minangkabau. The success of life must have a positive impact or benefit for the family and the nagari. There are several reasons for merantau and the various forms of *merantau* that have occurred among the Minangkabau people (Zahari, 2021, hal. 25).

Merantau is one of the work ethics of the Minangkabau people. As stated by Patji (2020: 83-84), ethos is a description of behaviour, ways of acting, or the most comprehensive idea about the world order of life, which is based on cultural values. In other words, ethos is an evaluative aspect as a fundamental attitude of themselves and their world (Minangkabau people), reflected in life. *Merantau* for the Minangkabau people is a place to train themselves to learn to live independently. This is revealed in the following pantun.

Karatau madang di hulu	'Go upstream madang'
Babuah babungo balun	'Because it has not yet borne fruit and blossomed'
Marantau Bujang dahulu	'Go far away you young man'
Di rumah baguno balun	'Because in the village you can't do anything'

The culture of migrating as a characteristic of the Minangkabau people is recorded in the lyrics of Minangkabau songs sung and popularised by Elly Kasim and Tiar Ramon, including the songs *Kelok-44, Tinggalah Kampuang, Langkisau, and Baa Co Iko Bana.*

Kelok-44 is a road trip route from Bukittinggi to Maninjau Lake. Kelok-44 is 10km long with a downhill road contour and has 44 turns. During the journey, travelers will enjoy stunning views of rice fields, Maninjau Lake, and Bukit Barisan landscape. The natural beauty of Kelok-44 is captured in the lyrics of Kelok-44.

The lyrics of Kelok 44 tell the story of someone about to leave his hometown with a beautiful view. Kelok 44 belongs to Agam Regency, West Sumatra Province. Minangkabau people are one of the ethnic groups with a *merantau* tradition. The tradition of *merantau* has also brought most of the Minangkabau people to inhabit areas outside of West Sumatra, even outside Indonesia.

One of the businesses that many Minangkabau people do is a restaurant business known as Padang restaurant. Padang restaurants can be found in various cities in Indonesia. A joke about Padang restaurants shows how wide the area of expansion of the Minangkabau people is, namely, "If people could inhabit the moon, there would also be Padang Restaurants" *Merantau* has indeed been ingrained in the Minangkabau people since the beginning. The purpose of *merantau* also varies. However, trading is one of them that is quite prominent. Where there is a location for trading, Minangkabau people can be easily found. There is another joke related to this trade about Minangkabau people. "Minangkabau people are one step ahead of the Chinese" (Meigalia, 2019).

The lyrics of Kelok 44 describe a young man from Tanjung Raya, Agam Regency, who is about to merantau. Minangkabau people go far away from their hometowns to make a living. If they succeed in their business overseas and have much money, they will return to their hometown. This is illustrated in the first stanza of the song Kelok 44 in (5a) below.

(5a)	*Maluncua denai nak lakeh*	'I'm rushing to leave soon'
	Ndeh mande tolong doakan	'Oh mother please help me with your prayers'
	Nan kok mujua Bundo malapeh	'May I go with your blessings'
	Bak ayam pulang kapauikan	'Like a hen coming home to roost'

The Minangkabau song *Kelok* 44's lyrics are written as rhyming pantun a-b-a-b. The rhyme is found in the suffixes -eh in *lakeh-malapeh* and *-kan* in *pray-kapauikan.* The cover of pantun (5a) *Maluncua denai nak lakeh* and *Ndeh mande tolong doakan* depicts a Minangkabau youth who will travel overseas to try his luck in order to meet his needs. He asks his mother for prayers to reach his goal and make a lot of money to get what he wants.

Meanwhile, in the content of the *pantun Nan kok mujua Bundo malapeh* and *Bak ayam pulang kapauikan,* the lyricist uses expressions that contain non-propositional meaning. Nan kok mujua Bundo malapeh contains a non-propositional meaning 'if he is lucky, he succeeds overseas' and the expression *Bak ayam pulang kapauikan* contains a non-propositional meaning 'as desired'.

(5b)	*Di kelok ampek puluah ampek*	'On the winding road 44'
	Denai bamulo barangkek	'I started to leave'
	Tinggalah kampuang sanak sudaro	'I left my village and my family'
	Denai ka barangkek ka tanah Jao	'I went to the island of Java'

The story of a young Minangkabau man from Tanjungraya District, Agam Regency, West Sumatra Province, is told on the cover of *pantun* (5b). Most young Minangkabau people are willing to move to Java and leave their beautiful hometown and family members, and this is done so that they can make money and improve their lives.

The song Kelok 44 tells about the culture of Minangkabau people and how they used to move around. *Merantau* is a piece of local wisdom for Minangkabau people. It is a way of thinking about their culture in the form of trying their luck and coming back home with success.

6. Non-propositional Meaning in Tinggalah Kampuang Song Lyrics

In addition, the lyrics of the song *Tinggalah Kampuang*, composed by Syahrul Tarun Yusuf, encode the migration tradition of Minangkabau people. This song has a beautiful arrangement of lyrics and is accompanied by melodious music, which makes it incredibly moving and capable of penetrating the listeners' hearts. This occurs because the lyrics of the song *Tinggalah Kampuang* depict the reality of the lives of Minangkabau people, who have a migration culture or tradition. *Perantau* (migrants from Minangkabau) always experience homesickness, which can be alleviated by listening to traditional Minangkabau songs.

Tinggalah Kampuang's lyrics are in the form of *pantun* rhyming a-b-a-b. This song's lyrics tell the story of a Minang youth from the Ranah Balingka who leaves his hometown to merantau (. Balingka is a village in the Agam Regency of West Sumatra, close to Mount Singgalang. This is expressed in the *sampiran* (prefatory statement) (6a), which includes *Tinggalah kampuang ranah Balingka* and *Gunuang Singgalang (ondeh) lai ka manjago*. According to what is stated in the proposition, both propositions have propositional meaning.

(6a) *Tinggalah kampuang ranah Balingka*
Gunuang Singgalang (ondeh) lai ka manjago
Oi mandeh kanduang tolong jo do'a
Antah pabilo (ondeh) kito basuo
'Goodbye to my village'
'Mount Singgalang will take care of you'
'Oh, my mother, please always pray for me'
'I do not know when we will meet again'

The contents of the *pantun* reveal that the mother's prayer determines a child's success. Therefore, a child generally asks his mother to pray for him. This was done because he believed that a child's success is related to a mother's prayer. The *pantun* (6a) also describes how a child feels when he is separated from his mother and leaves his beautiful hometown to change his destiny for the better by *merantau*. The lyrics of this song also reveal that a mother's prayer determines a child's success. Therefore, the proposition in the contents of the pantun, namely the proposition *Oi mandeh kanduang tolong jo do'a* encodes a non-propositional meaning in the form of 'a mother's prayer determines the success of a child' and the proposition *Antah kapan (ondeh) kito bertemu* encodes a non- propositional in the form of 'uncertainty when children and their mothers will be able to meet again because the Minangkabau people have a philosophy of *merantau* and will not return to their hometown before they are successful.'

The child's uncertainty about being able to reunite with his mother is also expressed in the cover of the following *pantun* (6b).

(6b)	*Takadia untuang kok lai ka mujua*	'If only my destiny would be good'
	Bilo masonyo kito basuo	'We will meet again someday'
	Sadangnyo arek tali jo buhua	'When the rope is tightly tied to the gusset'
	Bakarek rotan kini jadinyo	'Like a rattan cut now it becomes'

Pantun (6b) also rhymes a-b-a-b, with the word *mujua* in the first line and *buhua* in the third line, *basuo* in the second line, and *jadinyo* in the fourth line. In the prefatory statement, the lyricist uses the proposition *Takadia untuang kok lai ka mujua* 'If only my destiny would be good'. The proposition contains a non-propositional meaning: 'if you are lucky, *merantau* can change your fate for the better.' Meanwhile, the proposition *Bilo masonyo kito basuo* 'We will meet again someday' contains a non-propositional meaning: '*Perantau Minang* will return home and meet their mothers after succeeding overseas.'

The content part of the pantun expresses that leaving hometown, mother, and siblings is not easy because it will cause sadness. However, Minang youth must do it. This is encoded in the proposition *Sadangnyo arek tali jo buhua* 'When the rope is tightly tied to the gusset' and the proposition *Bakarek rotan kini jadinyo* 'Like a rattan cut now it becomes'. The proposition contained in the *pantun* is categorized as simile, *Bakarek rotan*, which encodes the non-propositional meaning 'to separate'.

7. Non-propositional Meaning in Langkisau Song Lyrics

Next, the song Langkisau, sung and popularised by Elly Kasim in the 80s, tells the story of the purpose of Minangkabau people going overseas. We can see this in the lyrics of Langkisau (7a) below.

(7a)	*Ndeh oi Langkisau bukik Painan*	'Oh, Langkisau Hill in Painan'
	Batampek mandi pincuran mandam	'There is a bathing place called Mandam shower'
	'Elok ka rantau kito bajalan	'It's better to go overseas'
	Kok lai tabungkik butang tarandam	'May the submerged trunk be awakened'

The lyrics of the song *Langkisau* (7a) are *pantun* consisting of four lines and rhymes a-b-a-b. *Langkisau* is a hill located in Painan City. From Langkisau Hill, we can see beautiful views, such as white sandy beaches and Painan city. The natural beauty seen from Langkisau Hill is revealed in the lyrics of the song Langkisau in the first stanza (7a) in the proposition *Ndeh oi Langkisau bukik Painan*. The use of *Ndeh oi (ondeh oi)* in the proposition is an interjection commonly used by Minangkabau people to express admiration for the beauty of the natural scenery they see.

In the content of the pantun, there is a Minang proverb *Kok lai tabangkik batang tarandam,* which encodes the non-propositional meaning 'to raise the dignity of the family'. The content of the *pantuns Elok ka rantau kito bajalan* and *Kok lai tabangkik batang tarandam* encode the non-propositional meaning '*merantau* is one of the efforts to raise the family's dignity'.

Meanwhile, the second stanza of the *Langkisau* song lyrics reveals that *perantau* always misses their hometowns. This is revealed in the content of the following *pantun* (7b).

(7b)	*Langkisau bukik Langkisau*	'Langkasau Hill, the Langkiau'
	Tanang aie di talao	'My hometown in Talao'
	Tangiang kampuang maimbau	'I heard my hometown calling'
	Taganang si aie mato	'Tears in my eyes'

The natural beauty of Bukit Langkisau makes Minangkabau *perantau* from Pesisir Selatan long for home. *Tangiang kampuang maimbau* 'I heard my hometown calling'encapsulates this.

The proverb Bak *ayam pulang ka pautan* appears in the third stanza of the Langkisau song lyrics, in (7c). This proverb expresses the non-positional meaning 'as desired'.

(7c)	*Ndeh oh badabuah lah ombak mahampeh*	'Oh, the waves are crashing'
	Batu kureta mamanciang ikan	'Fishing on the Batu Kereta Island'
	Jikok lai mujua bundo malapeh	'May I go with your blessings'
	Bak ayam pulang ka pautan	'Like a hen coming home to roost'

CONCLUSION

Minangkabau pantun in the lyrics of Minangkabau songs on the Pop Minang Album, published by Tanama Record and sung by Elly Kasin and Tiar Ramon, generally discusses life issues relating to romance and the customs of merantau (migrating). The words of the Minangkabau song are composed of pantun consisting of six lines that rhyme a-b-c-a-b-c and pantun consisting of four lines that rhyme a-b-a-b. The natural scenery of the Minang scenery is described in general terms on the prefatory statement. In contrast, the pantun contains statements in parables that compare the behaviour of plants and animals to that of humans. The combination of landscape as the prefatory statement and flora and fauna as the pantun's content demonstrates that Minangkabau people consistently apply their life philosophy, "alam takambang jadi guru," to their use of language.

Pantun, in the lyrics of Minangkabau songs, uses many expressions in similes that analogize human behaviour with animal and plant behaviour. These analogies are classified as metaphorical icons. Metaphorical icons widely used in the lyrics of Minangkabau songs are animal names, such as hen, alang, cikok, and musang, and plant names siriah leaves and areca nut. Expressions that use hen lexemes are found in the lyrics of Ayam Den Lapeh, Usah Diratoki, Sayang Tak Sudah. In the song lyrics Ayam Den Lapeh, the lexeme ayam encodes the non-propositional meaning of 'a lover or life partner'.

Meanwhile, in *Usah Diratoki*, the lyricist uses the idioms *ayam putiah* and *ayam tapauik*. The idiom *ayam putiah* in the proposition *Iyo sarik baa yam putiah* encodes the non-positional meaning of 'a young girl who is very beautiful, very good, very smart or a respected girl'. In contrast, the idiom *ayam tapauik* in the proposition *Ayam tapauik disembanya* encodes the non-positional meaning of 'someone's wife, husband, or fiancée is taken by someone else'. In addition, in the lyrics of *Usah Diratoki*, the metaphors *alang* and *cikok* are also found. Using the lexeme *alang* in the proposition *Iyo buruak lakunyo alang* encodes the non-propositional meaning of 'wealthy men or men with power'. *Alang manyemba* encodes the non-propositional meaning 'an ordinary man who likes to snatch other people's lovers or wives'.

Additionally, the idiom *daun siriah* in the proposition *Ulah rayu si daun siriah* encodes the non-propositional meaning 'a person who takes someone's companion (lover, husband, or wife), popularly referred to as a third person', yielding *Bacarai pinang jo tampuaknyo. Bacarai pinang jo tampuaknyo* encodes the non-propositional meaning 'the separation of the loving relationship between lovers or husband and wife'.

The lyricist of *Sayang Tak Sudah* employs the similes *ayam* and *musang* in his lyrics. In the proposition, both words are used: *Ayam sikua musang kok banyak.* The non-propositional meaning of 'a girl who is someone's fiancée or sweetheart' is encoded by the lexeme *ayam* in the proposition. In contrast, the lexeme *musang* in the proposition refers to 'an unmarried man'.

The term *ayam* appears in the lyrics of *Kelok-44* and *Langkisau* as well. The lexeme *ayam* is employed in the term *ayam pulang kepauikan* in the proposition *Bak ayam pulang kapauikan,* encoding the non-propositional meaning 'as desired' in both song lyrics. Also, the expression *tabangkik batang tarandam* appears in the lyrics of *Langkisau*. The expression appears in the proposition *Kok lai tabangkik batang tarandam,* conveying the non-propositional meaning 'to raise the family's dignity'.

References

Astuti, D. P. J. (2020). Semiotika Pantun Minang pada Masyarakat Minangkabau Kota *Bengkulu. Disastra: Jurnal Pendidikan Bahasa Dan Sastra Indonesia, 2*(1), 43. https://doi.org/10.29300/disastra.v2i1.2708

Ermitati. (2014). "Pengungkapan Budaya Suku Anak Dalam melalui Kosakata Bahasa Kubu." *Kandai, 10*(2), 153--164. http://ojs.badanbahasa.kemdikbud.go.id/jurnal/index.php/kandai/article/viewFile/319/138

Evans, V. (n.d.). *COGNITIVE LINGUISTICS AN INTRODUCTION.* EDINBURGH UNIVERSITY PRESS.

Fauconnier, G. (n.d.). *Mapping in ThoughtAnd Language.* Cambridge University Press. https://doi.org/https://doi.org/10.1017/CBO9781139174220

Gani, E. (2012). Kajian Terhadap Landasan Filosofi Pantun Minangkabau. *Komposisi: Jurnal Pendidikan Bahasa, Sastra, Dan Seni.* https://doi.org/10.24036/komposisi.v10i1.49

Ghani, K. A. (2021). SEMANTIK BANDINGAN: PENGENALAN KEPADA TEORI PENGADUNAN KONSEPTUAL. INTERNATIONAL JOURNAL OF HUMANITIES, *PHILOSOPHY AND LANGUAGE (IJHPL), Volume 4 I,* 28--51. https://doi.org/DOI 10.35631/IJHPL.414003

Humaedi, M. A. (2020). *Bahasa dan Budaya Dayak Santos bagi Persatuan Bangsa* (M. A. Humaedi (ed.); Pertama, p. 272). LIPI Press. lipipress.lipi.go.id

Kecskes, I. (2008). Dueling contexts: A dynamic model of meaning. *Journal of Pragmatics.* https://doi.org/10.1016/j.pragma.2007.12.004

Kecskes, I., & Kecskes, I. (2014). Politeness and Impoliteness. In *Intercultural Pragmatics.* https://doi.org/10.1093/acprof:oso/9780199892655.003.0010

Lyons, J. (1996). *Linguistic Semantics An Intoduction* (Kedua). Cambridge University Press.

Meigalia, E. (2019). *Minangkabau dalam Lirik Lagu* (Pertama). LPPM Univaersitas Andalas.

Navis, A. A. (1984). *Alam Takambang Jadi Guru.* Grafiti Pers.

Ristianti, D. H. (2018). *PSIKOLOGI LINTAS BUDAYA* (Solihin (ed.); kedua). LP2 IAIN CURUP. www.iaincurup.ac.id

Wulansari, D. (2016). Bahasa Pantun Dalam Makna Dan Budaya Masyarakat Me-. *Jurnal Society, VI*(1), 1–13. https://society.fisip.ubb.ac.id/index.php/society/article/download/31/19/%0A%0A

Zahari, M. (2021). *Peredupan Rasa Keminangan* (Pertama). Citra Hasta Prima.

The Vitality of Pannei
A Marginalized Language among its Community

Jusmianti Garing(jusm001@brin.go.id) | **Hastianah**(hast004@brin.go.id)
Buha Aritonang(ppid@brin.go.id) | **Nuraidar Agus**(nura026@brin.go.id) | **Musayyedah**(musa003@brin.go.id)
National Research and Innovation Agency, Archaeological, Language and Literature Research Organization

INTRODUCTION

Pannei language is one of the marginalized languages in Polman Regency, West Sulawesi Province, Indonesia. The marginalization occurs because speakers of this language gravitate to ignore its use in all communication situations, such as communication in family, environment, school, and others. It is concerning because the Pannei language has experienced degradation in its use, especially in the daily life of the Pannei people. Consequently, it is imperative to complete all research areas to protect this language and ensure that speakers can continue to use it in all contexts. If not, the Pannei language will be marginalized by its speakers and may even disappear in the future.

The Pannei language as identity of local community speaks in three sub-district, i.e., Mapilli, Tapango, and Matangnga Sub-district. In each of these sub-districts, the Pannei language speakers are scattered again in various villages, namely the Villages of Bulo, Pulliwa, Sabura, Karombang, Riso, Kaliambua, Tapango, Tuttula, Bussu, Mambu Tapua, Babba Tappua Lili, and Rangong. For more details about the speech area of the Pannei language, see Map 1 below.

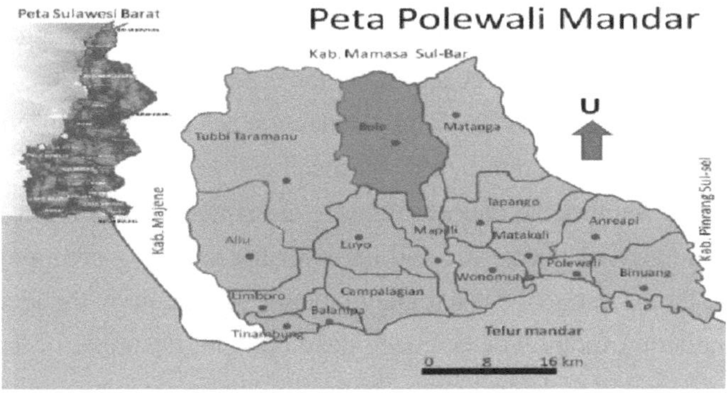

Map 1. Map of Polewali Mandar

Bulo sub-district was divided from the Mapili sub-district and is a village that is the youngest sub-district in Polewali Mandar, which is the axis between Matangga and Wonomulyo (see Map 2). The Bulo Village route can also be an alternative for those who want to visit Mamasa Regency. However, for now, Bulo District is an area that is still very underdeveloped due to its geographical location in the mountains. Bulo Subdistrict is a fertile area for plants and offers many agricultural goods that can be used. It hopes that the Polewali Mandar government can pay attention to the trans route between Matangga and Bulo to create a community that can help each other in the context of an advanced Polewali Mandar. The obstacle for the workers and farmers is the challenging road to pass.

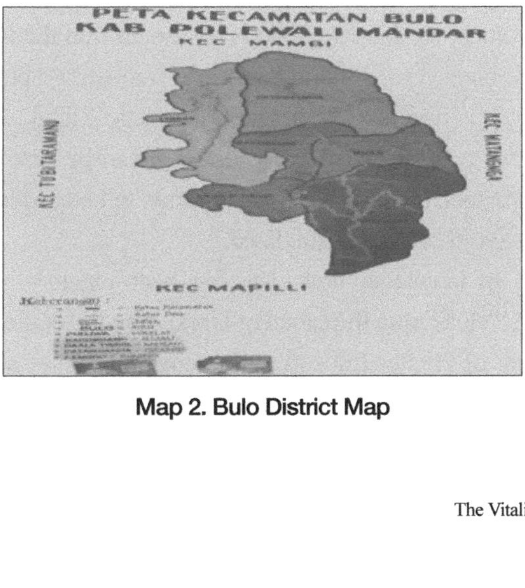

Map 2. Bulo District Map

The three sub-districts distribution of language speakers suggests that the Pannei language is safe according to the criteria for its vitality. However, this does not mean that the Pannei language has not experienced a shift or even extinction. Therefore, a more specific study or research is needed to determine whether the Pannei language has shifted. The life force of the Pannei language is a necessity and hope for the speaking community because the Pannei language is a regional identity, particularly the identity of the Pannei community. For language development, the study of language vitality is essential to determine the probability that a language will continue to be used and sustainable in the future. The vitality study is equivalent to being conducted to find out how far languages can survive—considering the influence of globalization today, which bombards all aspects of life, including the language aspect that threatens the existence of languages, especially regional languages. Therefore, efforts to maintain and preserve regional languages are essential due to the regional languages have the position and function as symbols of regional pride, regional identity, means of communication within the family, and supporting facilities of regional culture and language.

In addition, assessing a language's vitality is essential to prevent it from changing or even going extinct or being marginalized by the speakers. Once a language changes or is in danger of going extinct, it loses its ability to survive among its speakers and moves to the margins. That is, a language that is extensively spoken has changed to the point where it is in danger of disappearing, indicating that its speakers no longer find the language profitable and have chosen to use another, more frequently spoken language instead. Hence, it is necessary to assess a language's vitality to determine whether it is changing or endangered so that it can be cared for and preserved. By doing this, the language can continue to be used by its speakers and, of course, avoid being marginalized.

The vitality of languages nowadays has been extensively researched, with one study, "Measuring the Level of Upholding the National Language Among Institute of Higher Education Students" (Tohar et al., 2017). The analysis's findings indicated that IHE students speak Malay with a high level of fluency and recognition. The sophistication of their linguistic use, however, is only moderate. Gobbo (2021) wrote "Coolification and Language Vitality: The Case of Esperanto. The results show that Esperanto is a non-threatened language that can exist even if intergenerational transmission occurs outside family use. Another study was conducted by Andriyanti (2019) titled "Language Shift among Javanese Youth and Their Perception of Local and National Identities" The results show that the majority of young people with Javanese parents indicated that Bahasa Indonesia was their first language. It denotes a weaker intergenerational transfer of Javanese. Then, Agus, N et.al. (2019) wrote "Vitalitas Bahasa Limola." They stated that the vitality of the Limola language in the North Luwu Regency has decreased. Another study titled "Vitalitas Bahasa Ternate di Pulau Ternate" was conducted by Maricar & Duwila (2017). The study results find that the Ternate language's vitality is in the worrying category. A recent study had conducted by Bouchard (2022) and Hj. Mahali et al. (2022). Bouchard wrote "The vitality of Angolar: A study of attitudes on São Tomé Island." The finding illustrates how beliefs held by Angolares and the Forros, the predominant ethnolinguistic group of So Tomé Island, may adversely affect the preservation of Angolar Creole. While Hj. Mahali et al. (2022) wrote "The Domains and Language Choice Among the Young Murut Generation in Keningau District, Sabah." The findings showed that when Murut youths interact with many people regularly, language preferences have changed among them. The youthful generation's primary language for communication with family members, aside from English, is their mother tongue and the Sabah Malay dialect. When interacting with friends, however, the Sabah Malay dialect is employed. The education sector has the same scenario. It is evident from the analysis's results that the younger Murut generation will "alter" their language use to suit their requirements or environment.

The Pannei language is a minority language that appears marginalized since its native speakers frequently ignore using it daily. It marginalizes because this language is only spoken by a tiny portion of the population and is not frequently used or acknowledged in formal situations, educational institutions, the media, or other facets of public life. Marginalization can occur for a variety of reasons, including historical, political, economic, or cultural factors. Marginalized languages often face challenges in maintaining their vitality and preserving their unique cultural heritage, as they may be replaced by more dominant languages or face pressures to assimilate into the dominant group's culture. It can lead to a language shift, where younger generations may need to learn or use the marginalized language as their primary means of communication.

Hence, it is vital to preserving this language from a young age through research, particularly on the Pannei language's vitality, to determine whether it is in excellent condition. Regarding previous studies, the language vitality of the Pannei language has ever researched yet. So, The main topic of this study is the vitality of the Pannei language as a marginalization language in West Sulawesi. This study aims to highlight the degree of Pannei language survival. The findings of this study contribute to the academics can utilize it to advance linguistics, particularly in language planning and marginal language policy. In addition, it also contributes to the local government to preserve and maintain local languages from an early stage.

Vitality is a study that focuses on the ability of a language to survive. Vitality means the ability to survive and vitality (Soo Ying et al., 2015). Language vitality is a sign of language sustainability and the extent to which maintenance actions are required (Ehala, 2010). Vitality is not a property of the language itself or the population that speaks it but rather a description of the relationship between language, its speakers, and its broad linguistic, social, and political context (Chayinska et al., 2022; Meek, 2019; Pivot & Bert, 2017). Therefore, vitality reflects how language ecology impacts individual languages and their speakers (Grenoble & Whaley, 2005, 2021; M. P. Lewis & Simons, 2011). Many measure vitality on a unilinear continuum from safe (multiple variants) to extinction (Grenoble & Whaley, 2005; Roche, 2017; Simons & Lewis, 2013). Language's vitality shows how language is used as a means of communication in various social contexts for specific purposes (Clément & Norton, 2021; Costley et al., 2022; Julio & Tudela-isanta, 2022; Peng et al., 2016; Shulman et al., 2011). The most significant parameter of language vitality in daily use at home. A language with high vitality will spread widely across all generations (Bunck et al., 2020; Komondouros & McEntee-Atalianis, 2007; Retinskaya, 2021; Song & Zhu, 2016), both within and outside the home.

Giles et al. in Candrasari & Nurmaidah (2018), initially discussed language's vitality which later became important because it is a benchmark for maintaining a language by measuring the use of language as a daily communication tool in various social contexts and various purposes. High-vital languages have a chance of surviving, while low-vital languages are thought to be doomed to extinction. Meanwhile, Casquite & Young (2017), Maricar & Duwila (2017), and Nagy (2018) said that all generations use the language to be healthy and have high vitality. Therefore, concerning the vitality of language, Aritonang (2016) explains the speed of language extinction between generations of speakers based on the sociolinguistic hypothesis that if one language only uses speakers aged 25 years and over and those aged below no longer use it, The next 75 years—three generations—the language will be in danger of extinction. A language is likely to go extinct in the next 50 years—two generations—if people only speak it above the age of 50 and those under that age no longer use it. If a language is actively used only by speakers aged 75 years and over and speakers aged below it are no longer proficient in using it, especially in the family domain, it is likely that in the next 25 years—a generation—the language will be (threatened) extinct. According to a more precise statement, the language is vanishing faster the younger the speakers are since they cannot communicate in their mother tongue.

UNESCO, together with international linguist groups in 2002 and 2003, formulated the criteria for determining language vitality to assist the government in making policies for handling language in their country. In this case, UNESCO in M. P. Lewis & Simons (2011), together with international linguist groups, set nine criteria to measure the vitality of a language, namely the number of speakers, the proportion of speakers in the total population, the availability of teaching materials, language response to new media, the type and quality of documentation, language attitudes and government and institutional policies, the transition of the domain of language use, the attitudes of community members towards their language, and the transmission of language between generations. Based on these criteria, UNESCO and the international linguist group divide the vitality of language into six groups namely (1) extinct languages, namely languages without speakers; (2) nearly extinct languages, namely languages with a maximum of ten speakers, all of whom are older generations; (3) seriously endangered languages, namely languages with a large number of speakers, but their children no longer use the language; (4) threatened languages (endangered languages), namely languages with speakers of children, but tend to decline; (5) potentially endangered languages, i.e., languages with many children speaking, but which do not have official or prestigious status; and (6) languages that are not in risk of extinction, specifically those with excellent transmission to new generations (Ulfa, 2019). From several concepts, theories, and criteria for language vitality put forward by several research experts, this study applies language vitality criteria based on the findings of endangered languages. Another regulation that conveys preserving the local languages as national cultural treasures had mentioned in the Constitution of Paragraph 2, Article 32, 1945. The passage emphasizes that the Indonesian people must uphold, respect, and preserve regional languages. For regional languages to persist in the community of speakers, it is up to all of us to respect, preserve, develop, and promote them.

PANNEI VITALITY AS A MARGINALIZED LANGUAGE

The analysis results highlighted that ten indicators classified into four criteria determined the vitality of the Pannei language. The four criteria are incredibly critical and threatened, decreasing, endangered, stable and steady but endangered with extinction. These findings significantly impact the Pannei language's existence, making the Pannei language a marginal language in thier community.

The results show that each indicator has a different tendency for the percentage of respondents who preferred responses to each statement item. It can be seen in the following table.

Table 1. Pannei language vitality results in ten variables.

Num	Indicator Type	Pannei Language Vitality Criteria	Continuum Line	Total Score	Score Minimum-Maximum
1	Language transmission among speakers	Stable and steady, but endangered	1a	6567	1800—9600
2	Number and proportion of speakers	Endangered	2a	652	360—1800
3	Language usage	Decreasing	3a	8635	3120—15600
4	Domain and new media	Extremely critical and threatened	4a	954	600—3000
5	Language and literacy teaching material availability	Extremely critical and threatened	5a	626	480—2400
6	Government attitude and regulation	Decreasing	6a	2592	1080—5400
7	Speaker's attitude	Stable and steady, but endangered	7a	6759	1800—9000
8	Type and documentation quality	Extremely critical and threatened.	8a	726	600—3000
9	Language contact	Decreasing	9a	2023	720—3600
10	Bilingualism	Decreasing	10a	2716	840—4200

1. Language Transmission among Speakers

To determine the criteria for the Pannei language vitality based on the dimensions/indicators of the language transmission among speakers of Pannei speakers refers to the frequency value of the respondent's answer choices the language transmission among speakers by counting the 120 respondents, fifteen statement items, and five scales with, the total score are 8567. The series of numbers are entered into the following final calculation.

= Score Percentage

= (Total Score: Maximum Score) × 100%

= (6567 : 9600) × 100%

= 68.41%

The score of 68.41% lies in the stable and steady area but is threatened with extinction, with a total score of 6567. The expected ideal score for this indicator is 9600. So, the vitality of language transmission among speakers of Pannei is stable and steady but endangered. Here are the Continuum Lines 1 and 1a.

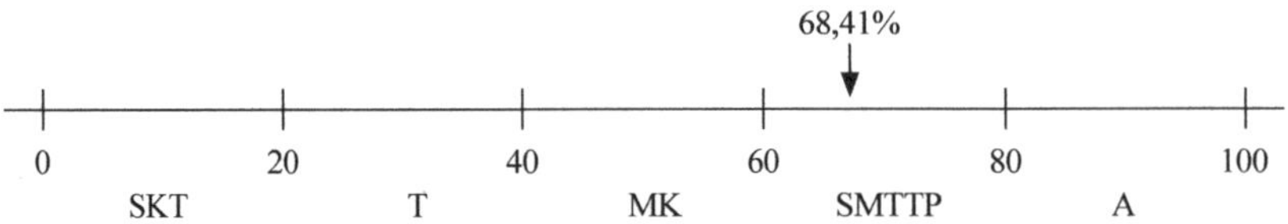

Continuum Line 1: Position and Interpretation of Likert Scale Range Language Inheritance Among Pannei Language Speakers Across Generations

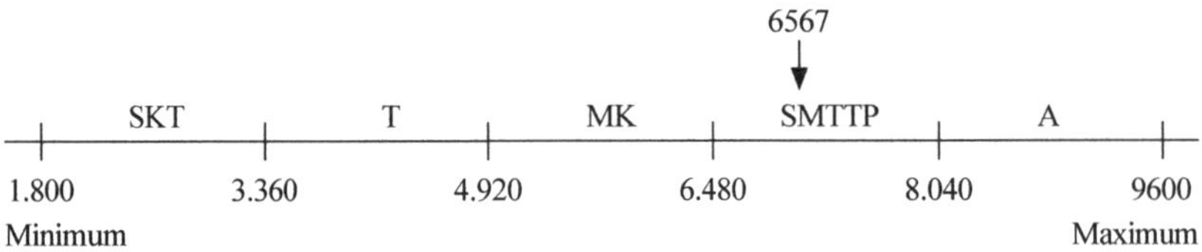

Continuum Line 1a: Position and Interpretation of Likert Scale Range Language Vitality Indicator Based on Language Inheritance Between Generations of Pannei Language Speakers

The vitality of the Pannei language with indicators of transmission among speakers with the criteria of experiencing stability and stability but being threatened with extinction. This criterion results from the frequency of responses to statements from individuals between the ages of 60 and 20 years. Over 60 years old, they teach their children the Pannei language and communicate with other speakers their age. However, at the age of 20 and under, this language inheritance does not occur. Speakers aged 60 and over rarely use this language when communicating with speakers aged 20. It indicates no intergenerational transmission between the ages of 60 to 20 years. Transmission occurs only among those aged 60 years and over. It shows that the resilience of this language could not be stronger, so it is a language that is marginalized among its speakers.

2. Number and Proportion of Speakers

To determine the criteria for the Pannei language vitality based on the dimensions/indicators of the number and proportion of Pannei speakers refers to the frequency value of the respondent's answer choices and the number and proportion of Pannei speakers by counting the 120 respondents, three statement items, five scales with a total score are 652. The series of numbers are entered into the following final calculation.

= Score Percentage

= (Total Score: Maximum Score) × 100%

= (652 : 1800) × 100%

= 36.22%

The score of 36.22% stands in the threatened area, with a total score of 652. The expected ideal score for this indicator is 1,800. It seems far from the ideal target score of 1800. Thus, the vitality of the number and proportion of Pannei speakers is considered endangered. Here are the Continuity Lines 2 and 2a.

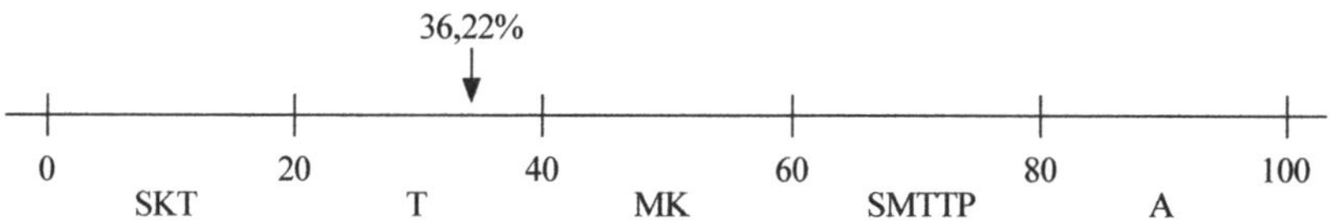

Continuum Line 2: Position and Interpretation of Likert Scale Range Number and Proportion of Pannei Language Speakers

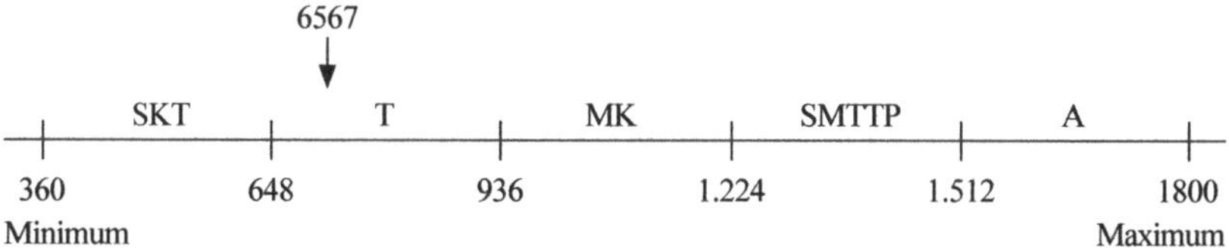

Continuum Line 2a: Position and Interpretation of the Likert Scale Range Language Vitality Indicator Based on the Number and Proportion of Pannei Speakers

The vitality of the Pannei language with indicators of the number and proportion of speakers is an endangered criterion. It is based on the fact that although the number of speakers of Pannei is more than other regional languages in the Pannei speech area, they rarely use Pannei in their daily communication or their environment, so this language is categorized as an endangered language. It is supported by measuring the vitality of the Pannei language that has been carried out. It means the speakers of this language do not have a positive attitude toward their language. Although there are still many of them, the vitality results show that this language is in a critical condition regarding the number of speakers. As a result, the Pannei language's current position is in the category of a language that its speakers marginalize.

3. Language Use

To determine the criteria for Pannei language vitality based on the dimensions/indicators of the language used refers to the frequency value of the respondent's answer choices regarding language use by counting the 120 respondents, 26 statement items, and five scales with the total score are 8635. The series of numbers are entered into the following final calculation.

= Score Percentage

= (Total Score: Maximum Score) × 100%

= (8635 : 15600) × 100%

= 55.35%

The score of 55.35% locates in the regressed area, with a total score of 8635. The expected ideal score for the indicator is 15600. Following the total score, the vitality of the language use of the Pannei language is classified as decreasing. It can show by the following Continuum Lines.

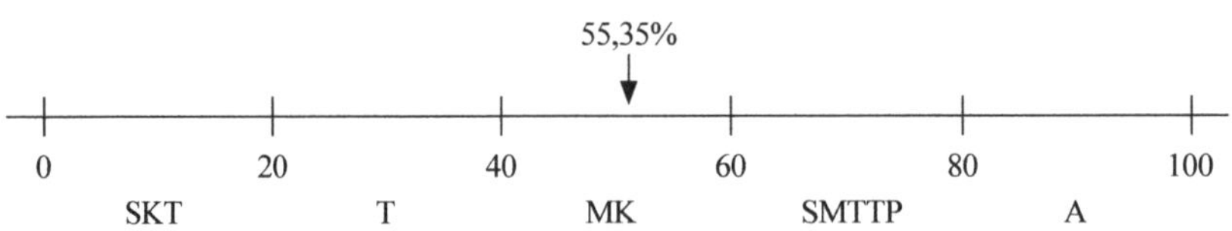

Continuum Line 3: Likert Scale Range Position and Interpretation Locations Where Pannei Is Spoken

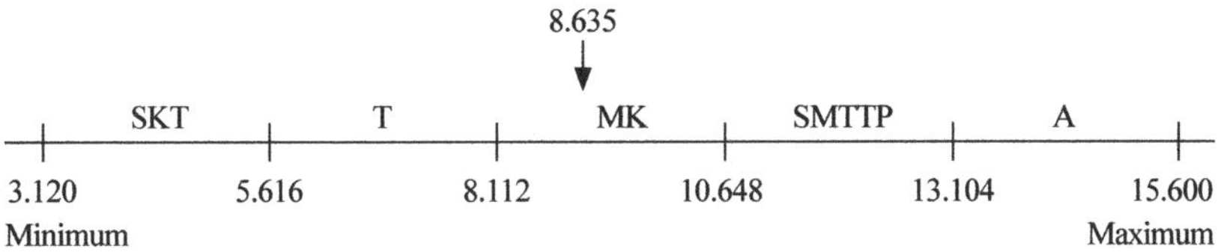

Continuum Line 3a: Position and Interpretation of the Likert Scale Range Language Vitality Indicator Based on Pannei Language Use Areas

The Pannei language vitality finds in the inclination always to use the Pannei language when speaking to parents; neighbors older than the speaker; husband/wife; siblings; relatives (uncle, aunt); and participating in religious activities at home. In contrast, they have proven never to use the Pannei language when speaking to doctors/midwives/nurses, to teachers outside the classroom during teaching and learning activities; to the village; to pray; to sub-district offices; and rarely use the Pannei language to fellow students when speaking outside the classroom during teaching and learning activities; and rarely uses Pannei language in bargaining activities at the stall. It means that the language use indicator in the Pannei language is decreasing. The Pannei language is only used at home, but it is never used outside the home. This indicator also shifts the condition of this language, particularly its use in society, so it is heading toward a language that will be forgotten or marginalized by its speakers.

4. Domain and New Media

To determine the criteria for the Pannei language vitality regarding the indicator of the domain and new media, it refers to the frequency value of the respondent's answer choices regarding the domain and new media by counting the number of 120 respondents, five statement items, and five scales with the total score are 954. The series of numbers are entered into the following final calculation.

= Score Percentage

= (Total Score: Maximum Score) × 100%

= (954 : 3000) × 100%

= 31.8%

The score of 31.8% lies in the threatened area, with a total score of 954. The expected ideal score for this indicator is 3000; however, the total score obtained is only 954. It's very far from expectations to an ideal score of 3000. The Pannei language is classified as critical and threatened. See the Continuum Lines 4 and 4a next.

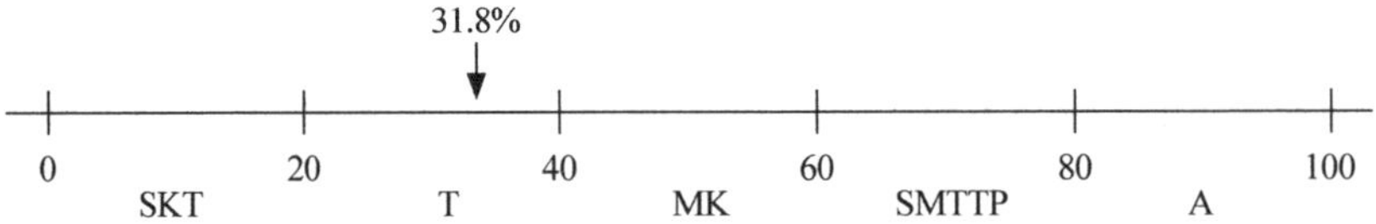

Continuum Line 4: Position and Interpretation of Likert Scale Range on Emerging Domain and New Media in Pannei Language

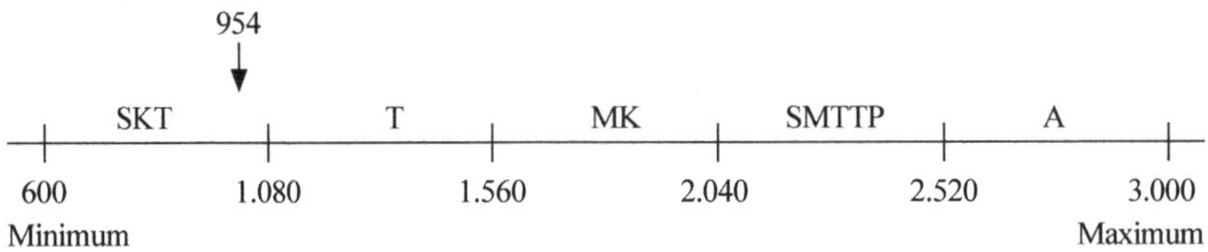

Continuum Line 4a: Position and Interpretation of Likert Scale Range Language Vitality Indicator Derived from the Pannei Language Domain and New Media

Domain and new media indicators with the criterion of language vitality are highly very critical and threatened due to the propensity of speakers of other languages not to visit areas where the Pannei language has spoken. It is also caused by the lacking of use of the Pannei regional language in broadcast media (television, radio), print media (newspapers, magazines), and translation of books in Indonesian and foreign languages (English, Arabic, Chinese) into Pannei (social media). These results are evidence that the condition of the Pannei language today has experienced a shift, and it is possible that in the next few years, this language will experience an endangered vitality if domains such as the media do not use Pannei as a language in conveying information to its people. It also characterizes that the Pannei language is a regional language not paid much attention to or marginalized, let alone used by the speaking community.

5. Language and Literacy Teaching Material Availability

To determine the criteria for the Pannei language vitality based on the dimensions/indicators of language and literacy teaching materials availability, of course, it refers to the frequency value of the respondent's answer choices regarding the availability of language and literacy teaching materials by counting the number of 120 respondents, four statement items, and five scales with, the total score are 626. The series of numbers are entered into the following final calculation.

= Score Percentage

= (Total Score: Maximum Score) × 100%

= (626 : 2400) × 100%

= 26.08%

The score of 26.08% stands in the threatened area, with a total score of 62. The ideal score for the indicator is 2400, but the total score obtained is only 626. The numbers series are inserted into the following Continuum Lines 5 and 5a.

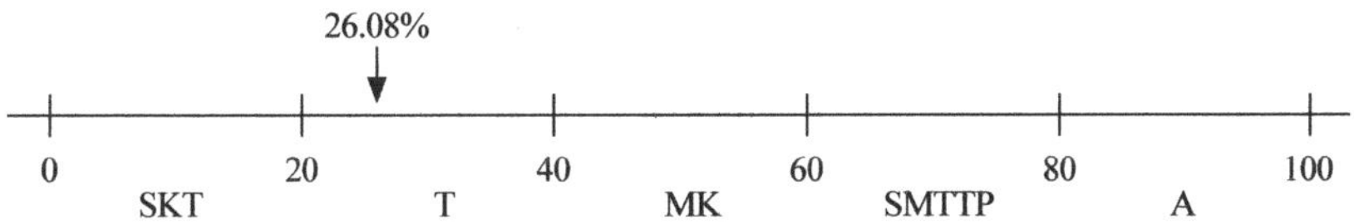

Continuum Line 5: Position and Interpretation of Likert Scale Range on Language and Literacy Teaching Material Availability

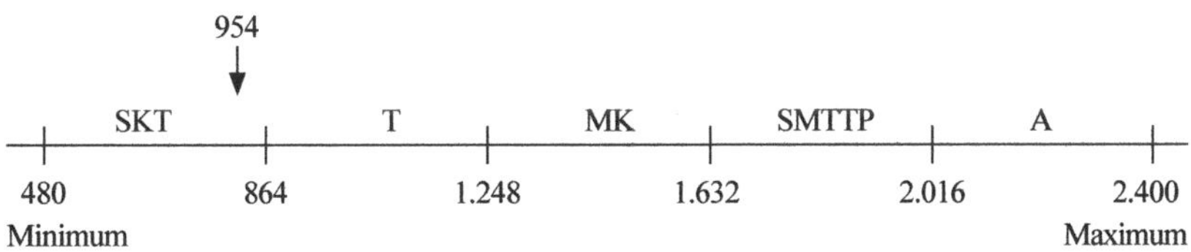

Continuum Line 5a: Position and Interpretation of Likert Scale Range on Indicator of Language Vitality Based on the Availability of Language and Literacy Teaching Resources

Under the total score on Continuum Line 5, adjusted for the total score on Continuum Line 5a, the vitality of the availability of language and literacy teaching materials are classified as critical and threatened. No documentation has been produced from learning materials in the Pannei language. In addition, the need for schoolbooks written in the Pannei language, include of a Pannei script/writing system, inadequate teaching materials for Pannei language learning, and the absence of reading materials contributed to the condition of this language being critical. That is the way; the Pannei language has recently been in a critical and threatening condition. It proves that the Pannei language is not considered an essential language for the Pannei people. The unavailability of documentation in teaching materials indicates that the Pannei language is critical because neither the local government nor the people care about their language anymore. It means that the Pannei language is automatically marginalized by its community.

6. Government Attitude and Regulation

To determine the criteria for the Pannei language vitality based on the dimensions/indicators of the government attitude and regulation, of course, it refers to the frequency value of the respondent's answer choices by counting the number of 120 respondents, nine statement items, and five scales with, the total score are 2592. The series of numbers are entered into the following final calculation.

= Score Percentage

= (Total Score: Maximum Score) × 100%

= (2592: 5400) × 100%

= 48%

The score of 48% occurs in the declining area, with a total score of 2592. The expected ideal score for this indicator is 5,400; however, the total score obtained is only 2592. By the total score gained, government attitude and regulation vitality are classified as decreasing. Here are the continuum lines 6 and 6a.

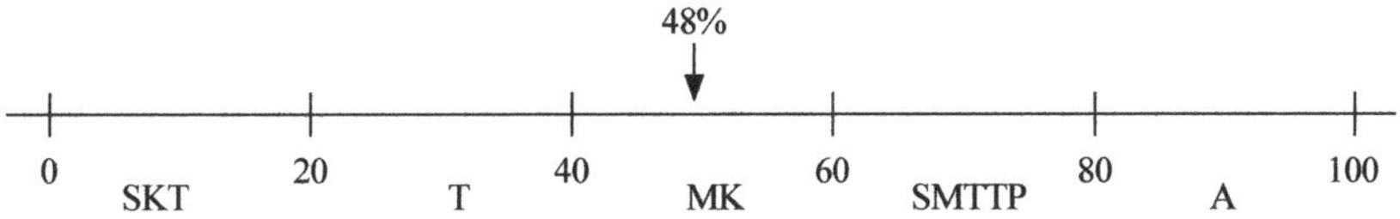

Continuous Line 6: Position and Interpretation of Likert Scale Range Government Attitude and Regulation

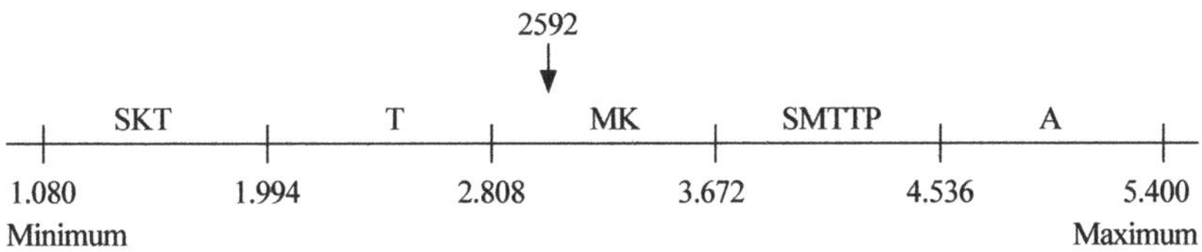

Continuous Line 6a: Position and Interpretation of Likert Scale Range Language Vitality Indicator Based on Government Attitude and Regulation

It is also happening in the indicators of government attitudes and regulations with criteria that have decreased or warning due to the tendency only to make local regulations to protect and not use the Pannei language. The government has never used the Pannei regional language at the district/city level or at the village/sub-district level to appreciate the use of the Pannei regional language. In addition, there are no regional restrictions that restrict the use of the Pannei language, nor are there any regional regulations that mandate the use of the Pannei language on specific days in government and office settings. The government's attitude that pays less attention to the Pannei language in the form of regulations makes it not maintained and gravitate to be marginalized by its users. Nonetheless, they enormously respect the use of the Pannei language and eagerly anticipate its regulation. It means the region's government has good respect and support to arrange the regulation related to the Pannei language maintenance. However, they do not realize the regulation, so this indicator has not provided better results.

7. Speaker's Attitude

To determine the criteria for the Pannei language vitality based on the dimensions/indicators of the speaker's attitude, of course, it refers to the frequency value of the respondent's answer choices by counting the number of 120 respondents, fifteen statement items, and five scales with, the total score are 6759. The series of numbers are entered into the following final calculation.

= Score Percentage

= (Total Score: Maximum Score) × 100%

= (6759 : 9000) × 100%

= 75,1%

The score of 75.1% happens in the stable area but is endangered. The expected ideal score for these items is 9000, and the total score obtained is 6759. By the total score, the vitality of the speaker's attitude is stable and steady but endangered. Here are the continuum lines 7 and 7a.

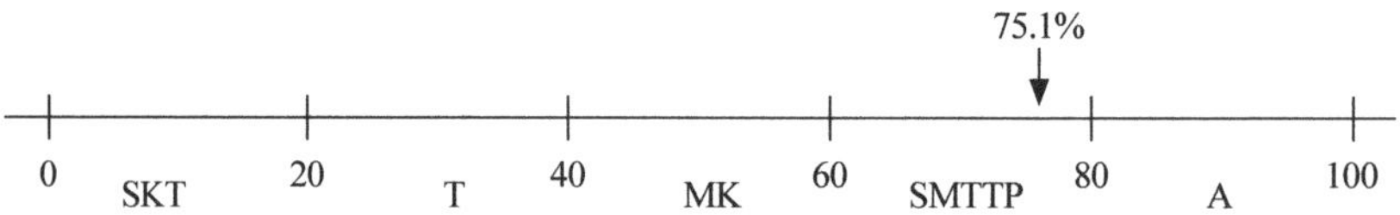

Continuum Line 7: Position and Interpretation of Likert Scale Range Presenter's Attitude

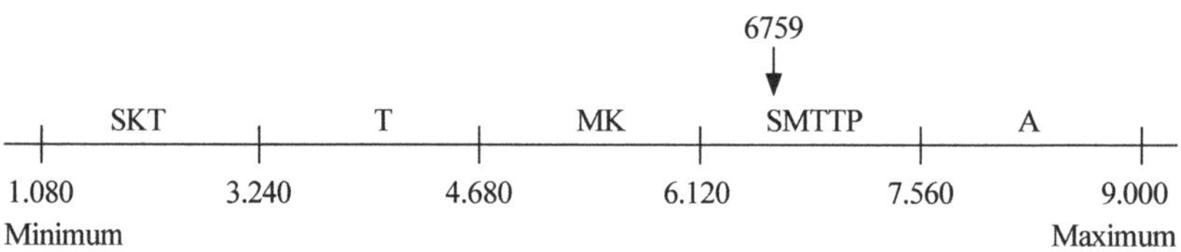

Continuum Line 7a: Position and Interpretation of the Likert Scale Range Based on Language Vitality Indicators of Speakers' Attitude

Another indicator of the Pannei language's vitality is the speakers' attitude. This indicator is stable but threatened with extinction. It is due to the tendency that the Pannei language can demonstrate the identity of the Pannei ethnic area, a means of communication between individuals, families, and communities in the region and that children must master the language. The lexicon of Pannei is more accessible to acquire than that of Indonesian. However, they disagree that Pannei is more advantageous than

Indonesian. They concur and believe that the Pannei language will be able to evolve with the times, and it is significant in the regional context relative to Indonesia. They also endorse that the Pannei language makes it simpler to explain emotions than Indonesian, and they are proud to use the Pannei language. Even though this indicator is categorized as stable, the vitality indicator results for the speaker's attitude are endangered. It means that the Pannei language, on the other hand, believes this language will develop in the future. However, the Pannei language will be seriously threatened if stakeholders and the people themselves do not have a positive attitude toward their language, so the speakers will slowly marginalize this language.

8. Type and Documentation Quality

To determine the criteria for the Pannei language vitality based on the dimensions/indicators of the type and quality of documentation, of course, it refers to the frequency value of the respondent's answer choices by counting the number of 120 respondents, five statement items, and five scales with, the total score are 726. The series of numbers are entered into the following final calculation.

= Score Percentage

= (Total Score: Maximum Score) × 100%

= (726 : 3000) × 100%

= 24,2%

The score of 24.2% falls in the threatened area, with a total score of 726. The expected ideal score for this indicator is 3000. Regarding the total score, the vitality of the type and quality of documentation is classified as critical and threatened. The Continuum Lines are following.

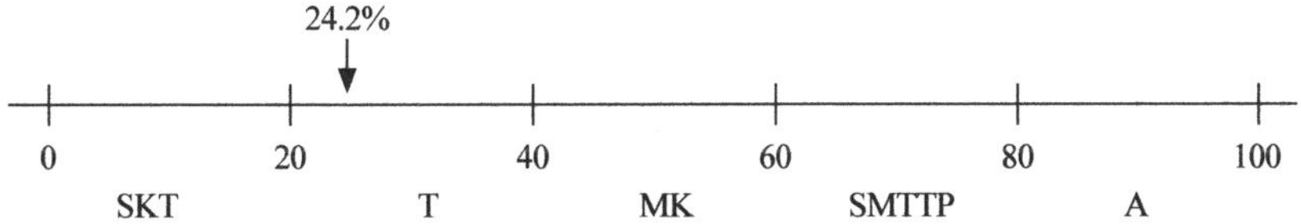

Continuum Line 8: Position and Interpretation of Likert Scale Range Type and Documentation's Quality

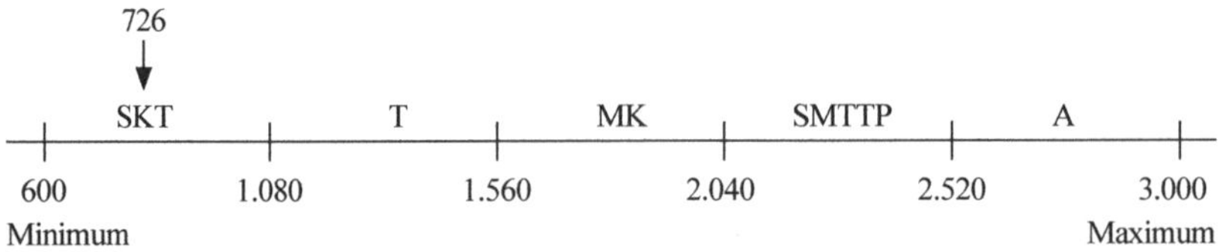

Continuum Line 8a: Position and Interpretation of Likert Scale Range Language Vitality Indicators by Type and Document Quality

In addition, the tendency of the Pannei language to deficiency dictionaries, teaching materials, documentation of sound recordings and pictures/videos, and documentation of grammatical sketches or word lists poses a danger to the indicators of the type and quality of documentation. It corresponds to the criteria for language vitality. In other words, the type and documentation quality of the Pannei language needs to be documented, either written or oral. Its condition causes the Pannei language to be in critical condition and threatened. This condition also hurts the current status of the Pannei language. By looking at such conditions, the Pannei language is indeed marginalized from the presence of other languages used in terms of the type and quality of documentation.

9. Language Contact

To determine the criteria for the Pannei language vitality based on the dimensions/indicators of the language contact, of course, it refers to the frequency value of the respondent's answer choices by counting the number of 120 respondents, six statement items, and five scales with, the total score are 2023. The number series is entered into the following final calculation.

= Score Percentage

= (Total Score: Maximum Score) × 100%

= (2023 : 3600) × 100%

= 56,1%

The score of 56.1% appears in the declining area, with a total score in 2023. However, the expected ideal score for this indicator is 3600. Thus, under the total score, the vitality of language contact is classified as decreasing.

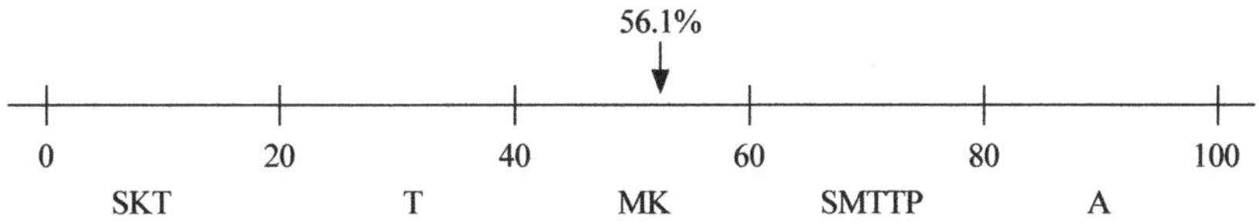

Continuum Line 9: Position and Interpretation of Likert Scale Range towards language contact

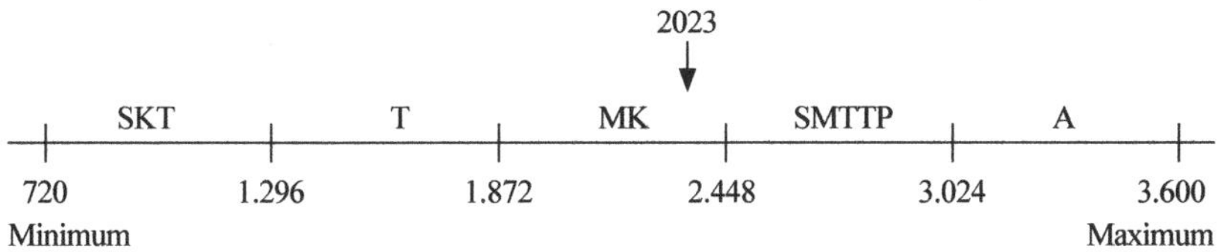

Continuum Line 9a: Position and Interpretation of Likert Scale Range on Indicator of Language Vitality Based on Language Contact

Regarding the Continuum above, the language contact indicator is decreasing based on respondents who have communicated with speakers of other languages. They can easily access other areas in the respondent's village, which pass by four-wheeled vehicles, and respondents have enjoyed mass media broadcasts in other languages. Language interaction happens when several speakers of various languages visit the respondent's village. Language contact can also affect the existence of the Pannei language. The existence of interaction with speakers of other languages allows this language to decrease because there is no concern about continuing to use the Pannei language in the speech area. As a result, the Pannei language became marginalized by the presence of other languages.

10. Bilingualism

To determine the criteria for the Pannei language vitality based on the dimensions/indicators of bilingualism, of course, it also refers to the frequency value of the respondent's answer choices by counting the number of 120 respondents, seven statement items, and five scales with the total score are 2716. The numbers series is entered into the following final calculation.

= Score Percentage

= (Total Score: Maximum Score) × 100%

= (2716 : 4200) × 100%

= 64,6%

The score of 64.6% occurs in the declining area, with a total score of 2716. The ideal score for this indicator is 4200, but the total score obtained only is 2716. Following the total score obtained, the vitality of bilingualism is classified as decreasing.

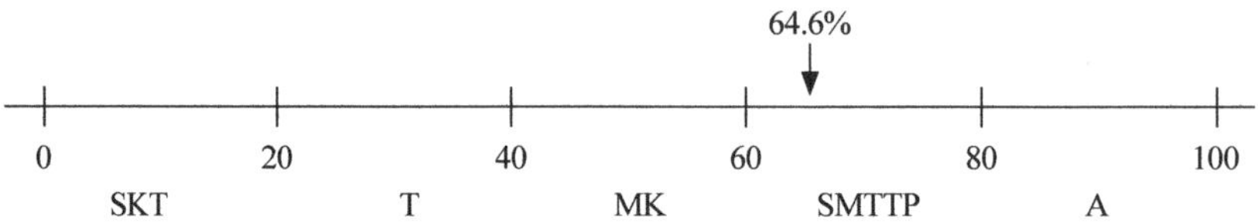

Continuum Line 10: Position and Interpretation of Likert Scale Range on Bilingualism

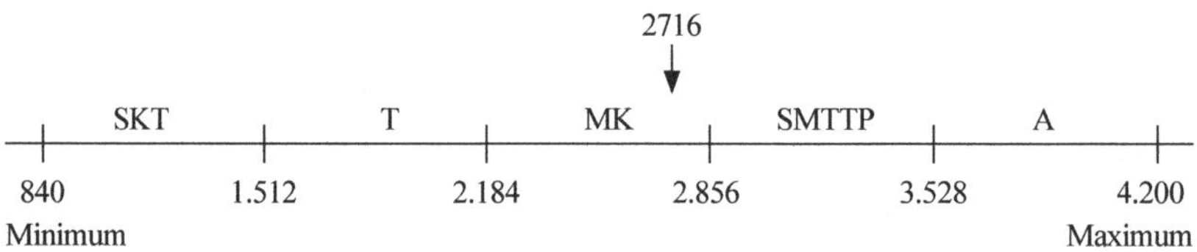

Continuum Line 10a: Position and Interpretation of Likert Scale Range Indicators of Language Vitality Based on Bilingualism

Referring to the Continuum of bilingualism, the Pannei language vitality includes indices of bilingualism based on the tendency to use Pannei and other languages, notably Indonesian and foreign languages, which is decreasing. Respondents often use other regional languages but rarely use Indonesian and foreign languages. However, they understand and can speak Indonesian well but not foreign languages. It meant that the Pannei languages could have done better due to the presence of languages other than the Pannei languages within their territory. The Pannei language is experiencing a shift because of its bilingualism. They are not only able to communicate in the Pannei language, but they also master other languages, such as Indonesian and other regional languages that are close to their area of speech. This bilingualism can trigger the Pannei language to become marginalized in its speech area.

The ten indicators as a criterion for determining the vitality of the Pannei language are still challenging because the ten indicators have different criteria. However, it is possible to determine the vitality of the Pannei language based on the calculation of the total score of each indicator according to the number of statement items for each indicator. The total score of each indicator indicates it is 32,250, which is almost close to the total score of the vitality of the Pannei language simultaneously is 32,786. By dispositioning the total score of all indicators at 32,250 against the interval distance of Continuum Line 11, it turns out that the vitality of the Pannei language has the same criteria for experiencing a decline, as shown in Continuum 11.

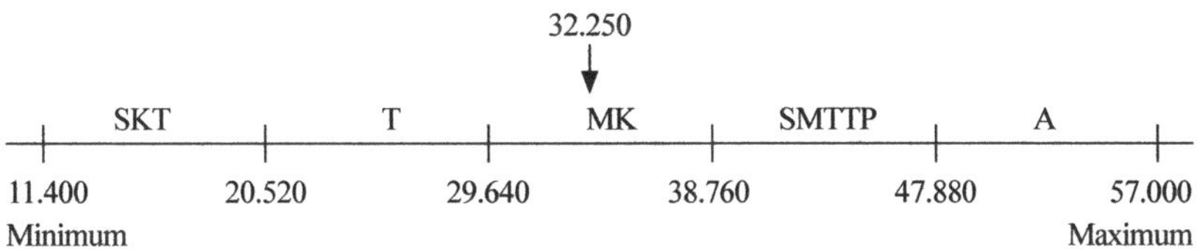

Continuum Line 11:
Position and Interpretation of Likert Scale Range
Based on the Total Value of the 10th Statement Item Frequency Indicator

Pannei language vitality is determined by ten indicators classified into five criteria. The five criteria are endangered, declining, critical and threatened, stable and stable, threatened with extinction, and safe. However, in the end, only four criteria were found. This study did not find one criterion, namely the safe category. That is, the current Pannei language needs to be more secure. The four criteria in the domain and new media, the type and quality of documentation, and available literacy teaching materials are three indicators of critical and threatened vitality.

Furthermore, indicators of the number and proportion of speaking languages are endangered criteria. Meanwhile, indicators of bilingualism, attitudes and government regulations, language use, and language contact, a measure of linguistic vitality, are decreasing criteria. Meanwhile, indicators of language transmission between speakers and speakers' attitudes are stable and consistent but are in danger of extinction. The results of this Continuum show that the Pannei language is in an insecure state and makes this language marginalized by its speakers.

CONCLUSION

To sum up, the Pannei language is currently precarious or unsafe, necessitating more language development or research from various scientific viewpoints. Regarding the result of vitality, the Pannei language is categorized as one of the marginal languages in its community. It occurs because the people in this area seldom use the Pannei language daily. The community avoids using this language even in their family, environment, and school. This way, organizing the Pannei language documentation and utilizing it as a basis for regulations protecting the language as a part of the Pannei community's identity will be possible. These findings relate to the regulation that the Indonesian government had made that the regional languages of Indonesia must be safeguarded, respected, and preserved. As Indonesian citizens, we are all responsible for preserving regional identities, such as local languages. Research on the vitality of regional languages in Indonesia is crucial since it determines a language's future viability and can determine Indonesia's community identity. The most important thing is that the local language can become the host in its speech area. It means that regional languages still exist in their speaking communities and are not marginalized by the presence of other languages in their speech areas.

Measuring the vitality of a language, mainly in marginalized languages such as Pannei, is one of the efforts to preserve regional languages from an early age. In this way, the shift and endangered of the language can be avoided so that it is possible that languages whose position has shifted or endangered, like Pannei, can return to being safe. Thus, the Pannei language has a significant chance of being used by the broader community so that Pannei does not become a language its speakers marginalize. Efforts to promote and preserve marginalized languages include language revitalization programs, community-based language education, language documentation and preservation projects, and technology to support language learning and communication.

References

Agus, N et.al., 2019. (2019). *Laporan Hasil Penelitian Vitalitas Bahasa Limola.*

Andriyanti, E. (2019). Language Shift among Javanese Youth and Their Perception of Local and National Identities. *GEMA Online Journal of Language Studies, 19*(3), 109–125. https://doi.org/10.17576/gema-2019-1903-07

Aritonang, B. (2016). Kriteria Vitalitas Bahasa Talondo. *Ranah: Jurnal Kajian Bahasa, 5*(1), 8. https://doi.org/10.26499/rnh.v5i1.34

Bouchard, M. (2022). *The vitality of Angolar A study of attitudes on São Tomé Island. 1*(March), 160–188.

Bunck, A. C., Baeβler, B., Ritter, C., Kröger, J. R., Persigehl, T., Pinto Santos, D., Steinmetz, M., Niehaus, A., Bamberg, F., Beer, M., Ley, S., Tiemann, K., Beerbaum, P., Maintz, D., & Lotz, J. (2020). Structured Reporting in Cross-Sectional Imaging of the Heart: Reporting Templates for CMR Imaging of Cardiomyopathies (Myocarditis, Dilated Cardiomyopathy, Hypertrophic Cardiomyopathy, Arrhythmogenic Right Ventricular Cardiomyopathy and Siderosis). *RoFo Fortschritte Auf Dem Gebiet Der Rontgenstrahlen Und Der Bildgebenden Verfahren, 192*(1), 27–37. https://doi.org/10.1055/a-0998-4116

Candrasari, R., & Nurmaidah. (2018). *Model Pengukuran Vitalitas Bahasa: Teori dan Aplikasi pada Penelitian Bahasa-Bahasa Nusantara* (Dr. Khalsiah (ed.)). CV. Sefa Bumi Persada.

Casquite, M., & Young, C. (2017). Hearing local voices, creating local content: Participatory approaches in orthography development for non-dominant language communities. *Creating Orthographies for Endangered Languages,* 54–68. https://doi.org/10.1017/9781316562949.003

Chayinska, M., Kende, A., & Wohl, M. J. A. (2022). National identity and beliefs about historical linguicide are associated with support for exclusive language policies among the Ukrainian linguistic majority. *Group Processes and Intergroup Relations, 25*(4), 924–940. https://doi.org/10.1177/1368430220985911

Clément, R., & Norton, B. (2021). Ethnolinguistic Vitality, Identity and Power: Investment in SLA. *Journal of Language and Social Psychology, 40*(1), 154–171. https://doi.org/10.1177/0261927X20966734

Costley, T., Kula, N., & Marten, L. (2022). Translanguaging spaces and multilingual public writing in Zambia: tracing change in the linguistic landscape of Ndola on the Copperbelt. *Journal of Multilingual and Multicultural Development,* 1–21. https://doi.org/10.1080/01434632.2022.2086985

Damanik, J. (2009). *PENGARUH PUPUK HIJAU KRINYU (Chromolaena odorata L.) TERHADAP PERTUMBUHAN DAN PRODUKSI JAGUNG* (Zea mays L.) SKRIPSI.

Ehala, M. (2010). Refining the notion of ethnolinguistic vitality. *International Journal of Multi-*

lingualism, 7(4), 363–378. https://doi.org/10.1080/14790711003637094

Fishman, Joshua, A. (1997). *reversing-language-shift-Josua-Fishman.pdf.* British Library.

Gobbo, F. (2021). Coolification and language vitality: The case of esperanto. *Languages, 6*(2). https://doi.org/10.3390/languages6020093

Grenoble, L. A., & Whaley, L. J. (2005). Saving languages: An introduction to language revitalization. *Saving Languages: An Introduction to Language Revitalization,* 1–231. https://doi.org/10.1017/CBO9780511615931

Grenoble, L. A., & Whaley, L. J. (2021). Toward a new conceptualisation of language revitalisation. *Journal of Multilingual and Multicultural Development, 42*(10), 911–926. https://doi.org/10.1080/01434632.2020.1827645

Hj. Mahali, S. N., Tamby Omar, A., & Mee, W. M. (2022). Domain dan Pemilihan Bahasa Generasi Muda Murut di Daerah Keningau, Sabah (The Domains and Language Choice Among the Young Murut Generation in Keningau District, Sabah). *GEMA Online® Journal of Language Studies, 22*(3), 119–138. https://doi.org/10.17576/gema-2022-2203-07

Julio, N. E., & Tudela-isanta, A. (2022). *Cuadernos Europeos de Deusto Alba Milà-Garcia* (Vol. 04, Issue Julio).

Komondouros, M., & McEntee-Atalianis, L. J. (2007). Language attitudes, shift and the ethnolinguistic vitality of the Greek orthodox community in Istanbul. *Journal of Multilingual and Multicultural Development, 28*(5), 365–384. https://doi.org/10.2167/jmmd483.1

Lewis, M., & Clark, W. (2011). Assessing endangerment: Expanding Fishman's GIDS. *In Travels to the Source of the Missouri River* (Issue April 2010). https://doi.org/10.1017/cbo9780511783364.003

Lewis, M. P., & Simons, G. F. (2011). Ecological Perspectives on Language Endangerment: Applying the Sustainable Use Model for Language Development. *A Colloquium Presented at the Annual Conference of the American Association for Applied Linguistics, March.* http://www-01.sil.org/~simonsg/presentation/Applying the SUM.pdf

Malik, A. (2018). Pengantar Statistika Pendidika: Teori dan Aplikasi. In *PENERBIT DEEPUBLISH.* PENERBIT DEEPUBLISH.

Maricar, F., & Duwila, E. (2017). Vitalitas Bahasa Ternate Di Pulau Ternate. *Etnohistori, IV*(2), 136–151.

Meek, B. A. (2019). Language Endangerment in Childhood. *Annual Review of Anthropology, 48,* 95–115. https://doi.org/10.1146/annurev-Anthro-102317-050041

Meor Osman, W. R., Abdul Wahab, H., Gedat, R., Mustafa, R., Kamil, S. M., Baharudin, R., & Abdullah, S. (2022). Tahap Penggunaan dan Sikap Terhadap Bahasa Kebangsaan di Bandaraya Kuching, Sarawak (A Study on the Standard of National Language Usage in Kuching City, Sarawak). *GEMA Online® Journal of Language Studies, 22*(2), 160–184. https://doi.org/10.17576/gema-2022-2202-09

Nagy, N. (2018). Linguistic attitudes and contact effects in Toronto's heritage languages: A variationist sociolinguistic investigation. *International Journal of Bilingualism, 22*(4), 429–446. https://doi.org/10.1177/1367006918762160

Peng, J., Choo, K. K. R., & Ashman, H. (2016). Bit-level n-gram based forensic authorship analysis on social media: Identifying individuals from linguistic profiles. *Journal of Network and Computer Applications, 70*. https://doi.org/10.1016/j.jnca.2016.04.001

Pivot, B., & Bert, M. (2017). Orthography creation for postvernacular languages: Case studies of Rama and Francoprovençal revitalization. *Creating Orthographies for Endangered Languages,* 276–290. https://doi.org/10.1017/9781316562949.014

Retinskaya, T. I. (2021). Ardennes regiolect: Functioning and vitality evaluation. *Acta Linguistica Petropolitana, 17,* 169–183. https://doi.org/10.30842/alp23065737172169183

Roche, G. (2017). Linguistic vitality, endangerment, and resilience. *Language Documentation and Conservation, 11*(August), 190–223.

Setiawati, E., Ardhian, D., Widodo, W., & Warsiman, N. (2019). Vitalitas Bahasa, Diglosia, Dan Ketirisannya: Pemertahanan Bahasa Manduro Di Desa Manduro, Kecamatan Kabuh, Kabupaten Jombang, Jawa Timur. *Widyaparwa, 47*(2), 116–127. https://doi.org/10.26499/wdprw.v47i2.293

Shulman, J. L., Collins, K. A., & Clément, R. (2011). In Consideration of Social Context: Re-examining the Linguistic Intergroup Bias Paradigm. *Journal of International and Intercultural Communication, 4*(4), 310–332. https://doi.org/10.1080/17513057.2011.595498

Simons, G. F., & Lewis, M. P. (2013). The World's Languages in Crisis: A 20-year Update. *Responses to Language Endangerment: In Honor of Mickey Noonan, October 2011,* 3–20.

Song, J., & Zhu, Y. (2016). Attitude, maintenance, and use of Beijing dialect and Putonghua among younger generation Beijing-born residents. *Journal of Asian Pacific Communication, 26*(1), 32–55. https://doi.org/10.1075/japc.26.1.02son

Soo Ying, H., Swee Heng, C., & Nadzimah Abdullah, A. (2015). Language Vitality of Malaysian Languages and Its Relation to Identity. *GEMA Online ® Journal of Language Studies, 15*(2), 119–136.

Tohar, S. N. A. M., Halim, A. A., & Samsu, K. H. K. (2017). Pengukuran tahap pemartabatan bahasa kebangsaan dalam kalangan mahasiswa institusi pengajian tinggi. *GEMA Online Journal of Language Studies, 17*(2), 105–122. https://doi.org/10.17576/gema-2017-1702-07

Ulfa, M. (2019). Eksistensi Bahasa Daerah di Era Disrupsi. *Stilistika: Jurnal Pendidikan Bahasa Dan Sastra, 12*(2), 197–207. https://doi.org/10.30651/st.v12i2.2948

Windiyani, T. (2012). Instrumen untuk Menjaring Data Interval, Nominal, Ordinal, dan Data tentang Kondisi, Keadaan, Hal Tertentu dan Data untuk Menjaring Variabel Kepribadian. *Jurnal Pendidikan Dasar, 3*(5).

Javanese Song Metaphors in Dongkrek Art as a Reflection of Local Wisdom of the Mejayen Community

Dwi Wahyuni(dwiw006@brin.go.id) | **Ery Agus Kurnianto**(erya002@brin.go.id)
Ahmad Zamzuri(ahmad.zamzuri@brin.go.id) | **Siswanto**(sisw014@brin.go.id)
Agus Sri Danardana(agus150@brin.go.id)
National Research and Innovation Agency, Archaeological, Language and Literature Research Organization

INTRODUCTION

According to Geertz (Rachmawati, 2017), local wisdom is a traditional cultural element rooted in community life. Local wisdom can be grouped into two aspects, namely: (1) abstract in the form of ideas, thoughts, and intellect and (2) concrete in the form of artifacts. This local wisdom can be obtained from generation to generation through various things, one of which is through regional arts. The development of regional arts is certainly motivated by the meaning, function, and culture of the people in the region (Irianto, 2017). Regional arts are passed down to the next generations through traditions. The inheritance must of course adhere to a number of rules, norms, and forms of artistic expression in order to maintain the local wisdom contained therein.

Along with the times, the inheritance of traditions has experienced significant obstacles. According to Pereira (Irianto, 2017), one of the obstacles to the inheritance of traditions in this modern era is the fading of local wisdom that is naturally attached to the community that owns the tradition. Furthermore, if this condition is left unchecked, the extinction of a regional art is inevitable. The most worrying impact of the fading of local wisdom is the emergence of marginalized cultures. Based on the Big Indonesian Dictionary (2016), the definition of marginal is remote; poor. So, marginal culture is a culture that is remote or marginalized. In this research, marginal culture can also be interpreted as a culture that is almost extinct. One example of a marginalized culture is dongkrek art, which is one of the regional arts originating from Mejayan Village, Mejayan District, Madiun Regency, East Java.

The causes of the near extinction of dongkrek art are not much different from the causes of the extinction of other regional arts, namely the lack of public and government attention and the entry of foreign cultures into Indonesia. According to (Wahyuningsih, Prabawati, & Febriary, 2012) dongkrek art was once almost extinct because it only remained in two places in Madiun Regency. However, the emergence of dongkrek art activist associations can save dongkrek from extinction. The problem is that these associations have not yet become permanent organizations. Their performance activities are also still limited due to constraints in procuring dongkrek facilities and equipment. Wahyuningsih, et al. (2012) also added that another obstacle faced by dongkrek art activists is the lack of public appreciation for these art activists. These obstacles are the main cause of dongkrek art becoming marginalized again.

Actually, there have been efforts made to maintain dongkrek art, such as increasing the function of the art. Basically, dongkrek art is a ritual art. However, the addition of entertainment functions is done to attract people, especially the younger generation. The addition of the function of dongkrek art into entertainment art can be seen in the addition of suko pariksuko dance. Initially, in dongkrek art, the song sung was *Sekar Gambuh.* The song is sung at the opening of the dongkrek performance. However, after the addition of the Suko Pariksuko dance, the dancers also sing other songs, such as Ngluri Kabudayan, Rohing Dalu, and dolanan songs. The dolanan songs sung include *Cublak-Cublak Suweng, Buto Galak, Ilir-Ilir, Sluku Bathok, Jamuran,* and *Cenkir Legi* (Margarita, 2022). The selection of these songs is not without reason because the cultural markers attached to dongkrek art are not only found in the dance and music performances, but also the lyrics of the songs sung. The songs were chosen because the lyrics are considered to reflect the local wisdom of the Mejayan community.

The reflection of local wisdom in the songs sung in dongkrek art can be seen from the metaphors in the lyrics. The lyrics contain principles, rules, and advice in life that are dominated by metaphors in conveying the message. Lakoff and Johnson (Wulandari, 2017) explain that metaphors arise due to the limitations of human language so that metaphors are needed to convey unlimited human thoughts. Based on this, this study will identify the metaphors contained in the songs sung in dongkrek art and explain the reflection of local wisdom reflected in the metaphors. The reflection of local wisdom will later act as a characteristic of the Mejayan community and can contribute to the cultural heritage of the archipelago.

The method used in this research is a qualitative method that comes from the text and aims to find out the complexity of the data used as the object of research (Hancock, Ockleford, & Windridge, 2001). The source of the research data is the lyrics of *Sekar Gambuh, Lir Ilir,* and *Cublak-Cublak Suweng* songs sung in dongkrek art. The collected data will be classified based on the content of the songs that contain metaphors. Furthermore, each lyric containing metaphors will be analyzed using Lakoff and Johnson's conceptual metaphor theory and Cruse and Croft's image scheme. The identification of the form of source domain, target domain, and metaphor image scheme using these theories will be used to see the reflection of local wisdom of the Mejayan community as the ultimate goal of this research.

Similar research related to dongkrek art has been conducted by Affandi and Subiyantoro (2018). The study used folklore as the object of research. In addition, the purpose of the study was to determine the first level of meaning using Roland Barthes' semiotic theory. In the results of his research, it is stated that there are cultural values in the form of educational values, morals, leadership, heroism, and aesthetics contained in the art of dongkrek. Another research is a study written by Hanif, et al. (2019) which results in the development of an internalization model of the values contained in dongkrek art. The research is a type of Research and Development (R&D) using the internalization model development procedure which is analyzed for effectiveness using descriptive statistics. To complement these two studies, this research focuses on the reflection of local wisdom contained in the metaphors of the lyrics sung in the art of dongkrek. Thus, in addition to different research objects, this study also uses different methods and approaches in looking at cultural elements in dongkrek art.

DISCUSSION

The discussion in this study will focus on determining the source domain, target domain, and image scheme contained in the lyrics of the songs sung in dongkrek art. There are three songs that will be analyzed, namely songs entitled *Sekar Gambuh, Lir Ilir,* and *Cublak-Cubla Suweng*. The three songs are organized based on knowledge mapping to see the same scheme from the source and target domains. Based on the source and target domains, the conceptual metaphors can be concluded. Furthermore, the conceptual metaphors that have been known can be associated with the local wisdom reflected in them.

1. Sekar Gambuh

Gambuh is one of the macapat songs. According to Wirodono (Margarita, 2022) the word *gambuh* comes from *gampang nambuh*, which is an attitude that shows arrogance because it has power or is also known as a challenging attitude. In addition, gambuh can also mean meeting or finding something after a long search. The search in question can be in the form of identity, ideals, and God. Based on these two meanings, gambuh in dongkrek art is related to the origin of the art. It is told that there was a figure called Eyang Palang who had the courage to challenge the giant who brought the plague to Mejayan Village. In his efforts to expel the giant, Eyang Palang received help from God, which was an answer to the prayers of the people of Mejayan at that time.

Sekar Gambuh is sung by the singer or host at the opening of a dongkrek performance. Sekar Gambuh is sung at the beginning because it contains the history of dongkrek art so that people who watch are expected to know the origin of dongkrek art. In addition to the history of dongkrek art, Sekar Gambuh shows the local wisdom of Mejayan people which is reflected through metaphors in the lyrics. The following is a mapping of metaphors in the lyrics of Sekar Gambuh in the art of dongkrek as a reflection of the local wisdom of the Mejayan community.

Table 1. Metaphorical Mapping of Sekar Gambuh

Data	Source Domain Metaphor		
1.	*Sekar Gambuh amurwani atur* (Tembang Gambuh begins the conversation)		
	Source Domain Tembang Gambuh a. Tembang macapat b. There are stipulations on the number of lines, syllables, etc. Begins a. Getting started b. Precede The conversation a. Conversation b. Performed by two or more people	**Target Domain** Challenge a. Call to war b. Things that need to be addressed Challenging a. Inviting to war b. Against Meeting a. Encounters b. Two or more things come together	**Image Schematic** Identity: matching (The same scheme for one thing as another)
2.	*Priya luhur kang yasa* (A noble man who is powerful)		
	Source Domain A noble man a. Noble man b. Kind c. Respected Powerful a. Possess strength b. Beyond the nature of nature (supernatural)	**Target Domain** Leader a. Guide a group of people b. Giving hints c. Possessing power d. Respected Leadership a. Ability to direct a group of people b. There is power c. There is responsibility	**Image Schematic** Identity: matching (The same scheme for one thing as another)

The conceptual metaphors found in Sekar Gambuh are structural metaphors derived from the mapping between aspects of the source and target domains. The similarity of the conceptual structure between the source and target domains is the existence of an identity element that distinguishes one element from another, which is explained as follows. The source domain of *Sekar Gambuh amurwani atur*, which means that the song gambuh begins the conversation, has the target domain of a challenge to conduct a meeting. The two domains show an identity image scheme with a match subtype that shows the same scheme between *tembang gambuh* and challenge, begins with challenging, and conversation with meeting. As explained earlier, gambuh means challenging attitude so there is a match between gambuh song and challenge. Furthermore, conversation is a concrete form of meeting. The process of conversation in the lyrics is done by starting with tembang gambuh which is a concretization of the meeting carried out by challenging.

Then, the lyrics *priya luhur kang yasa* which means a noble man who is powerful represents a leader who has a leadership spirit. The image scheme in the second data is identity with a match subtype that shows the same scheme between the noble man with the leader and powerful with leadership. The noble man is a concretization of the form of a leader. Powerful is a depiction of the leadership spirit that must be possessed by a leader.

The metaphors described above also explain the realm of life of the Mejayan people. In the analysis, the realms of Mejayan people's lives that are seen are the realm of society and the realm of religion and belief. Metaphors that show the realm of society are seen in the first data, namely in the lyrics of *Sekar Gambuh amurwani atur* which means that the song gambuh begins the conversation. Sekar Gambuh is a Javanese song which is an example of a macapat song. In connection with this, it can be seen that the realm of society shown through the lyrics is the Mejayan community which is part of Javanese society. In addition, there is the realm of religion and belief seen in the second data, namely in the lyrics priya luhur kang yasa which means a noble man who is powerful. The metaphor contained in the lyrics shows that the people of Mejayan have a belief that there are noble, great, or chosen people who have magic or *kanuragan*. It is represented by priya luhur or noble men.

Furthermore, the conceptual metaphors in Sekar Gambuh reflect the local wisdom of the Mejayan community in the form of values, namely chivalry and leadership. According to Kamus Besar Bahasa Indonesia (2016), chivalry is an attitude of bravery. In Sekar Gambuh, this attitude is shown in the lyrics of *Sekar Gambuh amurwani atur*, which means that the song gambuh begins the conversation. As explained earlier, this metaphor represents an encounter that is conducted in a challenging manner. Challenging here can be correlated with courage, which is a reflection of the local wisdom of the Mejayan people who have a brave nature in facing a threat or problem.

Another local wisdom found in Sekar Gambuh is the value of leadership. According to Thoha (Wulandari, 2017) leadership is an activity to influence the behavior of others to be directed to achieve certain goals. The value of leadership in Sekar Gambuh is shown in the lyrics *priya luhur kang yasa* which means a noble man who is powerful. The metaphor contained in the lyrics contains the value of leadership with the noble man as a representation of the leader and sakti as a representation of leadership. Leaders who have a leadership spirit can be correlated with the value of leadership which is a reflection of the local wisdom of the Mejayan community led by a *Palang* (head of village) who has the ability to direct its citizens to certain goals for the common good.

2. Lir Ilir

Tembang Lir Ilir is a Javanese song created by Raden Syahid, later known as Sunan Kalijaga. This song was used by Sunan Kalijaga as one of the media for Islamic propagation (Mukhlasin, 2019). The content of the song Lir Ilir is in the form of advice and messages about life. In addition to advice, in the song Lir Ilir can be seen the local wisdom of the Mejayan community which is reflected through metaphors in the lyrics. The following is a mapping of metaphors in the lyrics of Lir Ilir in dongkrek art as a reflection of the local wisdom of the Mejayan community.

Table 2. Lir Ilir Metaphor Mapping

<table>
<tr><th>Data</th><th colspan="3">Source Domain Metaphor</th></tr>
<tr><td>1.</td><td colspan="3">Ilir-ilir, lir ilir tandure wis sumilir
(Wake up, wake up the plant has bloomed)</td></tr>
<tr><td></td><td>Source Domain
Wake up
a. Standing up (from sitting/sleeping)
b. Awake (from sleep)
c. Awake (from unconsciousness)
Plants
a. Plants that are planted
b. Need water
c. Need fertilizer
d. May be infested with pests
Has bloomed
a. Starting to grow
b. Grow buds/flowers/other plant parts
c. Fertile</td><td>Target Domain
Rise
a. Wake up from laziness
b. Fighting
c. Remember/confess/repent
Human
a. Growing from child to adult
b. Have a need to live
c. Can get down and make mistake
Energized
a. There is a will
b. Emerging power
c. Live well</td><td>Image Schematic
Identity: superimposition
(Two entities of the same type, but each with unique characteristics)</td></tr>
<tr><td>2.</td><td colspan="3">Tak ijo royo-royo taksengguh temanten anyar
(Has turned green like a newlyweds)</td></tr>
<tr><td></td><td>Source Domain
Has turned green
a. Turns green
b. Fertile
c. Dense leafy Newlyweds
a. New status
b. Party</td><td>Target Domain
Improving
a. Change for the better
b. Live well
c. Full of good deeds
New life
a. Start something new
b. There is a spirit
c. Achieving happiness</td><td>Image Schematic
Identity: matching
(The same scheme for one thing as another)</td></tr>
<tr><td>3.</td><td colspan="3">Mumpung padhang rembulane, mumpung jembar kalangane
(While the moon still shines brightly, while there is still plenty of free time)</td></tr>
<tr><td></td><td>Source Domain
Moon
a. Earth's natural satellite
b. Around the earth
c. Seen at night Shine
a. Luminous
b. Emitting light</td><td>Target Domain
Time
a. A time
b. Continues to pass
c. Opportunity, chance, and tempo
Free time
a. Leisure
b. Vacant (still occupiable)</td><td>Image Schematic
Identity: matching
(The same scheme for one thing as another)</td></tr>
</table>

The conceptual metaphor contained in the song Lir Ilir is a structural metaphor obtained from the mapping results between aspects in the source and target domains. The similarity of the conceptual structure between the source and target domains is the existence of an identity element that distinguishes one element from another, which is explained as follows. The source domain of *ilir-ilir, lir ilir tandure wis sumilir* which means wake up, wake up the plant has blossomed has a target domain of rise, rise up humans must be enthusiastic. The two domains show an identity image scheme with a superimposition subtype that shows two entities, namely plants and humans, which are the same type (both living things), but have their own unique characters. Plants have characters, such as needing water, fertilizer, and can be attacked by pests, while humans have characters, such as having various needs for life and can fall down or make mistakes. Furthermore, waking up is a concrete form of rising up and blossoming is a concrete form of being vibrant.

The source domain is *tak ijo royo-royo taksengguh temanten anyar* which means that it has become green like a new bride and groom, while the target domain has improved like having a new life. The image schema in the second data is identity with a match subtype that shows the same schema between has turned green and improving and newlyweds and new life. Has turned green is a concretization of getting better. Newlyweds is a representation of a new life that will begin when someone is willing to change for the better.

The lyrics *mumpung padhang rembulane, mumpung jembar kalangane* mean while the moon is still shining brightly, while there is still plenty of free time. Based on the lyrics, there are source domains, namely the moon and shine, with target domains, namely time and leisure. The image scheme in both domains is identity with a match subtype that shows the same scheme between moon and time and shine and leisure. The moon, which is a celestial body, is a concretization of time (period) which continues to pass as the moon continues to circle the earth. In addition, shining is a concrete form of leisure which explains that as long as the moon is still shining as a representation of as long as time is still free (still exists).

The metaphors described above also explain the realm of Mejayan people's lives. In the analysis, the realm of Mejayan people's lives that can be seen is the economic realm. Metaphors that show the economic realm are seen in the first and second data, namely in the lyrics *ilir-ilir, lir ilir tandure wis sumilir tak ijo royo-royo taksengguh temanten anyar* which means wake up, wake up the plants have blossomed and have turned green like a new bride. Plants that have blossomed and have turned green are representations of rice plants in rice fields. In this regard, it can be seen that the economic domain shown through the lyrics is the livelihood of the Mejayan people, namely as farmers. Margarita (2022) mentioned that the majority of Mejayan people have a livelihood as farmers because the location is in the form of rice fields with soil conditions that are very suitable for food crops, especially rice.

Furthermore, the conceptual metaphor in the song Lir Ilir reflects the local wisdom of the Mejayan community in the form of moral values. According to Kamus Besar Bahasa Indonesia (2016), moral values are teachings about good and bad that are generally accepted regarding actions, attitudes, obligations, and so on. In the song Lir Ilir, this value is shown by the three lyrics in the data in table 2. Based on the explanation of the metaphors in the three data, it can be seen that the representation of moral values is shown by a passionate attitude for a new and better life as long as there is still time or opportunity. This moral value is a reflection of the local wisdom of the Mejayan community which teaches to use time as well as possible in terms of goodness.

3. Cublak-Cublak Suweng

Cublak-Cublak Suweng is one of the traditional songs sung in Dongkrek to accompany the suko pariksuko dancers. This song was created by one of the Walisongo figures, who spread Islam in Java. Like the song Lir Ilir, the song Cublak-Cublak Suweng is also one of the songs used as a medium for da'wah (Ariesta, 2019). This song contains moral values that are closely related to religious teachings and Javanese culture. In addition, there is local wisdom of the Mejayan community that is reflected through metaphors in the lyrics. The following is a mapping of metaphors in the lyrics of Cublak-Cublak Suweng in dongkrek art as a reflection of the local wisdom of the Mejayan community.

Table 3. Metaphorical Mapping of Cublak-Cublak Suweng

<table>
<tr><th>Data</th><th colspan="3">Source Domain Metaphor</th></tr>
<tr><td>1.</td><td colspan="3">Cublak-cublak suweng
(Earring holder)</td></tr>
<tr><td></td><td>Source Domain
Earrings
a. Jewelry
b. Ear-mounted</td><td>Target Domain
Treasure
a. Tangible and intangible assets
b. Owned by someone</td><td>Image Schematic
Identity: superimposition
(Two entities of the same type, but each with unique characteristics)</td></tr>
<tr><td>2.</td><td colspan="3">Suwenge teng gelenter
(Earrings are scattered)</td></tr>
<tr><td></td><td>Source Domain
Earrings
a. Jewelry
b. Ear-mounted Scattered
a. Messy
b. Irregularly located</td><td>Target Domain
Treasure
a. Tangible and intangible assets
b. Owned by someone Everywhere
a. Scattered
b. Available in various places</td><td>Image Schematic
Identity: matching
(The same scheme for one thing as another)</td></tr>
<tr><td>3.</td><td colspan="3">Mambu ketundhung gudel
(The smell addressed by gudel)</td></tr>
<tr><td></td><td>Source Domain
The smell
a. Smell
b. Can be picked up by the sense of smell Addressed
a. Approached
b. Visited
Gudel
a. Buffalo calf</td><td>Target Domain
Lust
a. Desire
b. Resides in the human soul Stupid people
a. No knowledge</td><td>Image Schematic
Identity: matching
(The same scheme for one thing as another)</td></tr>
</table>

The conceptual metaphor found in the song Cublak-Cublak Suweng is a structural metaphor obtained from the mapping between aspects of the source and target domains. The similarity of the conceptual structure between the source and target domains is the existence of an identity element that distinguishes one element from another, which is explained as follows. The source domain of *cublak-cublak suweng*, which means the place of earrings, has a target domain where there is treasure. The two domains show an identity image scheme with a superimposition subtype that shows two entities, namely earrings and treasure, which are of the same type (both valuable), but have their own unique characters. Earrings have characters, such as being a type of jewelry and being attached to the ear, while treasure has characters, such as tangible or intangible wealth and being owned by someone. Furthermore, earrings are a concrete form of treasure. The depiction that the earring is put in the ear is a representation that wealth is owned by someone.

The source domain of *suwenge teng gelenter*, which means that the earrings are scattered, has a target domain of treasure everywhere. The image scheme in the second data is identity with a match subtype that shows the same scheme between earrings and treasure and scattered with everywhere. Earrings are a concretization of the form of treasure, while scattered is a representation that treasure can actually be obtained everywhere or around us.

The lyrics *mambu ketundhung gudel* means the smell of gudel. Based on the lyrics, there are source domains, namely smell, addressed, and gudel, with target domains, namely lust and stupid people. The image scheme in the third data is identity with a match subtype that shows the same scheme between *smell* and *addressed* also *gudel* and stupid people. Smell is a concretization of lust that resides in the human mind. Smell can basically be a fragrant or foul aroma that can be captured by the human sense of smell, but smell is often identified with an unpleasant aroma. The same applies to lust. Lust is a desire, which can be positive or negative. However, the term lust is often identified with something negative. So, smell and lust have the same schema. Furthermore, gudel is a concrete form of stupid people. Gudel means buffalo calf which is also a term for a stupid person. Thus, gudel in the lyrics represents a stupid people who only indulges in lust or desires that are not good.

Furthermore, the conceptual metaphor in the song Cublak-Cublak Suweng reflects the local wisdom of the Mejayan community in the form of the value of self-control. According to Ronen (Wulandari, 2017), self-control is a process that individuals do on the basis of their will and thoughts. In other words, a person can refrain from negative behavior. In the song Cublak-Cublak Suweng, this value is shown by the three lyrics in the data in table 3. Based on the explanation of the metaphors in the three data, it can be seen that the representation of the value of self-control is shown by refraining from the temptation of worldly treasures represented by the lyrics *suwenge teng gelenter* which means that the earrings are scattered. Someone who cannot control themselves is identified with gudel or buffalo children. In Javanese culture, gudel is a term for stupid people. Thus, the value of self-control in the song Cublak-Cublak Suweng is a reflection of the local wisdom of the Mejayan community that teaches to be able to control themselves from indulging in lust or desires that are not good, such as greed, cruelty, and others.

CONCLUSIONS

Dongkrek art is a regional art originating from Mejayan Village, Mejayan District, Madiun Regency which is included in the marginal arts. This art is almost extinct due to the lack of appreciation from the community and government towards art activists and the preservation of the art. In fact, a local art is attached to the local wisdom of the local community which becomes the identity of the community. The local wisdom of the Mejayan community in Dongkrek art is reflected through metaphors in the songs sung in the art. The songs sung include Sekar Gambuh, Ngluri Kabudayan, Rohing Dalu, and dolanan songs. The dolanan songs sung include *Cublak-Cublak Suweng, Buto Galak, Ilir-Ilir, Sluku Bathok, Jamuran,* and *Cenkir Legi*. The reflection of local wisdom contained in these songs acts as a characteristic of the Mejayan community that can contribute to the cultural heritage of the archipelago.

Based on the results of the analysis of the source domain, target domain, and image scheme, it can be concluded that the conceptual metaphor contained in the songs sung in dongkrek art is a structural metaphor. The image schemes found in the songs are identity image schemes with the subtypes of match and superimposition. Based on the metaphor, the realm of Mejayan people's life that is reflected is the realm of society in the form of Gambuh song as a Macapat song which illustrates that Mejayan people are part of Javanese society, the realm of religion and belief in the form of Mejayan people's belief in kanuragan or magic, and the economic realm in the form of Mejayan people's livelihood as farmers. Furthermore, the metaphors in the songs sung in the dongkrek art reflect the local wisdom of the Mejayan community in the form of values, including chivalric values, leadership values, moral values, and self-control values. This local wisdom is inherent in dongkrek art. So, the community and the government must work together to preserve the art of dongkrek because if this art becomes extinct, the local wisdom inherent in it will also disappear.

References

Affandi, A. R., & Subiyantoro, S. (2018). Pemaknaan Tingkat Pertama (Denotatif) Cerita Rakyat Dongkrek di Kabupaten Madiun. *Jurnal Persona, 4*(2), 41-50.

Ariesta, F. W. (2019). Nilai Moral dalam Lirik Dolanan Cublak-Cublak Suweng. *Jurnal Ilmu Budaya, 7*(2), 188-192.

Azhar, F. (2021). *Peribahasa Metaforis Bahasa Mbojo Beranah Air, Api, dan Tanah.* Depok: Universitas Indonesia.

Bahasa, B. P. (2016). *Kamus Besar Bahasa Indonesia.* Retrieved April 7, 2023, from https://kbbi.kemdikbud.go.id/

Hancock, B., Ockleford, E., & Windridge, K. (2001). *An introduction to qualitative research.* Trent focus group.

Hanif, M., Hartono, Y., & Wibowo, A. M. (2019). Pengembangan Model Internalisasi Nilai Kesenian Dongkrek Guna Meningkatkan Ketahanan Budaya Siswa SMA. Gondang: *Jurnal Seni dan Budaya, 3*(2), 134-143. doi:https://doi.org/10.24114/gondang.v3i2.14252

Irianto, A. M. (2017). Kesenian Tradisional sebagai Sarana Strategi Kebudayaan di Tengah Determinasi Teknologi Komunikasi. *Jurnal Nusa, 12*(1), 90-100.

Margarita, A. (2022). *Perubahan Bentuk Kesenian Dongkrek dalam Budaya Masyarakat Desa Mejayan Kabupaten Madiun.* Surakarta: Institut Seni Indonesia.

Mukhlasin, A. (2019). Pendidikan Karakter Pemimpin Melalui Tembang Dolanan (Analisis Tembang Lir Ilir Karya SUnan Kali Jaga). *Jurnal Warna, 3*(1), 41-49.

Rachmawati, D. K. (2017). Kearifan Lokal dalam Leksikon Ritual Kesenian Ogoh-Ogoh di Pura Kerthabumi Dusun Bongso Wetan Desa Pengalangan Kecamatan Menganti Kabupaten Gresik-Jawa Timur. *Parole: Journal of Linguistics and Education, 5*(2), 129-144.

Wahyuningsih, S., Prabawati, S. P., & Febriary, I. (2012). *Revitalisasi Seni Pertunjukan Dongkrek sebagai Upaya Penguatan Identitas Daerah dan Pengembangan Aset Wisata Budaya di Kabupaten Madiun Jawa Timur.* Surakarta: Universitas Negeri Sebelas Maret.

Wulandari, A. (2017). Kearifan Lokal Orang Jawa dalam Metafora Novel Para Priyayi Karya Umar Kayam. *Sasdaya: Gadjah Mada Journal of Humanities, 1*(2), 164-183.

Gugon Tuhon in the Perspective of Generation Z in Wonosobo Regency

Harini(hari052@brin.go.id) | **Kustri Sumiyardana**(kustri.sumiyardana@brin.go.id)
Sriyono(sriy009@brin.go.id) | **Sri Nardiati**(srin008@brin.go.id)
M. Yasif F. Mifthah(muha271@brin.go.id)
National Research and Innovation Agency, Archaeological, Language and Literature Research Organization

INTRODUCTION

Gugon tuhon is advice that contains taboos or prohibitions that are passed down from generation to generation by word of mouth. Gugon tuhon is a Javanese belief that has been passed down from generation to generation. Gugon tuhon is often called superstition (Setiawan, 2019). Javanese people are afraid of receiving bad consequences if the prohibition is violated. Gugon tuhon is one of the Javanese cultures in the form of myths (Dewi & Sugiarti, 2020). However, the myths in gugon tuhon are in the form of virtuous advice that if obeyed will bring goodness. Therefore, gugon tuhon is one of the Javanese cultures that has noble values (Kurniawati & Widhyasmaramurti, 2019). In a study conducted by Budiono, gugon tuhon in Javanese society has the vaclue of love, politeness, health, order, and perfection (Budiono, 2015).

The meaning contained in gugon tuhon is hidden (Khasanah & Ernawati, n.d.). This is probably because children will not understand if the cause-and-effect relationship of a prohibition is clearly explained. For example, when parents forbid children to eat drupes and their seeds, "*Yèn mangan sêmangka, nangka sabrang, sawo bangsanipun kêcik, aja nganti katut isine, mundak thukul ana ngêmbun-êmbunan.*" The meaning of the sentence is that if you eat watermelon, soursop, and sawo, such as little sawo, don't eat the seeds, they will grow on your head. The point of the gugon tuhon is to advise children to be careful when eating fruits with seeds. The seeds should not be swallowed because they can choke or cause digestive problems. However, young children cannot understand if explained about the dangers of choking or indigestion. Therefore, something that is easily understood by children is chosen, namely that the seeds will grow in the fontanel.

Another example of gugon tuhon is as follows. "*Yen mangan aja karo ngadek, mengko ndak wetenge dawa*", meaning that if you eat not while standing, your stomach will become long. After being given such advice, children will rethink eating while standing because the advice also mentions the consequences (Dwiguna, 2017). Furthermore, Dwiguna explained that the real meaning of the gugon tuhon is that eating while standing will cause the food being eaten to fall to the floor, either because it is nudged by someone else or because the hand grip is not strong enough. In addition, Javanese people consider eating while standing as an impolite behavior. In terms of health, eating while standing can also lead to a distended stomach because it eats more. This distended stomach is what is meant by a long stomach in the gugon tuhon above.

Javanese society uses gugon tuhon as a method of teaching manners and ethics to children or the younger generation. Usually, gugon tuhon is taught by grandparents to their grandchildren or fathers and mothers to their children. They consider giving advice in the form of gugon tuhon as part of their role as parents. Gugon tuhon is not only given as a theory, but is taught directly to children when they make a mistake. For example, if a child sits in front of the door, and her grandmother sees it, her grandmother will immediately say, *"Aja njagong nang ngarep lawang, mengko ndak ora sida diusamar"*. So gugon tuhon is not given by parents to their children in a formal method, but informally and taught directly in practice. This makes gugon tuhon an effective way for parents in Java to teach ethics to their children.

However, the changing conditions of the world make human attitudes also change. This change can usually be seen in each generation. Generation is a term to refer to a group of people who were born in the same time span. Each generation has different characters and perspectives on things. Generational groups can be used as a tool to analyze changes in views over time, such as formative experiences, people's views of the world, how people deal with problems, and also how people interact with the life cycle and aging (Dimock, 2019). If in previous generations gugon tuhon was still fully believed, it would certainly be different from the current generations. The more advanced the world becomes, the more the human mindset changes. Modern humans are required to think logically, realistically and rationally. Nowadays, many children consider gugon tuhon as a mere threat because it is irrational. In fact, according to some Javanese people today, believing in gugon tuhon is considered a setback (Budiono, 2015). People who believe in gugon tuhon are considered backward because they believe in things that cannot be accepted by common sense. This is especially true for children born in the age of technology, such as Generation Z.

Generation Z or commonly referred to as GenZ are children who are still growing and developing. This generation is also called the post-millennial generation. They are the most diverse generation and can master technology very well because from birth they have been side by side with technology. GenZ is characterized as impatient, individualistic, independent, highly demanding, materialistic, and recognize themselves as realistic and flexible (Dreyer & Stojanová, 2023).

According to some demographers and researchers, the earliest start of this generation's birth span was in 1991 and the latest in 2004 (Giachino et al., 2023). However, experts have different opinions regarding the birth span of GenZ. According to the Pew Research Center, there is no definitive threshold for determining the age range of generations after the Boomers (Dimock, 2019). However, Dimock classifies the age range for GenZ as people born between 1995 and 2012. This age range is also used by researchers in Indonesia to refer to genZ in Indonesia (Nadila, 2022).

This research wants to examine the views of GenZ in Wonosobo, a city far from Yogyakarta which is the center of Javanese civilization, towards gugon tuhon. From this research, it can also be seen what gugon tuhon is still known in Wonosobo Regency, as well as the percentage of understanding, belief, and implementation of gugon tuhon by GenZ in Wonosobo Regency.

Gugon tuhon comes from two words, gugon (from the root word gugu affixed with -an) and tuhon (from the root word tuhu affixed with -an). According to the Baoesastra Djawa Dictionary (Porwadarminta, 1939), 'gugu' means miturut marang pitutur (to believe in advice), while 'tuhu' means real, temen (to do carefully). If seen from the word-for-word meaning, gugon tuhon means believing in a piece of advice and taking that advice seriously.

Gugon tuhon is divided into three types, namely gugon tuhon kang salugu, gugon tuhon that contains wasita sinandhi, and gugon tuhon that includes wewaler (prohibition) or pepecuh (Padmosoekotjo, 2009). Gugon tuhon kang salugu is gugon tuhon that is as it is. Usually, gugon tuhon salugu comes from fairy tales. For example, *"Yen turu wayah maghrib, mengko dipangan bethara kalla"* which means 'if you sleep at maghrib time, you will be eaten by Bethara Kalla'. Bethara kalla is an evil giant in Javanese fairy tales. The advice contains a prohibition against sleeping at maghrib time. Maghrib time is the time when Muslims pray maghrib. If you sleep at maghrib time you will miss the maghrib prayer. Therefore, parents forbid sleeping at maghrib time. Gugon tuhon wasita sinandhi is advice whose essence is kept secret. The advice is not given openly but is hidden and replaced with words that contain threats. An example of gugon tuhon salugu is *"Aja ngidoni sumur, mundhak lambene suwing"*. This means, don't spit into the well, you'll end up with a cleft lip". The essence of the advice is that people should not spit into the well because the well is a source of water that is used by residents for their daily needs, including ablutions, bathing, cooking needs, washing, and others. It would be inappropriate if the water used for food and hygiene by the villagers was polluted with saliva. From a health perspective, saliva that enters the well can contaminate the water with bacteria. As is known, saliva is a source of transmission of various diseases. Finally, gugon tuhon wewaler, which is gugon tuhon that contains a prohibition or taboo on doing something. For example, *'Ora kena ngundhuh mantu pas nas'e wong tua'*. The gugon tuhon forbids the marriage of a child on the day of his or her parents' death. For example, if a parent dies on Saturday Wage (Javanese calendar), then the person should not marry their child on Saturday Wage. The advice is actually so that people always remember their parents, even though they have died. So if you want to hold a celebration or have fun, don't do it on the day of your parents' death.

Every utterance contained in gugon tuhon contains good advice so that there is meaning from each utterance. The meaning in gugon tuhon speech will be analyzed using pragmatics theory according to Levinson (1983). According to Levinson, to know the meaning of utterances spoken by speakers, we must know the meaning of words and grammatical relationships between words and also draw conclusions that will be the link between what is said and what is assumed (Levinson, 1983). Speakers also have a purpose when telling gugon tuhon to their speech partners. The intention of the speaker to say an utterance is called an illocutionary speech act. The expected effect of speech in gugon tuhon is called perlocutionary speech acts (Saifudin, 2019).

This research uses descriptive qualitative research methods. The subject of this research is GenZ in Wonosobo Regency, namely children born from 1995 to 2013. The respondents of this research amounted to 224 people. The data of this research are 10 gugon tuhon sayings obtained from the website www.sastra.org as a reference source. This website was chosen because it contains complete Javanese language and culture and is widely used as a reference by researchers and the public in finding references about Javanese language or culture. This website is managed by Yayasan Sastra Lestari. Ten gugon tuhon data were analyzed using Levinson's (1983) pragmatic theory to determine their meaning. Generation Z's views on gugon tuhon will be analyzed from the questionnaire results. The questionnaire consists of two parts. The first part contains the respondent's personal data to obtain factual data about the respondent's background. The second part contains a list of questions regarding the understanding of gugon tuhon, namely: whether they have heard it, whether they understand what it means, whether they believe it, whether they do it, who said it, and the reason for doing it. The questionnaire was distributed online using google form to shorten the time and make it easier for respondents to fill in the data because it can be done anytime and anywhere.

DISCUSSION

Based on the results of data analysis, it can be explained that of the 224 respondents selected, 55.4% were female and 44.6% were male. Most of the respondents were the first child with a total percentage of 42.5%, followed by the second child with 33.6%. Fathers' occupations were mostly farmers and mothers' occupations were mostly housewives. Most respondents were still in school and unmarried. They live with their nuclear family, namely their parents and brothers or sisters.

Of the 224 respondents, 94.6% use Javanese for daily communication at home, and the rest use Indonesian. They also use Javanese when communicating with friends at school. However, when communicating with teachers most respondents used Indonesian.

GenZ in Wonosobo Regency's Perception of Gugon Tuhon

Looking at the theory of speech acts according to Austin (1962), there are illocutionary and perlocutionary speech acts in the 10 gugon tuhon in this study. The utterances in gugon tuhon are illocutionary speech acts because they are not only a statement of prohibition but also expect the speech partner to stop doing the prohibited thing. Gugon tuhon is usually spoken by speakers when they see their partners doing things that are prohibited according to gugon tuhon. Therefore, the intention of the speech is to tell the speech partner to do something according to what is contained in the gugon tuhon. The speech in gugon tuhon also contains perlocutionary speech acts. The existence of a cause-and-effect relationship in gugon tuhon can give influence to the speech partner so that he will think again to do it. Furthermore, the speech partner will decide to obey this prohibition or ignore it. To be able to know the meaning in gugon tuhon, it needs to be described pragmatically.

Furthermore, the results of the questionnaire will be displayed in the form of a table containing indicators of listening, understanding, believing, and doing. The hearing indicator is used to see the existence of gugon tuhon in Wonosobo Regency. The more people who have heard a gugon tuhon indicates the stronger the existence of the gugon tuhon in Wonosobo Regency. The understand indicator is used to find out how many respondents understand the meaning of gugon tuhon. The believe indicator is used to see how many respondents believe the cause-and-effect relationship in gugon tuhon. The do indicator is used to see how many respondents want to obey and carry out gugon tuhon. After that, the reasons why respondents perform gugon tuhon and who are the informants who tell gugon tuhon to respondents will be elaborated.

1. Aja njagongi bantal, mengko ndak wudunen

'Don't sit on the pillow, you'll get boils',

The Gugon tuhon 'aja njagongi bantal, mengko ndak wudunen' can be understood as follows.

The word *'njagongi bantal'* refers to the act of sitting on a pillow and the word *'wudunen'* refers to an illness, namely boils. The meaning of the gugon tuhon is a prohibition not to sit on a pillow because pillows contain bacteria that if attached to the skin can cause skin diseases, such as boils. Pillows harbor a lot of bacteria because when people fall asleep on pillows, they sometimes drool. This drool or saliva makes the pillow a hotbed of bacteria. In addition, there are times when people who have traveled will feel hot and tired and sleep using a pillow. Eventually the pillow will contain many bacteria that can cause skin diseases.

In addition, the pillow is a place to support the head. In Javanese society, the head is something that is honored. Javanese people will get angry if their head is held, especially by a younger person, because it is considered disrespectful. Duduk is the activity of placing the buttocks in a place. Sitting on a pillow means putting the buttocks on top of the head. Meanwhile, the butt is a part of the body that is considered inappropriate and has a negative impression for Javanese people. Therefore, placing the buttocks in the place of the head is impolite and unethical so that sitting on a pillow is prohibited.

The following are the results of the analysis of the views of genZ in Wonosobo Regency on the gugon tuhon.

Table 1. Njagongi Bantal

Indicator	Number (%)
Heard	99.1
Understand	92
Believe	51.1
Implement	87.9

Based on table 1 above, it can be seen that almost all GenZ in Wonosobo have heard of gugon tuhon njagongi bantal. This can be seen in the number of percentages that reached 99.1%. Most of them, 92%, understand the gugon tuhon. However, only a few believed in the gugon tuhon. Only half of the respondents believed in the gugon tuhon, 51.1%. Even so, there are still quite a lot of people who practice this gugon tuhon. As many as 87.9% of the total respondents practiced the gugon tuhon. As many as 70.1% of the respondents answered that the reason they keep doing it is because they know that the actions prohibited in the gugon tuhon are not good. A total of 35.3% do it because they are afraid that it will actually happen, 8.5% of respondents do it because they are afraid of the person who said the gugon tuhon, and the rest for other reasons. This means that the gugon tuhon 'njagongi bantal' still exists in Wonosobo Regency, as evidenced by the number of GenZ in Wonosobo who have heard the gugon tuhon. They understand it well, but some of them do not believe in the gugon tuhon. This means that the reasons contained in the gugon tuhon cannot be accepted by their minds.

Looking at who told the gugon tuhon 'njagongi bantal', 35.3% answered that they heard the gugon tuhon from their mother, 33.9% from their grandmother, and the rest from others, meaning that mothers and grandmothers are the people who most often teach the gugon tuhon.

2. Yen madhang ora dientekake, mengko pitike mati

'If you don't finish eating, the chicken will die'

The Gugon tuhon *'Yen madhang ora dientekake, mengko pitike mati'* can be understood as follows.

The word *'madhang ora dientekake'* refers to the act of taking too much food and not being able to finish it. The word *'pitike mati'* refers to the death of the pet chicken so that it no longer has chickens. The meaning of the gugon tuhon is the prohibition not to take food excessively so as not to waste it. Wasting food is the same as wasting fortune. Javanese people believe that people who waste the fortune that has been given by God will find it difficult to get fortune. In this case, the death of a pet chicken is considered a loss of fortune. Chickens are Javanese pets that are usually fed from household leftovers. The existence of chickens is very valuable for Javanese people, especially in ancient times, because they can be sold or slaughtered for side dishes.

The following are the results of the analysis of GenZ in Wonosobo Regency's understanding of the gugon tuhon *'madhang ora dientekake'*.

Table 2. Madhang Ora Dientekake

Indicator	Number (%)
Heard	71.4
Understand	64.3
Believe	32.6
Implement	61.2

Based on table 2 above, it can be seen that almost all GenZ in Wonosobo have heard gugon tuhon *'madhang ora diientekake'*. This indicates that the gugon tuhon is still widely circulated in Wonosobo. This can be seen in the total percentage which reached 96.9%. Most respondents, 84.4%, said they understood the gugon but did not believe in it. This means that the reasons contained in the gugon tuhon cannot be accepted by their minds. Even so, there are still quite a lot of people who practice this gugon tuhon. A total of 82.1% of respondents practiced this gugon tuhon. However, even though they do not believe in it, they still practice the gugon tuhon. A total of 67% of respondents answered that the reason they still carry it out is because they know that the actions prohibited in the gugon tuhon are indeed not good. A total of 21% did it because they were afraid it would actually happen, 6.7% of respondents did it because they were afraid of the person who said the gugon tuhon, and the rest answered for other reasons.

Looking at who said the gugon tuhon 'madhang ora dientekake, 44.6% answered that they heard the gugon tuhon from their mother, 30.8% from their grandmother, 7.1% from their father, and the rest from others, meaning that mothers and grandmothers are the people who most often teach the gugon tuhon. In this gugon tuhon, quite a lot of respondents heard it from their fathers. This is because this gugon tuhon is related to pet chickens. Usually the person who takes care of pet chickens is the father, so it is natural that fathers take an active role in telling the gugon tuhon madhang ora dientekake to their children compared to other gugon tuhon.

3. Aja njagong nang tengah lawang, mengko ndak ora sida dilamar

'Don't sit in front of the door or you won't get proposed to'

The Gugon tuhon *'Aja njagong nang tengah lawang, mengko ndak ora sida dilamar'* can be understood as follows.

The word *'njagong nang tengah lawang'* refers to the act of sitting in front of an open door and the word *'ora sida dilamar'* refers to a failure because people do not come to propose. The meaning of the gugon tuhon is the prohibition not to sit in front of the door because it prevents people from entering the house. The door is the place where people go out or enter the house. If someone sits in front of the door, it will interfere with the mobility of people who will pass through the door.

The following are the results of the analysis of GenZ in Wonosobo Regency's understanding of the gugon tuhon *'njagong nang tengah lawang'*.

Tabel 3. Njagong Nang Tengah Lawang

Indicator	Number (%)
Heard	71.4
Understand	64.3
Believe	32.6
Implement	61.2

Based on the table above, it can be seen that most GenZ in Wonosobo have heard gugon tuhon 'madhang ora diientekake'. This can be seen in the number of percentages that reached 71.4%. This means that this gugon tuhon is circulating in Wonosobo Regency. Not only had they heard of it, 64.3% of them also understood it. However, most did not believe in the gugon tuhon and only 32.6% believed in it. This means that the reasons contained in the gugon tuhon cannot be accepted by their minds. Even so, there are still quite a lot of people who practice this gugon tuhon. A total of 61.2% of respondents practiced this gugon tuhon. A total of 48.7% of respondents answered that the reason they keep doing it is because they know that the actions prohibited in the gugon tuhon are not good. As many as 29.6% do it because they are afraid that it will actually happen, 6.7% of respondents do it because they are afraid of the person who said the gugon tuhon, and the rest answered for other reasons.

Seen from who said the gugon tuhon 'njagong nang tengah lawang', 27.2% answered that they heard the gugon tuhon from their grandmother, 22.8% from their grandmother, 8.9% from their father, and the rest from others, meaning that mothers and grandmothers are the people who most often teach the gugon tuhon, followed by father or father.

4. Yen nyapu ora resik, mengko bojone godhegen

'If you don't sweep cleanly, you'll get a husband with sideburns/feathers'

The Gugon tuhon *'Yen nyapu ora resik, mengko bojone godhegen'* can be understood as follows.

The word *'nyapu ora resik'* refers to the act of cleaning the floor using a broom but there is still trash left behind. Meanwhile, the word *'bojone godhegen'* refers to a husband whose face is full of sideburns so that it looks unclean. In ancient times, Javanese people considered a man whose face was full of sideburns as someone who did not keep clean. The meaning of the gugon tuhon is the suggestion to do something seriously so that what is done is not in vain. If sweeping is not done seriously the floor will remain dirty so that what has been done is in vain. Women who do not sweep cleanly are also considered unable to maintain cleanliness. A clean man does not want to marry a woman who cannot maintain cleanliness. Therefore, in the gugon tuhon it is said that a woman who does not sweep cleanly will get a husband who is not clean either.

The following are the results of the analysis of GenZ in Wonosobo Regency's understanding of the gugon tuhon *'nyapu ora resik'.*

Table 4. Nyapu Ora Resik

Indicator	Number (%)
Heard	88.8
Understand	77.2
Believe	36.2
Implement	83

Based on the table above, it can be seen that most of the GenZ in Wonosobo have heard gugon tuhon nyapu ora resik. This can be seen in the number of percentages which reached 88.8%. This means that the gugon tuhon is circulating in Wonosobo Regency. Not only have they heard, 77.2% of them also understand or comprehend this gugon tuhon. However, genZ in Wonosobo did not believe in the gugon tuhon and only 36.2% believed in it. This is because the consequences in the gugon tuhon cannot be accepted by their minds. Even so, there are still quite a lot of people who carry out this gugon tuhon. A total of 61.2% of respondents practiced this gugon tuhon. Most of them answered that the reason they keep doing it is because they know that the actions prohibited in the gugon tuhon are not good. As many as 30.8% did it because they were afraid it would actually happen, 10.3% of respondents did it because they were afraid of the person who said the gugon tuhon, and the rest answered for other reasons.

Seen from who said the gugon tuhon, 37.5% answered that they heard the gugon tuhon from their mother, 19.6% from their grandmother, and the rest from others, meaning that mothers and grandmothers are the people who most often teach the gugon tuhon.

5. Aja cok sangga uwang (sanggawang), mengko ndak nyangga wirang

'Don't sit on your chin, you'll get embarrassed'

The Gugon tuhon *'aja cok sangga uwang, mengko ndak nyangga wirang'* can be understood as follows.

The word *'sangga uwang/sanggawang'* refers to the act of sitting relaxed while resting one's chin on one's hand, while the word 'nyangga wirang' refers to a situation that makes one embarrassed. People who like to rest their chins on their hands or daydream indicate that they are lazy. This is contrary to the hardworking character of Javanese people. People who are lazy and do not want to work will not get fortune so that their lives will be difficult. People who do not want to work so that they cannot live a decent life like others will be scorned by others. This will make the person embarrassed because they are the subject of public gossip.

The following are the results of the analysis of GenZ understanding in Wonosobo Regency of the gugon tuhon *'sangga uwang'*.

Table 5. Sangga Uwang (Sanggawang)

Indikator	Jumlah (%)
Dengar	56.7
Paham/Mengerti	42.4
Percaya	33
Melaksanakan	46.9

Based on the table above, it can be seen that some GenZ in Wonosobo have heard of gugon tuhon sangga uwang. This can be seen in the number of percentages which reached 56.7%. Most of them do not understand the meaning of gugon tuhon and also do not believe in it. 39.7% do it because they know that sangga uwang is a bad thing to do, 23.7% do it because they are afraid it will actually happen, and 11.6% do it because they are afraid of the person who said the gugon tuhon.

Looking at who told the gugon tuhon 'sangga uwang', 18.7% answered that they heard the gugon tuhon from their grandmother, 17% from their mother, 9.8% from their grandfather, and the rest from others, meaning that mothers and grandmothers are the people who most often teach the gugon tuhon, followed by grandfathers.

6. Aja adus lebar ashar, mengko ndak mati tanggung

'Don't bathe after asr or you'll die in middle age'

The Gugon tuhon *'Aja adus lebar ashar, mengko ndak mati tanggung'* can be understood as follows.

The word *'adus lebar ashar'* refers to an act of bathing done in the afternoon, which is marked by the asr prayer time. The word *'mati tanggung'* refers to a situation where a person dies in middle age. *'Tanggung'* means halfway. *'Mati tanggung'* means dying at an age that is not young but not old either or is called middle age. At this age, people are usually having fun living life. At middle age, the human economy is just starting to settle, already has children who are still cute, and life is starting to stabilize. The meaning of the gugon tuhon is the advice to bathe before the afternoon, let alone the night because it is not good for health and can cause death. According to some research, bathing in the afternoon will bring disease.

The following are the results of the analysis of GenZ's understanding of the gugon tuhon *'adus lebar ashar'* in Wonosobo Regency.

Table 6. Adus Lebar Ashar

Indicator	Number (%)
Heard	51.8
Understand	44.6
Believe	26.3
Implement	34.8

Based on the table above, it can be seen that some GenZ in Wonosobo have heard gugon tuhon adus lebar ashar. This can be seen in the number of percentages that reached 51.8%. Most of them do not understand the meaning of the gugon tuhon, do not believe in it, and do not carry out the gugon tuhon. Only 37.5% of respondents do it because they know that wide asr adus is a bad thing to do, 25.9% do it because they are afraid it will really happen, and 8.5% do it because they are afraid of the person who said the gugon tuhon. This means that the gugon tuhon is difficult to understand and the reasons contained in the gugon tuhon cannot be accepted by their minds.

In terms of who told them the gugon tuhon *'adus lebar ashar'*, 19.6% said they heard the gugon tuhon from their grandmother, 15.2% from their mother, 8.9% from their neighbor, and the rest from others. This means that grandmothers and mothers are the people who most often teach the gugon tuhon, followed by neighbors.

7. Aja mangan iwak tlampik, mengko ndak ditampik wong lanang/wong wedok

Do not eat the tlampikan part of the chicken or the tip of the wing, it will be rejected by a boy/girl.

The Gugon tuhon *'Aja mangan iwak tlampik, mengko ndak ditampik wong lanang/wong wedok'* can be understood as follows.

The word *'mangan iwak tlampik'* refers to the act of eating the end of a chicken wing. This part contains only bones and skin. The words *'ditampik wong lanang/wong wedok'* refer to a rejection by the opposite sex. The meaning of the gugon tuhon is the prohibition to eat the tip of the chicken wing because this part has no meat, only bones and skin. If you insist on eating the tlampik part, it is feared that you will choke because of its small size and hard and sharp texture. In addition, eating the tlampik part of the chicken will be considered greedy because it eats chicken to parts that are not suitable for human consumption. Greedy people are certainly not liked by others, especially by partners. Therefore, in the gugon tuhon it is said that people who eat the tlampik part of the chicken will be rejected by the man or woman they love because their loved ones will not like their gluttony.

The following are the results of the analysis of GenZ's understanding of the gugon tuhon *'mangan iwak tlampik'* in Wonosobo Regency.

Table 7. Mangan Iwak Tlampik

Indicator	Number (%)
Heard	54
Understand	42
Believe	32.1
Implement	47.8

Based on the table above, it can be seen that some GenZ in Wonosobo have heard the gugon tuhon 'mangan iwak tlampik'. This can be seen in the number of percentages that reached 54%. Most of them do not understand the meaning of the gugon tuhon and also do not believe in it but still carry out the gugon tuhon. Based on the results of the questionnaire, 29.9% of GenZ in Wonosobo carry out the gugon tuhon because they know that mangan iwak tlampik is a bad thing, 32.6% do it because they are afraid it will really happen, and 9.8% do it because they are afraid of the person who said the gugon tuhon.

Looking at who told the gugon tuhon 'mangan iwak tlampik', 22.3% answered that they heard the gugon tuhon from their mother, 20.1% from their grandmother, 7.6% from their father, and the rest from others. This means that mothers and grandmothers are the people who most often teach the gugon tuhon, followed by fathers.

8. Aja mangan iwak brutu, mengko ndak getun mburi

'Do not eat the brutu/butt part of the chicken, you will regret it later'.

The Gugon Tuhon *'aja mangan iwak brutu, ndak getun mburi'* can be understood as follows.

The word *'mangan iwak brutu'* refers to the act of eating chicken by the buttocks. The word *'getun mburi'* if interpreted literally means regret in hindsight. This word refers to the condition of a person who experiences a regret for the actions he has taken. The meaning of the gugon tuhon is the prohibition to eat chicken buttocks because it is not good for health. Chicken butt is the part of the chicken that has a high fat content because this part only contains skin, fat, and young bones. The fat in this part can cause various diseases, such as cholesterol. The disease will not come immediately after we eat it. However, if we often eat this part of the chicken, over time the effect will be felt and the body will become sick. After experiencing illness, people will only regret eating unhealthy foods. Regret is useless if you are already sick.

The following are the results of the analysis of GenZ's understanding of the gugon tuhon *'mangan iwak brutu'* in Wonosobo Regency.

Table 8. Mangan iwak brutu

Indicator	Number (%)
Heard	65.6
Understand	52.2
Believe	40.2
Implement	55.8

Based on the table above, it can be seen that most of the GenZ in Wonosobo have heard the gugon tuhon *'mangan iwak brutu'*. This can be seen in the number of percentages that reached 65.6%. Some of them do not understand the meaning of the gugon tuhon and also do not believe in it. Compared to the other gugon tuhon, the gugon tuhon *'mangan iwak brutu'* has a higher percentage of belief. 55.8% of respondents still carry out the gugon tuhon even though they do not understand or believe in it. Based on the results of the questionnaire, 35.3% of GenZ in Wonosobo carry out the gugon tuhon because they know that mangan iwak brutu is a bad thing, 31.7% do it because they are afraid it will really happen, and 12.5% do it because they are afraid of the person who said the gugon tuhon. From the respondents' answers, we can know that the gugon tuhon *'mangan iwak brutu'* still exists in Wonosobo although only some have heard of it. Although they do not understand and do not believe in the gugon tuhon, most of them still do it.

In terms of who told them the gugon tuhon *'mangan iwak tlampik'*,

29.5% said they heard the gugon tuhon from their mother, 21.9% from their grandmother, and the rest from others. This means that mothers and grandmothers are the people who most often teach the gugon tuhon.

9. Nak saur ora milu pasa, mbesuk dadi uler jedhung

'If you participate in sahur but do not fast, you will become a jedhung caterpillar (a caterpillar as big as a mattress)'

The Gugon tuhon *'Nak saur ora milu pasa, mbesuk dadi uler jedhung'* can be understood as follows.

The word *'saur ora milu pasa'* refers to a situation where a person has done sahur but he still eats during the day because he is not fasting. The word *'ulat jedhung'* refers to an animal that looks like a caterpillar but is as big as a mattress. You could say it is a giant caterpillar and its existence is a myth. The meaning of the gugon tuhon is the recommendation to fast, especially if there is an intention to fast, which is indicated by doing sahur or eating before fasting. People who have eaten sahur but do not fast means that they increase the intensity of their eating so that it will increase the calories that enter their body. The calories that enter the body become excessive, causing the body to become fat like a caterpillar that is as big as a mattress. Caterpillars that are as big as mattresses certainly cannot move much because their body size is too large. By imagining being a jedhung caterpillar, it is hoped that it can influence children, make children afraid, so that children will continue their intention to fast.

The following are the results of the analysis of GenZ understanding in Wonosobo Regency of the gugon tuhon *'saur ora pasa'*.

Table 9. Saur Ora Pasa

Indicator	Number (%)
Heard	36.6
Understand	29
Believe	22.8
Implement	35.3

Based on the table above, it can be seen that most GenZ have never heard of the gugon tuhon *'saur ora pasa'*. This can be seen in the number of percentages which is only 36.6%. They also do not understand the meaning of the gugon tuhon and also do not believe in it. Most of them also do not practice the gugon tuhon. There were only 35.3% who practiced the gugon tuhon. Based on the results of the questionnaire, 35.7% of GenZ in Wonosobo who carry out the gugon tuhon because they know that 'saur ora pasa' is a bad thing, 21.4% do it because they are afraid it will really happen, and 8.5% do it because they are afraid of the person who said the gugon tuhon. This means that the gugon tuhon 'saur ora pasa' still exists in Wonosobo but is rarely spoken. They do not understand and do not believe in the gugon tuhon, but a small number still do it. This means that the gugon tuhon is not acceptable to the minds of GenZ in Wonosobo.

In terms of who told them the gugon tuhon *'saur ora pasa'*, 14.3% said they heard the gugon tuhon from their grandmother, 12.5% from their mother, and the rest from others. This means that grandmothers and mother are the people who most often teach the gugon tuhon.

10. Aja nyabet nganggo sada, mengko ndak gering taun

'Don't hit with a stick, it will cause chronic pain'

The Gugon tuhon *'Aja nyabet nganggo sada, mengko ndak gering taun'* can be understood as follows.

The word *'nyabet nganggo sada'* refers to an act of hitting another person using a stick. Children usually like to play with sticks and hit them around, including their friends. The word *'gering taun'* refers to an illness that does not go away for years. The meaning of the gugon tuhon is a prohibition against hitting others with sticks because hitting with sticks can hurt others. Being hit with a stick feels more painful than using other objects. In this gugon tuhon, Javanese parents teach their children about the law of sowing and reaping, meaning that people will be rewarded for what they do. If you hurt other people, you will get a reply from God in the form of pain too.

The following are the results of the analysis of GenZ in Wonosobo Regency's understanding of the gugon tuhon *'nyabet nganggo sada'*.

Table 10. Nyabet nganggo Sada

Indicator	Number (%)
Heard	83
Understand	68.8
Believe	52.7
Implement	71.4

Based on the table above, it can be seen that most of the GenZ in Wonosobo have heard the gugon tuhon *'nyabet nganggo sada'*. This can be seen in the number of percentages that reached 83%. Most of them can understand the meaning of the gugon tuhon and also believe in it. Most of them implement the gugon tuhon. Based on the results of the questionnaire, 53.1% of GenZ in Wonosobo carry out the gugon tuhon because they know that nyabet nganggo sada is a bad thing, 39.7% do it because they are afraid it will really happen, and 6.7% do it because they are afraid of the person who said the gugon tuhon. This means that the gugon tuhon 'nyabet nganggo sada' still exists in Wonosobo, understood, believed, and implemented by most GenZ in Wonosobo.

Judging from who told the gugon tuhon 'nyabet nganggo sada', 28.6% answered that they heard the gugon tuhon from their mother, 22.3% from their grandmother, 8% from their grandfather, and the rest from others. This means that mothers and grandmothers are the people who most often teach the gugon tuhon, followed by grandfathers.

CONCLUSION

Based on the results of data analysis, it can be concluded that gugon tuhon still exists in Wonosobo because there are still many GenZ who have heard the gugon tuhon. Most of them do not understand and do not believe in gugon tuhon but they still carry out gugon tuhon. The reason they keep doing gugon tuhon is because they know that the prohibition in gugon tuhon is not good to do. But there are also those who do gugon tuhon because they are afraid that it will really happen and a small number do it because they are afraid of the person who said the gugon tuhon.

Although gugon tuhon is still often spoken in Wonosobo Regency, its existence will be threatened with disappearance if it is not considered. If you look at the relatively low understanding and level of trust of GenZ, there is a possibility that gugon tuhon will not be told to the next generation. This needs to be watched and considered so that gugon tuhon is preserved as part of Javanese culture.

Most of the GenZ in Wonosobo heard this gugon tuhon from their mothers and grandmothers. This means that women have an important role in preserving gugon tuhon as a culture to teach politeness and manners to children.

References

Budiono, T. (2015). Gugon Tuhon dalam Bahasa Jawa (Sebuah Tinjauan Etnolinguistik). *Ethnolinguistics.* https://www.academia.edu/40184101/GUGON_TUHON_DALAM_BAHASA_JAWA_Sebuah_Tinjauan_Etnolinguistik_

Dewi, N. N. A. K., & Sugiarti. (2020). Mitos Gugon Tuhon pada Serat Centhini I Gubahan Agus Wahyudi. *Jurnal Pembelajaran Sastra, 2*(1).

Dimock, M. (2019). *Defining generations: Where Millennials end and Generation Z begins.* https://www.pewresearch.org/fact-%0Atank/2019/01/17/where-millennials-end-and-generation-z-begins/: Washington D.C.: Pew Research Center

Dreyer, C., & Stojanová, H. (2023). How entrepreneurial is German Generation Z vs. Generation Y? *Procedia Computer Science, 217*, 155–164.

Dwiguna, P. M. (2017). *Pemahaman Anak terhadap Ajaran dalam Gugon Tuhon: Suatu Tinjauan Pragmatik.* Universitas Indonesia.

Giachino, C., Pucciarelli, F., Bollani, L., & Alessandro, B. (2023). Is Generation Z ready to fly into the space? The future of tourism is coming. *Futures, 145.*

Khasanah, I., & Ernawati, Y. (n.d.). KepercayaanMasyarakat Jawa dalam NovelPrau Layar Ing Kali Codedan Prau Layar Ing Kali Opak Karya Budi Sardjono (Kajian Antropologi Sastra). *Ejurnal.Unesa.Ac.Id.*

Kurniawati, D., & Widhyasmaramurti. (2019). Pragmatic Meaning of Baby Care Gugon Tuhon in Javanese. *International Review of Humanities Studies, 4*(2).

Levinson, S. C. (1983). *Pragmatics.* Cambridge Univercity Press.

Padmosoekotjo, S. (2009). Gugon Tuhon. *Jurnal Terjemahan Alam Dan Tamadun Melayu I*, 167–171.

Porwadarminta, W. J. S. (1939). *Baoesastra Djawa.* J. B. Wolters Uitgeversmaatschappij.

Saifudin, A. (2019). Teori Tindak Tutur dalam Studi Linguistik Pragmatik. *LITE, 15*(1).

Setiawan, K. E. P. (2019). *Maguti: Kajian Simbolisme Budaya Jawa.* CV. Kanaka Media.

Codeswitching by Bajo in Multilingual Community

A Study from Maringkik Island Village

Muhammad Shubhi(muhammad.shubhi@brin.go.id) | **Lalu Erwan Husnan**(lalu002@brin.go.id)
St. Raudloh(stra001@brin.go.id) | **Oldrie C. Sorey**(oldriesorey@gmail.com)
Siti Djuwarijah(siti083@brin.go.id)
National Research and Innovation Agency, Archaeological, Language and Literature Research Organization

INTRODUCTION

Multilingual environment or better known as multilingualism (Yakpo, 2015: 259--261). Multilingualism is a condition in which a society (everyone has different abilities at a certain level such as passively or actively using a language other than their mother tongue or first) could use more than one language. Under these conditions, the local language or the language used for the first time since birth (Velazquez, 2015: 189) is referred to as the mother tongue, which is the language used in the family sphere and tends to be in informal conditions. The second language is the language used by the community as a medium of communication with other people who have different cultures. This second language has a higher position in terms of its use and is considered more prestigious even though it is generally used by people for cross-cultural communication. The second language tends to be owned by the majority culture in a geography such as a district or province or a certain wider area.

In addition to the first and second languages which experience friction in terms of lingual and cultural, multilingual speakers usually also master a third language which is used as a medium of communication in formal situations including education. This third language is usually the language used in general or nationally (Paliwala, 2015: 208--209) and becomes the national identity, Indonesian. This language condition is experienced by the Bajo people in Lombok Island. They are required to carry out social adaptation in the form of language adaptation for educational reasons, meeting the needs of daily life, and as a cross-cultural communication strategy.

The Bajo people in Lombok Island have made settlements in the northern, western and southern coastal areas (Husnan et al., 2021). They generally make a living as fishermen. Every day they meet and interact with residents of the island of Lombok, namely the Sasak tribe, who speak the Sasak language. Interaction with other speakers (Sasak) occurs in markets, schools, government agencies, on the roads, and on the coast, especially ports. Then what are the domains of language used in Bajo community? Which language codes do they use? What types of codeswitching are used?

These questions have been tried to be answered through research conducted by Yosi and Sadia (2019), Khairunas (2017), Nurhamidah et al. (2018), Patmasari et al. (2022), Zainil (2019), dan Dewi (2021). Yosi and Sadia conducted a code-switching study on the dialogue used in the novel Game of Death written by Lexie Xu. The code-switching phenomenon in the novel's dialogue shows a tendency to use situations rather than metaphors. In addition, there are four types of codeswitching found, namely referential, metalinguistic, fatigue, and expression functions. Khairunas in his study on codeswitching on talk shows on NET TV found 62 data. There are three types of code switching found, namely 41 intra-sentential, 12 inter-sentential, and 9 extrasentential. In addition, the study also found reasons for using codeswitching, namely 30 data related to certain topics, 1 data quoting other people's statements, 5 data being empathetic towards something, 9 data interjection, 3 data repetition for clarification, 3 data for the purpose of clarifying the contents of the speaker's speech, and 9 identity expression data. Both studies are code switching found in print and electronic media, novels, and TV dialogues.

Nurhamidah et al. conducted a study of the debate on the use of codeswitching, whether it is good or not. The first opinion tends to think that codes switching is not good because it shows limitations in achieving learning targets. The second opinion holds that codeswitching is something good for learning. The research concludes that codeswitching is accepted as something useful considering that codeswitching has several functions for teachers. Namely to convey material and students receive material and communication in class. Patmasari et al. conducted a study of teacher and student perceptions of the use of codeswitching. Research shows that teachers use codeswitching for certain situations and specific reasons. They still emphasize the use of English as much as possible because the class target is English. The findings show that their students have positive attitudes and perceptions towards the use of code-switching in the EFL classroom. They assume that teachers should be welcome to use code-switching in EFL classrooms because it can help them (students) and maintain communication between teachers and students. Zainil also conducted a study on the code-switching phenomenon carried out by the teacher and his perceptions of the effectiveness of language learning related to the choice of language used. The study was conducted with the first language being Minang (L1) and the second language being Indonesian (L2). The research found that the function of the Indonesian language is as a medium of pedagogy and affective functions, namely grammar explanation, motivation, and encouragement. In addition, research also shows the use of L1 as a medium to maintain distance and closeness between teachers and students. The teacher in this context does reflexivity. The three studies related to perceptions of the use of codeswitching in the learning process in the classroom emphasize that codeswitching is needed for certain situations and specific purposes to support the communication process in class and the acceptance of learning material and reflexivity by the teacher.

Dewi conducted a study on the use of language in the form of code mixing, code switching, borrowing, pidginization, and creolization. Research shows the use of codes can vary with respect to language elements such as sentences, clauses, phrases, and words which have limitations considering the code chosen by speakers depending on the needs of speakers to communicate.

These studies show that linguistic phenomena in the form of code switching can be studied in media (novels and TV). These studies show that code switching is a strategy used in EFL classrooms for certain situations and specific purposes and involves the local first language (L1), second language (L2) (Indonesia), and foreign language (L3), English. This research is a study of code choice in multilingual situations with three languages. Is there another phenomenon in code choice in codes switching in EFL classrooms in multilingual situations (Ustunel, 2016: 115--117) with four languages, especially from the teacher's perspective.

This study is focus on codeswitching in Bajo's community (Ustunel, 2016: 50). It describes the types of codeswitching used by Bajo's speakers. They are multilingual. They could speak local language (Bajo); Bajo's second language (Sasak), and national language (Indonesian). They live in Maringkik Island Village. Most of them are Bajo. They use Bajo to communicate with the same ethnic backgrounds (Ustunel, 2016: 96). It is Bajo's local language which has been maintained by the speakers up to now. They use Sasak and Indonesian with people whose ethnic backgrounds are Sasak and others who live in Tanjung Luar village or other villages in Keruak district. Both are used for cross cultural communication and communication using national language.

In short, it is an interesting phenomenon to know the type of codes made by the Bajo's people. They can use one of them to have one or more goal for the sake of transferring information and fulfill their social need.

There are different aspects to code switching, namely linguistic, social, pragmatic, and cognitive. All of these factors have a role in the choice of code in a multilingual society (Tamargo et al., 2016: 6). The study of codes switching should not only be directed at the diversity of influencing factors but also different groups. In this context, Aabi quotes what Labov has said (1972: 457 in Aabi, 2020: 1) that codes switching from one language to another is governed by grammatical rules. Codeswitching is no longer considered only as language behavior but is motivated by something bigger, namely social, and cultural phenomena in the context of human interaction.

Aabi explained that the multilingual situation and cultural differences lead to the use (Albirini, 2016: 64) of more than one language (Ustunel, 2016: 27) at different levels and types (Aabi, 2020: 55). The study of codes switching in multilingual situations leads to three perspectives, namely linguistic, psycholinguistic, dan sociolinguistic (Stell and Yakpo, 2015: 1). The study of code switching in multilingual situations leads to three perspectives, namely linguistic, psycholinguistic, and sociolinguistic. The first perspective leads to universal grammar constraints on code switching. The second perspective focuses on how the linguistics of the bi/multilingual system is stored and accessed. The third perspective focuses on code-switching social motivations. The perspective adopted influences the methodological framework used. Regarding code switching in English Class, Ustunel (2016: 2) assumes that it is in a monolingual context where teachers and students share knowledge in the context of learning English as a foreign language.

Codeswitching is a common phenomenon in a bi- or multilingual community. It is the use of more than one codes by people (Grosjean in Liceras et al., 2016: 107), they must share the particular codes. However, there are some different viewpoints for codeswitching proposed by some linguists. Indeed, they give some underlined points to understand this sociolinguistic phenomenon.

To start this point, Poplack (in Migge, 2015: 86) classified codeswitching into three main classes. They are tag-switching, inter-sentential, and intra-sentential. The first one refers to the insertion of a tag in one language into utterance in another language or dialect. The second type is switching at sentence boundaries. It is the use of clauses or sentences of one language or dialect in another language or dialect which is usually done by quite fluent speakers. It is also called mechanical switching. The third type is switching in the middle of a sentence, the speaker is usually not aware of his/her switch. The switching occurs unconsciously to fill in unknown or unavailable terms in one language or dialect. It is also called code mixing, but the speaker in code mixing cannot momentarily remember the term in one language.

Codeswitching which is seen from linguistic varieties in bilingual or multilingual societies studied by Gardner-Chloros (in Backus, 2015: 24). They said that codeswitching is the use of linguistic varieties, indeed, in terms of languages or dialects in a conversation or sentence. It could influence everyone who is in contact.

Skiba (in Ustunel, 2016: 39) classified codeswitching based on the reasons of using it. He said that there are four reasons for someone employing codeswitching. First, codeswitching usually occurs when the speakers are upset, tired, or distracted in some manner. Second, codeswitching is used when someone wants to express their solidarity with a certain group. Third, codeswitching is used to exclude others who do not speak the language from a group of conversation. Four, codeswitching is used when the speaker wants to convey their message to the listeners. In this case, Hernandez-Campoy (2016: 45) said that multilingual people tend to switch their codes to mark formality, as well as dialectal case. Hernandes-Campoy also emphasized that these communities also try to maintain distance and identity through code choices. Related to learning in class. This has an impact on the authority to use the language Hernandez-Campoy (2016: 106--107) in educational field, there is one language with a certain more prestige status (formal-learning media) and other languages are in the status of a less prestigious language with use that is limited to certain domains and communities. The use of certain codes was also stated by Mendoza (2015: 80) that it was used as a way of showing group solidarity.

It is important to take a note that Indonesian is a dominant language used as a means of transferring knowledge at school. All the subjects except English must be in Indonesian. Sasak and Bajo are not dominant for they are only used to speak with Sasak speaker, and Bajo. Contact of those languages in term of codeswitching in EFL classroom can uses classification of codeswitching proposed by Poplack (in Migge, 2015: 86). In this context, codeswitching is a common phenomenon in the English classroom (Ustunel, 2016: 29), whether in the form of EFL, ESL, or English as Academic Language (EAL). In a situation like that described by Ustunel, it is like an English class for Bajo speakers. Interaction in the class is dominated by the target language (English) and students' first language (L1/native). Different situations faced by Bajo's students. They focus on the target language (English), in certain times and situations, use code-switching to their mother tongue (Bajo language as their native language), a second language (Sasak language as a cross-cultural language (L2), the language that dominates the area where they live), and the national language (Indonesian). as the national language and formal media for the delivery of knowledge in the world of education).

Method is a crucial problem in doing a sociolinguistic study. It must suit the goal of doing the study. To do that, it is important to choose the participant involved, how to collect the data, and how to analyze the data. Participants who are involved in this study are Bajo's people in Maringkik Island Village. The method used to choose the village is purposive for several reasons. First, there are some enclaves of Bajo in Lombok based on studies done by Language Office of West Nusa Tenggara since 2006—2008 (Husnan et al., 2021). Those enclaves are Bajo in Medana, Gili Indah Village, in North Lombok, Bajo in Tanjung Luar and Maringkik Island, in East Lombok, and Bajo in Awang, South Lombok, in Central Lombok. Of the enclaves, Bajo in Maringkik Island Village is the enclave which still maintains Bajo Language, it is in isolated area, small island. In contrast, many people cannot speak Bajo in South Lombok, but they still maintain some cultural events related to the sea culture. As result, this study proposed a proposal to have a study at some domain activities of Bajo in Maringkik Island Village. They are school, sport area, religious place (mosque), family, and street.

There are some methods used to collect the data. They are observation (Holmes and Stubbe, 2015: 13), recording and note taking, and interview. Observation is done in all domain activities. Recording is also done covering utterances produced by speakers (Whynot, 2016: 93). It has been done more than once. The recorder is put in a certain place and recognized by the speakers. They have been explained about the goal of the study. However, they heard aware of their utterances so that some of their utterances at the beginning of the conversation excluded from the data to be analyzed. In case of knowing the participants involved in the conversation, this study got the description of participants from key informants.

Data of this study is analyzed using some steps. They are diachronic, simple statistics, labeling, transcription, and classification. Diachronic used is padan (comparative) proposed by Mahsun (2019). This method is useful to know whether the code belongs to Bajo or other languages (Sasak and Indonesian). Techniques used for this method are comparative technique and contrasting technique. In other words, padan includes both comparative and contrastive analysis and determines whether the codes belonged to one of three languages or not.

DISCUSSION

The Bajo community in Pulau Maringkik Village must choose one or more codes (languages) that are mastered in the appropriate domain. The selection of these codes is greatly influenced by the participants, setting, objectives, and topics discussed. Here is the domain in question.

Table 1. Domain of choice of code (language) of the Bajo people

Domain	Address	Setting	Topic	Code
Education	Teacher-students	Elementary School	Tale	Indonesian
	Students	Elementary School	School subject	School subject
Religion	Religious leader	Mosque	Jumatan lecture	Indonesian
	Bajo's people	Mosque	Information	Bajo
Commerce	Sasak	Market	Fish	Sasak
Fishing	Bajo's people	Sea shore	Fishing	Bajo
Family	Parents	Home	Fish	Bajo
Friendship	Friends	Home	Chess	Bajo
Sport	Friends	Court	Volley	Indonesian

The table above shows that in formal situations, especially in schools which tend to go one way, the teacher chooses Indonesian as the code. During discussions between students, Indonesian was also an option. However, Bajo in informal situations in schools is used by teachers and students. In the mosque, the Imam uses Indonesian for sermons every Friday. However, information is informed from the mosque using the loudspeaker uses Bajo. In the fishing market, in Tanjung Luar Village, they use Bajo or Sasak (both). The use of Sasak for most of the participants in the market is Sasak ethnic background. Between fellow Bajo, they still use the Bajo language. Besides at school, Indonesian is also used in sports situations.

Example 1

Itu Atun bilangan *dangai arangna Atun*

That 2prs num what name-clt 2prs

(What is the number Atun what is the number Atun)

Example 2

Masih lohor ni jak, Waq ka*sini*

Still noon this father to here

(I thought my father was here)

Example 3

Niaq buatang no Amir. Jak **ke** tengaq no. ndek **ke samping** basaqn **ke samping** jak.

any passenger that 2prs bring to center that do not to side wet-clt to side if

(Amir, there are passengers. Bring the things to the center, do not to the either side of the boats, otherwise it will be wet)

The three languages (Bajo, Sasak, and Indonesian) are used by Bajo (Indonesia is in **bold** one, Sasak is underlined, and Bajo is italic). The three languages used have similar forms which indirectly support code switching from one language to another.

In example 1, the speaker said it in a formal situation in the teaching and learning process. The clause 'dangai arangna' can be replaced with clauses in Indonesian and Sasak 'apa namanya' and 'ape arann'. This means that the three hottest languages share the same pattern. These forms (equivalence constraints) cause an option to choose one of the codes in an appropriate time, setting, or addresser for a certain purpose. Example 2 is code switching from Bajo to Sasak and Indonesia. At this level, considering that the form is almost the same, the prefix 'ka' can be replaced with the prefix 'ke' in Indonesian and the prefix 'juk' in Sasak. The examples shown show how languages with similar forms affect code switching. However, code switching requires proficiency in two others than the first language (mother tongue). Example 3 shows the speaker's lack of knowledge of the language of his contact partner. The word 'jak' can be translated as 'if'. The first 'jak' is not acceptable but the second 'jak' is acceptable.

The following are the two common types of code switching found, namely intrasentential and intersentential.

Table 2. Intrasentential Codeswitching

Host	Guest language						Total	
	Indonesian		Sasak		Bajo		N	%
	N	%	N	%	N	%		
Indonesian	-	-	26	25	35	33.7	61	58.7
Sasak	14	13.4	-	-	6	5.8	20	19.2
Bajo	9	8.6	14	13.5	-	-	23	22.1
Total	23	72	40	38.5	41	39.5	104	100

Table 2 shows a total of 104 code switching using intrasentential. Of the total code switching, 58.7% were code switching from Indonesian to Sasak and Bajo. The second code switching was from Bajo to Indonesian and Sasak which reached 22.1%. The third is code switching from Sasak to Indonesian and Bajo which reaches 19.2%.

Table 3. Intersentential Codeswitching

Host	Guest language						Total	
	Indonesian		Sasak		Bajo		N	%
	N	%	N	%	N	%		
Indonesian	-	-	15	14.3	27	25.7	42	40
Sasak	18	17.2	-	-	12	11.4	30	28.6
Bajo	16	15.2	17	16.2	-	-	33	31.4
Total	34	32.4	32	30.5	39	37.1	105	100

Table 3 shows a total of 105 code switching using intersententional. Of the total code switching, 40% is code switching from Indonesian to Sasak and Bajo. Next is code switching from Bajo to Indonesian and Sasak which reaches 31.4%. The code switching from Sasak to Indonesian and Bajo reached 28.6%.

The above description shows that even though the Bajo people in Pulau Maringkik Village occupy settlements on a small island separated from the mainland of Lombok Island, which is dominated by ethnic Sasak, they have proficiency in the language of their contact partners and the national language (Indonesia). The language of their contact partners is their means of bonding in social life. One of the ways they use is to do code switching using the three languages they are fluent in. They use code switching from the formal domain of education and religion to the informal domain in their own environment and in an environment with a Sasak ethnic background, at a fish market in another village, namely the Fish Auction Place (TPI).

The ability to use another language as a code choice in certain situations shows the intense contact of the Bajo community in Pulau Maringkik Village with other communities as their contact partners. This is also indicated by the number of codeswitching used in the several domains studied, which shows an almost equal number between intrasentential and intersentential. This is possible considering that the three languages have forms that can replace each other.

CONCLUSION

The code switching used by the Bajo community in Pulau Maringkik Village is a manifestation of a multilingual situation. They have the competence to use three languages, one national language and the other two are the languages of their ethnicity and the ethnic language of their contact partners. Mastery of the three languages and the forms that can replace each other are supporting factors for the use of code switching in the speech domain of the Bajo people.

Apart from Indonesian being the national language, the need for mastering the language of their contact partners (Sasak) is motivated by factor that every day they meet and interact in one of the important domains to make ends meet, namely the Fish Auction Place (TPI) which is also adjacent to a shopping center. In that domain, the contact partner uses L2.

References

Aabi, M. (2020). *The Syntax of Arabic and French Code Switching in Morocco.* Palgrave Macmillan. https://doi.org/10.1007/978-3-030-24850-5

Albirini, A. (2016). *Modern Arabic Sociolinguistic: Diglossia, Codeswitching, attitudes and Identity.* Routledge Taylor & francis Group.

Backus, A. (2015). U Usage-based Approach to Code-Switching: The Need for Revonciling Structure and Function. In K. Stell, Gerald and Yakpo (Ed.), *Code-Switching between Structural and Sociolingusitic Perspectives* (pp. 1--19). De Gruyter.

Dewi, K. T. (2021). Language Use: Code Mixing, Code Switching, Borrowing, Pdiginization, and Creolization. *Yavana Bhasha: Journal of English Language Education, 4*(1), 34—44. https://doi.org/10.25078/yb.v4i1.2209

Hernandez-Campoy, J. M. (2016). *Sociolinguistic Styles.* Wiley Balckwell.

Holmes, Janet and Stubbe, M. (2015). *Power and Politeness in the Workplace:* A Sociolinguistic Analysis of Talk at Work (Second). Routledge Taylor & francis Group.

Husnan, Lalu Erwan; Raudloh, St; Inayatusshalihah, I. (2021). *Laporan Penelitian Kekerabatan Isolek* Bajo di Wilayah Nusa Tenggara Barat.

Khairunas, S. (2017). Code-Switching in TV Talk Show Program Entitled 'Sarah Sechan' on NET TV. *Proressive, 12*(2), 37—46.

Liceras, Juana M.; Fuertes, Raquel Fernandez; Klassen, R. (2016). Language Dominance and Language Nativeness: The View from English-Spanish Codeswitching. In M. C. P. Tamargo, Rosa E. Guzzardo; Mazak, Catherine M.; and Couto (Ed.), *Spanish-English Codeswitching in the Caribbean and the US* (p. 336). John Benjamin Pubslihing Company. https://doi.org/10.1075/ihll.11

Mahsun. (2019). *Metode Penelitian Bahasa* (III). Rajawali Press.

Mendoza, C. H. (2015). Pragmatic Functions and Cultural Communicative Needs in the Use of Innovative Quotatives among Mexican Bilingual Youth. In T. Potowski, Kim and Bugel (Ed.), *Sociolinguistic Change Across the Spanish-Speaking World: Case Study in Honor of Anna Maria Escobar* (p. 238). Peter Lang.

Migge, B. (2015). The Role of Discursive Information in Analyzing Multilingual Practices. In K. Stell, Gerald and Yakpo (Ed.), *Code-Switching between Structural and Sociolingusitic Perspectives* (pp. 185--206). De Gruyter.

Nurhamidah; Fauziati, Endang; and Supriyadi, S. (2018). Code-Switching in EFL Clasroom: Is it Good or Bad? *JEE: Journal of English Education, 3*(2), 78—88. https://doi.org/10.31327/jee.v3i2.861

Paliwala, A. B. (2015). Creaole/Superstrate Code-Switching: Structure and Consequences. In

K. Stell, Gerald and Yakpo (Ed.), *Code-Switching between Structural and Sociolingusitic Perspectives* (pp. 207--236). De Gruyter.

Patmasari, Andi; Agussatriana; and Kamaruddin, A. (2022). An Investigation of the use of Code-Switching in EFL Classroom: Attitudes and Perceptions. *ELS-JISH: ELS Journal on Interdisciplinary Studies in Humanities, 5*(2), 230—239. https://doi.org/10.34050/elsjish.v5i2.21006

Stell, Gerald and Yakpo, K. (2015). Elusive or Elf-Evident? Looking for Common Ground in Approaches to Code-Switching. In K. Stell, Gerald and Yakpo (Ed.), *Code-Switching between Structural and Sociolingusitic Perspectives* (pp. 1--18). De Gruyter. https://doi.org/9783110343540

Tamargo, Rosa E. Guzzardo; Mazak, Catherine M.; and Couto, M. C. P. (2016). Multiple Influencing Factors, Diverse Participants, Varied Techniques: INterdisciplinary approaches to the Study of Spanish-English Codeswitching. In M. C. P. Tamargo, Rosa E. Guzzardo; Mazak, Catherine M.; and Couto (Ed.), *Spanish-English Codeswitching in the Caribbean and the US* (p. 336). John Benjamin Pubslihing Company. https://doi.org/10.1075/ihll.11

Ustunel, E. (2016). *EFL Classroom Code-Switching*. Palgrave Macmillan. https://doi.org/10.1057/978-1-137-55844-2

Velazquez, I. (2015). Integrational Perceptions of Spanish Use and Viability in First-Generation Midwestern Latino Households. In T. Potowski, Kim and Bugel (Ed.), *Sociolinguistic Change Across the Spanish-Speaking World: Case Study in Honor of Anna Maria Escobar* (pp. 187--214). Peter Lang.

Whynot, L. A. (2016). *Understanding International Sign: Sociolinguistic Study*. Gallaudet University Press.

Yakpo, K. (2015). Code-swithcing and Social Change: Convergent Language Mixing in a Multilingual Society. In K. Stell, Gerald and Yakpo (Ed.), *Code-Switching between Structural and Sociolingusitic Perspectives* (pp. 259--288). De Gruyter.

Yosi, Ni Putu Diana and Sadia, I. G. (2019). An Analysis of Code Switching in Dialogue of the Indonesia Novel Permainan Maut by Lexie Xu. *Humanis: Journal of Arts and Humanities, 23*(3), 176—184. https://doi.org/10.24843/JH.2019.v23.i03.p02

Zainil, Y. (2019). Pedagogical Practices of Code-Switching in EFL Classroom in Padang, Indonesia. The First ELEHIC: *Social Sciences on Sustainable Development for World Challenge: The Ffirst Economics, Law, Education and Humanities International Conference,* 634643. https://doi.org/10.18502/kss.v3i14.4343

The Origin of Budong-budong and Topoyo Ethnicity in Central Mamuju Regency

Hasina Fajrin R.(hasina.fajrin.r@brin.go.id) | **Heksa Biopsi Puji Hastuti**(heks001@brin.go.id)
Firman A.D.(firm013@brin.go.id) | **Ratnawati**(ratn015@brin.go.id)
Sarwo Ferdi Wibowo(sarw004@brin.go.id)
National Research and Innovation Agency, Archaeological, Language and Literature Research Organization

INTRODUCTION

Central Mamuju Regency was once an area of Mamuju Regency, then expanded into a separate regency in 2012 through the Plenary Session of the House of Representatives of the Republic of Indonesia on the New Autonomous Region Bill. Central Mamuju Regency consists of five sub-districts: Pangale, Budong-Budong, Tobadak, Topoyo, and Karossa Districts. The capital of the district is Tobadak. Long before it became a separate district, Central Mamuju Regency has been one of the destination areas for transmigration since 1981. The transmigration program is still one of the flagship programs of the Central Mamuju Regency (Hanapi, 2022), so the Central Mamuju Regency is likened to a miniature Indonesia (Kominfo Mamuju Tengah, 2023). Various ethnicities and religions, such as Javanese, Balinese, and Lombok, transmigrated to Central Mamuju Regency (Dinas Tenaga Kerja dan Transmigrasi, 2022).

The symbol of Central Mamuju Regency represents the difference through a motto that reads *lallaq tassisaraq* (there are several different versions in writing) (Alimuddin, 2013). The motto is intended to mean "even though we are different or scattered in some places, we will not be separated," implying that the government and local people are aware of the multi-ethnic existence in the region. Cultural diversity refers to differences obtained culturally so that the emergence of majority and minority societies is inevitable (Parekh, 2006). Therefore, such differences need to be framed in brotherhood because inter-ethnic conflicts and misunderstandings are prone to occur, which can then threaten national disintegration. Ethnicity in this context follows the definition of Law of the Republic of Indonesia Number 40 of 2008 concerning the Elimination of Racial and Ethnic Discrimination (Penghapusan Diskriminasi Ras dan Etnis, 2008) which is defined as the classification of humans based on beliefs, values, customs, customs, norms, language, history, geography, and kinship.

Moreover, the issue of ethnicity is a sensitive matter in multicultural Indonesian society. In Indonesian historical records, many inter-ethnic conflicts occurred, such as Samawa and Balinese ethnicities in 1980 (Ardiansyah, 2010), Ambonese and Sambas ethnic conflict (Alqadrie, 1999), Chinese ethnic conflicts even with several other ethnicities, such as with Javanese in Surakarta in 1972-1998 and Bugis Makassar which also occurred repeatedly (Juditha, 2015; Putro et al., 2017). Recently, the world of social media was shocked because of a scientific article that discusses a specific ethnicity, and the ethnic support community does not approve of statements that are considered disparaging to the ethnicity. In fact, according to an official statement from the university, the recommendations in the paper encourage inter-ethnic appreciation and acceptance because diversity is necessary (Humas Unismuh, 2023).

The discourse on migrants and vulnerable indigenous people creates a dichotomy among ethnic groups that should be allowed to grow and develop appropriately in Indonesia because the law guarantees equality, freedom, justice, and universal human values according to the law. Inequality between migrants and indigenous people due to migration is the most common on record to Bertrand (2004). It is justified by Hos et al. (2022) that transmigration becomes a way for different ethnic backgrounds to meet and interact. These encounters often trigger dissociative social processes due to struggles for access to resources. Bertrand (2004) cites local processes such as transmigration as one of the causes of the formation of a critical juncture. This critical juncture relates to the historical moment when various groups questioned the national model and institutional order by mobilizing or renegotiating their position within the nation or even wanting to get out of the model.

Therefore, an understanding of ethnic identity is essential to discuss because by knowing their identity, they can counter threats from outside and make the identity an internal identity confirmation. With this threat, affirmation and re-articulation of consciousness become essential to new points of view and absorption of meaning that can counter and interrupt the dominant discourse (O'Reilly, 2004).

In Central Mamuju Regency, various ethnicities live, but in this paper, what will be discussed are Budong-Budong and Topoyo ethnicities. Research on the identity of the two ethnicities was sparked by a written statement stating that the Budong-Budong people were referred to as the Panasuan people who broke away (Laskowske, 2007). It is also confirmed in Ethnologue (2023) that Panasuan is a family of Seko languages. Meanwhile, oral literature data and websites found that the Budong-Budong ethnic group claimed to be the early ethnic group in the region and included the Topoyo ethnic group as part of their ethnicity.

Several studies on ethnicity in Central Mamuju Regency have been conducted. However, the study had a different focus. Dwi (2018) discusses the procession of the *Pamose* tradition, people's views on the tradition, and its existence in the modern era. Aksarin discusses similar studies but uses different loci and slight modifications in the problem statement. In his writings, Aksarin (2018) mentions three problem formulations and two of them are precisely the same as the research conducted by Dwi (2018). What is different is only the third question. He relates the implementation of the tradition from the point of view of the Islamic Aqedah. Both studies use traditions carried out by two different ethnicities. One mentions the implementation of traditions in Topoyo Village, and the other mentions the implementation of traditions by the indigenous people of Budong-Budong. The location is in two villages in the same district, namely Topoyo District.

Therefore, using oral data and pages that discuss the origins of the two ethnicities, this study aims to discuss how the Budong-Budong and Topoyo ethnicities construct their identity and why these ethnicities construct their identity as such. It is intended to get an idea of why the two ethnicities are considered different, as mentioned by previous studies, and to anticipate and prevent conflicts that have previously occurred in other regions in Central Mamuju Regency. At the same time, the area is still a new district, so it needs to reflect on areas that are also multi-ethnic. In addition, the transmigration program is continuing today because the number of natural resources is not comparable to that of human resources, so this identity is essential to avoid conflict.

Identity is the difference between one group and another. Identity is formed through historical experience, culture, religion, and belief. This identity is evident in language and other forms of expression, such as art, music, and oral literature. Identity and oral literature have an important role because, in social science, stories become a medium for understanding how people think and live their lives. In addition, the story of who and how a person exists in the world comes from the experiences and knowledge of the experiences of others that are often attached to where those experiences occur (Waite, 2022). It is in line with McAdams' (1996) statement that the stories told in a society profoundly affect its members and how its members think, feel, and behave, reflected in the literature of that culture.

Identity is divided into cultural and political identities. Cultural identity refers to the subject's position in social relations or interactions, while political identity relates to the sense of ownership of the subject's position in the sense of otherness (Barker, 2016). In relation to cultural identity, identity is connected through cultural boundaries because it has the same culture. In contrast, political identity relates to the same thing that is owned that distinguishes it from others (Weedon, 2004). Identity is always fragmented, unstable, never completed, and always in the process of representation (Hall, 2003) because the process of meaning cannot be separated from the social construction at that time, so the process of articulation or the process of connecting different elements to form a unity is always temporary.

This paper uses the qualitative descriptive method. The data source is an inventory of oral literature mapping in the Topoyo Regency carried out by Fajrin R. et al. (2020) and other written sources scattered on accessible pages. The data is read over and over again. After that, data in words, phrases, sentences, and discourses that can be used to describe ethnic identity, especially Budong-Budong and Topoyo in Central Mamuju Regency, are classified. However, the ethnicities discussed in this data are limited to Topoyo and Budong-Budong ethnicities. After classification, the relationship between data in the form of words, phrases, sentences, and discourses is then analyzed to obtain a description of the identity of the two ethnicities. Other research evidence supporting the description is also used to confirm the oral sources and the page.

DISCUSSION

The Origin of Topoyo and Budong-Budong from Oral Literature

Writings on the ethnic origins of Topoyo and Budong-Budong will be studied using oral literature that is still alive and developed in Topoyo and Budong-Budong society. Topoyo writing has various versions of Topoyo and Topoiyo. Topoyo is related to the region's name, while Topoiyo, interchangeably with Topoyo, is used in some references to refer to the name of the language. The origin story has two versions and uses two different languages, namely the Tangkou language and the Budong-Budong language. Based on oral literature data found, the Budong-Budong and Topoyo people were once one ethnicity. They are even likened to coming from the same root because of father and mother, such as oral data from interviews with Budong-Budong speakers.

Jari he onno Topoyo he kan rei memahenggoring rei nahameha ameambemehatu ameangudengopo ngaporei tonggo jari padau torronduwu nasitukartipirarro. Apahee to Topoyo kan termasuk tutuei. Jari mbelurunuperionu ti Topoyo nangappa jari nanjerinemalupai ko ada'adarei cerinupeo.

Translation

In the past, Tangkou was united with Topoyo; they had a father and a mother. Once upon a time, Topoyo also wanted to establish the Budong-Budong custom. Topoyo then asked the elders, including Tangkou, to establish the Budong-Budong custom. They were then told to go down. The parents also let them down.

Tangkou or Budong-Budong and Topoyo ethnicities used to have one ethnicity. Both ethnicities are described as having the same identity because they come from the same father and mother. However, they differ in terms of age. The Budong-Budong ethnicity is said to be older, implying that the ethnicity existed first. When the Topoyo ethnic wanted to secede to establish customs, they asked permission from the elders, including the Budong-Budong ethnicity. However, they may establish the same ethnicity as the Budong-Budong customs in areas different from Tangkou and Topoyo regions. Along the way, ethnicity grew and developed to adapt to new areas.

In the following quotation, in addition to mentioning having the same mother and father, the following quotation also explicitly mentions that the customs of the two ethnicities are one. Only the names of the villages differ, but in practice, they are the same. Topoyo ethnicity is attached to ethnic characters that never refuse. Therefore, the name Topoyo literally means a person who always says yes.

Jari hepedenitehaonu Topoyo palipurombelurolupeo caluppeikocaro iyyo. Jari hemo artino anue Topoyo pasalaniteao lukolupeko karo iyyo. Jari teha Topoyo. Lupongkorongonu malpongkoro biasa mapearenou ri ulu minyamboro rei naekomupakalu pongkoha tombongongolu konggori korommana. Jari nitarongho iyyo. Jari iyo tarru jari hemmopede negaramperionu tuu Topoyo.

Translation

It is usually expressed with "please come down". The people told to go down also said, "iyyo ." Finally, the custom was brought down to Topoyo. There is only one custom, which is the one in Tangkou Hamlet. However, because they brought the custom down, eventually, there was also a custom in Topoyo. The customs are the same, but the village's name is different. It is said that parents used to say to Topoyo, "you are here," and then answered, "iyyo ."Iyyo in Indonesian means yes. Finally, the village was named Topoyo.

The meaning that Topoyo people always believe in the origin story of Topoyo has implications for several things. First, they always say yes only to the Budong-Budong people because they have been allowed to have the same customs even though they are in different villages from Budong-Budong, like a younger brother who follows the words of his brother. Secondly, they always say yes because it accommodates the interests of the people they interact. Third, they always say yes because they recognize their ethnicity as immigrants in the area. Hence, they know to put themselves in the middle of the ethnicity that has come first, such as the oral literature that developed in the following Topoiyo language.

Topoiyo e rio turapa nambiboromeha repisamo keluargano rungono tetuakka nace'urongono tettue'i nalollo rongono naputi'i. Jadi downahende heitatuakka netuilongoro netuei karnololullu. Sehingga nambarioro permusuha ri Bamballoka naiyebabende. Arearehe nasipapattuino tuakono karena nihiriqi (cemburu) sehingga tottue na merencanakan ri daerah barat, Bamballoka.

Translation
Topoyo is an immigrant. In the past, in the western area, there were two brothers. The two had been married. His older brother married a black woman. The younger brother married a white and beautiful woman. The elder brother wanted to disturb his brother's beautiful wife. Because his elder brother was always annoying, his younger brother proposed to leave the place to avoid quarreling with the older brother. Then, he made a fortress in the west. The fort is made of banana stems, so it is named Bamballoka, the origin of Bamballoka.

The oral literature data indicate differences and similarities with the origin of the earlier Budong-Budong-speaking Topoyo. According to this oral literature, the Topoyo claim to be migrants, not natives. They were in

Budong-Budong because of conflicts in the previous region. The conflict is said to occur between a brother and sister. The two brothers had different fates. The older brother got a dark-skinned wife, while the younger brother was light-skinned. The difference in destiny triggers conflict in the form of jealousy. The elder brother wants to have the younger brother's wife. The younger brother and his wife decided to leave the region to avoid conflict. Initially, the husband and wife only intended to stop by Budong-Budong, as the following quote.

> *Nimbanngi yarosungoi manyiho nyalaroi pituhoi ri Budong- budong. Dona hende nanyambu ri Budong-budong rearemo herapa nabajikatuwaro nabiaro. Riosewattu naujorumbangi bengi nabuheuwei nabono naobebottojole pallapoboi. Taparikinonganai naobebottojole pallapoboi niolorongngianai padecengindulu jehe terenduruhe paturuhi rio naobebottojole pallapoboi ri solu. Niteatere berarti ri telapal ri solu. Sehingga niparenta masyarakano lokonambali todapa rindo solu. Nihomboro nonggo napatongko Budong-budong tangkou kudapaneuri solu. Tappa nalapor ngananauje mammano neneo rio toratapue. Angkianamo ye anano pandehai ane tunabui kohotureu anne tujakomuoloi. Jari dipandehai torapanuinge niatemenako tonadui apa todui. Jari yane todui allotorihui keangkapueku. Naratalluna sipacaka kupito. Nimba massukituing. Massukituing kami tongi usir mene ri oppoki. Abiceritonge hambibu kaummbenorongoki. Sehingga kiteha onihoni magaranotopongiapai to Budung-budung, Tangkou, namalako rena tindaane menutapo parenda. Nemba-nembaki teha muturui. Natehaturratamo Iyyo.*
>
> Translation
>
> The younger brother and his wife then ran to Budong-Budong by riding a mangiwang fish. In Budong-Budong, he only stayed over but set up huts and gardened. One night, it rained heavily. In the morning, corn stalks and fronds were washed away by water. People who are bathing look at this and wonder why there are corn and sago fronds washed away. Does this mean that people live in the river's upper reaches? Then, he reported to his parents. The people were then ordered to set foot, looking for people upstream, believing there must be someone. They

walked down the road by the river and found the village of Budong-Budong. Children are bathing in the river. The children ran to inform their parents that someone had arrived. His parents said, "Tell me if good people come here if bad people tell them to go home." Because the people who came said that they had nothing to fear because the people who came were good, they were finally called up to the house. The host then told him that they had come to find a living because they had been expelled from their village. People who own villages then say they can live in the village as long as they want to be governed. "What we do is also what you do ."The immigrant was willing to say, "iyo." Finally, the village was named Topoyo.

Based on the quote above, although the couple only intended to stop by, they made cottages and gardened. This house-making and gardening activity then revealed that someone must live near the river. Corn stalks and fronds washed away by water were found by residents living downstream. They then went along the river's edge to look for signs of life and found Budong-Budong. The couple then said that they had been expelled from their village. The natives then gave conditions to stay in the village as long as they wanted to be ruled. In addition to these conditions, Mahrul (2017) mentions other conditions, such as not being able to precede traditional rituals in Tangkou and not going beyond the plantations of the Tangkou people if they grow crops. Like the Budong-Budong version of Topoyo's origins, the Topoyo people agree to follow the conditions mentioned by the Budong-Budong ethnicity.

Implicitly, the first and second versions of Topoyo ethnic origins indicate that the Budong-Budong ethnicity includes the Topoyo ethnicity. Statements denying that the Topoyo ethnicity is not part of the Budong-Budong ethnicity are not found, even though they are immigrants. Mahrul (2017), in his writing, it is clearly stated that the Budong-Budong custom does live in three villages, namely Tangkou, Topoyo, and Tobadak. In the past, they lived in the river's upper reaches and named it Tangkou because when clearing land, the most common plant found was tangkou in the Budong-Budong language meaning nail. In addition, the statement immigrants show "knowing themselves" as people who migrate to people's villages so they are willing to follow the rules that apply in that place, such as the saying Where the earth is stepped on, where the sky is upheld well.

The origin of Topoyo and Budong-Budong from other sources

The origins of Topoyo and Budong-Budong are not only narrated in oral literature. Different versions of the oral literature already mentioned are found on a page. Unfortunately, only one version of the story is mentioned and written in Indonesian. However, this version is still important to discuss because the readership has more opportunities than the oral literature mentioned earlier. Besides, as Hall (2013) said, Although it is not canon literature, it still needs to be considered because of its continuous transmission. People are interested and even share the page. Many bloggers have shared the page version of the story without any modification of the content, but the author chose the page that wrote the story first. The page was written by a blogger named his blog Bumi Ngapaboa (Bumi Ngapaboa, 2011).

According to the author of the page, who introduces himself as Bumi Ngapaboa (2011), There used to be two brothers, one named Oiyo and the other named Oili. They are from Kaili. Oiyo's wife is lovely and is a nobleman descended from Mandar. Oiyo and Oili used to fish together in the river. However, that day Oili pretended to have a stomachache, so she did not go fishing, so Oiyo went alone. He managed to fish for a talking fish that gave him He managed to catch a talking fish and gave him a golden needle and a small machete as long as he did not kill the fish. When he returns home, he finds his wife crying while telling him that Oili, Oiyo's older brother, wants him as his wife. Oiyo was angry at that, and the small machete he carried became big. Before Oiyo and Oili's quarrel occurred, Oiyo's wife came to divorce and intended to leave the village so that there would be no bloodshed between the two brothers. He also went away from the fight. Oiyo then followed. The husband and wife then walked toward the sun until they finally met Budong-Budong village. They were then given a place and built a civilization called Topoyo. However, the civilization built was influenced by Kaili culture, Central Sulawesi.

Based on this representation of Topoyo and Budong-Budong ethnic identity, the early humans who founded Topoyo are said to have originated from Kaili before fleeing to Budong-Budong and had established contact with the Mandar kingdom through marriage. The statement also indicates that they recognize as immigrants. It is possible that the Budong-Budong people's acceptance and assistance to them while fleeing led them to claim later to be ethnic believers who obeyed the rules and orders that prevailed in Budong-Budong. Meanwhile, for Budong-Budong, they are part of the Budong-Budong people because they have married the daughter of a descendant of the Mandar kingdom. As stated by Sopu (2016), Central Mamuju was once a division of Mamuju Regency, part of Pitu Babana Binanga, which literally means seven estuarine kingdoms.

Cultural Identity of Budong-Budong and Topoyo

Language as one of the cultural identities is the most accessible identification for these two ethnicities. What is more, language research has been extensively conducted and well-documented. According to Grimes & Grimes (1987), Budong-Budong is a dialect of the Mamuju language spoken around the mouth of the Budong-Budong River in the Budong-Budong District. Valkama (1987) does not dispute the dialect grouping by Grimes & Grimes (1987), except the location of those dialects on the map needs to be revised. Further research conducted by Friberg & Laskowske (1989) categorizes Budong-Budong as a family of Seko languages, although they are very different. However, they claim that the categorization is still tentative. The more recent research conducted by Yamaguchi (2001) confirms that the Tangkou or Budong-Budong language is a dialect of the Mamuju family in West Sulawesi (formerly part of South Sulawesi). In its development, Badan Pengembangan dan Pembinaan Bahasa (2019) calls the Budong-Budong language its language.

From the results of the study, what somewhat raises a question mark is that the Budong-Budong language is identified as related to the Panasuan, which 72% (Friberg & Laskowske, 1989). The statement is like confirming the statement (Laskowske, 2007) that Budong-Budong is Panasuans who broke away because of language similarities. It is possible that the separation was also caused by religion because according to records from Friberg & Laskowske (1989), The majority religion of Panasuan at that time was Christianity, while Budong-Budong was Muslim (SIL International, 2023a).

Unlike the Panasuan, the Budong-Budong people include the Topoyo ethnicity even though the Topo yo language, commonly called Topoiyo, is a Kaili language family in Central Sulawesi(Friberg & Laskowske, 1989). Data-driven by Badan Pengembangan dan Pembinaan Bahasa (2019), Topoyo and Budong-Budong languages have a high percentage difference of isolects, which is 90 %. The difference is high enough to confirm that the two languages used by each ethnicity are indeed different. The area of speakers of the Topoiyo language is still more expansive than that of the Budong-Budong language. Valkama claims that only 11 households speak the Budong-Budong language. Moreover, language contact with transmigrants also makes the Budong-Budong language vulnerable to extinction because they must be multilingual to communicate with migrants who use different languages.

The Budong-Budong people consider the Topoyo people mothers and fathers. According to history, the kingdom of Mamuju was recorded as a member of the Pitu Babana Binanga federation in the XVI century (Kila, 2019), making the kingdom of Balanipa ama 'father' and the kingdom of Sendana as indo 'mother .'In addition, the kingdom of Mamuju is also said to have established contact with Kaili through trade (Sewang, 2018). In oral literature, it is mentioned that the relationship with Kaili was also established through marriage.

Therefore, the Budong-Budong people make Topoyo language a second language (SIL International, 2023c) because, in its development, the language is still more widely used (Badan Pengembangan dan Pembinaan Bahasa, 2019). Budong-Budong language is only spoken by people in Tabolang Village, Topoyo District, Central Mamuju Regency, West Sulawesi Province. In comparison, the Topoiyo language is still found in Tabolang Village, Salulebo Village, Topoyo, and Salupangkang.

Although they do not share a common language, the Budong-Budong ethnicity accommodates Topoiyo as a second language used in daily life, indicating that although they claim to be an ethnic group that came first, there is an inevitable shift due to contact with other languages. Moreover, Topoyo is also said to have Kaili's influence in implementing its traditions. In addition, the inter-ethnic marriage of Budong-Budong and Topoyo and geographical proximity are also ways for the two ethnicities to claim to be related. Marriage in any tradition is sacred, so when the two ethnicities are allowed to marry each other, they recognize the existence of an equal relationship between them.

Furthermore, the implementation of traditions such as pamose, still practiced by the Topoyo and Budong-Budong ethnicities, reinforces cultural identity as an ethnic group living around the river. In addition, they are also bound by an oath that reads:

hema koi ma rubu talli pambahifua?
rapa ndolu manu na bikka
ohe nasihafu pammaseno
kelor narattu katufua no.

Translation
Who broke the brother's blood oath?
Will break like a broken chicken egg
Scattered like rice
Like Moringa leaves fall, his life

The Budong-Budong and Topoyo ethnic communities who claim to have the same identity highly uphold this oath. They firmly believe the violator will never succeed because his life is like broken chicken eggs, scattered rice, and falling Moringa leaves. The metaphor describes a complicated life because it is impossible to pick up eggs that have been broken. Even if it is possible to collect scattered rice and Moringa leaves, one needs a long time. It was also impossible to take it whole again. These words are like a mantra for the local people imprinted in their hearts, so they do not do so.

CONCLUSION

The description of the origin of the Budong-Budong and Topoyo ethnicities using oral literature and stories found on the site generally has the same pattern; namely, the two ethnicities represent themselves as the same ethnicity on the one hand, as well as different on the other. The Budong-Budong ethnicity, which is also claimed by the Topoyo ethnic as indigenous people, slowly became a minority, so with the spirit of cultural identity included the Topoyo ethnicity as part of them. However, they need to find more similarities other than just being residents who first existed in the area, considering that Central Mamuju Regency is so open to the transmigration program, which has the potential to cause more ethnic people to come from outside than the original ethnicity. It is to strengthen their identity in facing challenges in the uncertain future.

This research has limited data sources because it is only through literature studies, so it requires more field data to confirm statements found in previous research that has yet to be answered.

References

Aksarin, A. (2018). *Tradisi Mamose Masyarakat Adat Budong-Budong di Desa Tabolang Kecamatan Topoyo Kabupaten Mamuju Tengah (Tinjauan Aqidah Islam)* [Undergraduate]. Universitas Islam Negeri Alauddin .

Alimuddin, M. R. (2013, December 16). *Menyoal Kalimat Lalla Tassisara' di Lambang Kabupaten Mamuju Tengah.* Mandar Untuk Nusantara Kebudayaan Mandar Dan Kebaharian Nusantara. https://ridwanmandar.blogspot.com/2013/12/menyoal-kalimat-lalla-tassisara-di.html

Alqadrie, S. (1999). Konflik Etnis di Ambon dan Sambas: Suatu Tijauan Sosiologis. *Antropologi Indonesia, 58.*

Ardiansyah, S. I. (2010). Konflik etnis samawa dengan etnis bali: tinjauan sosial politik dan upaya resolusi konflik. *Fakultas Ilmu Sosial Dan Ilmu Politik, Universitas Samawa, Sumbawa Besar, NTB, 23,* 4.

Badan Pengembangan dan Pembinaan Bahasa. (2019). *Bahasa Topoiyo.* Bahasa Dan Peta Bahasa Di Indonesia. https://petabahasa.kemdikbud.go.id/provinsi.php?idp=Sulawesi Barat

Barker, C. (2016). *Cultural Studies: Teori & Praktik.* Kreasi Wacana.

Bertrand, J. (2004). *Nationalism and Ethnic Conflict in Indonesia* (J. Ravenhill, Ed.; 1st ed.). Cambridge University Press.

Bumi Ngapaboa. (2011, January 28). *Sejarah Kampoeng Ngapaboa Topoyo.* Bumi Ngapaboa. https://bumingapaboa.blogspot.com/2011/01/sejarah-kampoeng-ngapaboa-topoyo.html

Dinas Tenaga Kerja dan Transmigrasi. (2022, February 23). *Pemberangkatan Transmigrasi Ke Mamuju Tahun 2021.*

Dwi, T. (2018). *Tradisi Pamose di Desa Topoyo Kecamatan Topoyo Kabupaten Mamuju Tengah* [Undergraduate]. Universitas Negeri Makassar.

Fajrin R., H., Ridwan, M., Jemmain, Rasyid, Abd., & Nasruddin. (2020). *Pemetaan Sastra di Kabupaten Mamuju Tengah.*

Friberg, T., & Laskowske, T. V. (1989). South Sulawesi Languages, 1989. In *NUSA: Linguistic Studies of Indonesian and Other Languages in Indonesia 31* (pp. 1–17). Universitas Katolik Atma Jaya. http://sealang.net/archives/nusa/pdf/nusa-v31-p1-18.pdf

Grimes, C. E., & Grimes, B. D. (1987). *Languages of South Sulawesi.* Dept. of Linguistics, Research School of Pacific Studies, Australian National University.

Hall, S. (2003). Representation: *Cultural Representations and Signifying Practices* (S. Hall, Ed.; 1st ed.). Sage Publications Ltd.

Hall, S. (2013). Stuart Hall Interview - 2 June 2011. *Cultural Studies, 27*(5), 757–777. https://

doi.org/10.1080/09502386.2013.773674

Hanapi, M. F. (2022, September 30). *Mamuju Tengah mengandalkan program transmigrasi bangun pertanian.* Berita. https://www.antaranews.com/berita/3148297/mamuju-tengah-mengandalkan-program-transmigrasi-bangun-pertanian

Hos, J., Kusujiarti, S., Upe, A., Arsyad, M., Dharta, F. Y., & Natanson, J. (2022). Conflict Management in Multi-ethnic Communities: A Case Study in Southeast Sulawesi, Indonesia. *Journal of International Migration and Integration, 23*(4), 1963–1985. https://doi.org/10.1007/s12134-021-00923-0

Humas Unismuh. (2023, April 11). *Skripsi Dianggap Menyinggung Suku Tolaki, Begini Klarifikasi Kaprodi Pendidikan Sosiologi Unismuh.* Berita Kampus. https://news.unismuh.ac.id/2023/04/11/skripsi-dianggap-menyinggung-suku-tolaki-begini-klarifikasi-kaprodi-pendidikan-sosiologi-unismuh/

Juditha, C. (2015). Stereotip dan Prasangka dalam Konfl ik Etnis Tionghoa dan Bugis Makassar. *Jurnal Ilmu Komunikasi, 12*(1).

Kila, S. (2019). Berdirinya Kerajaan Mamuju. Walasuji: *Jurnal Sejarah Dan Budaya, 10*(2), 155–172. https://doi.org/10.36869/wjsb.v10i2.16

Kominfo Mamuju Tengah. (2023, February 2). *33 Kerukunan duduk bersama membincang pembentukan Forkompak.* Berita Daerah. https://8enam.com/33-kerukunan-duduk-bersama-membincang-pembentukan-forkompak/

Laskowske, T. (2007). The Seko Languages of South Sulawesi: A Reconstruction *. *Studies in Philippine Languages and Cultures, 15*, 115–210. https://www.sil.org/system/files/reapdata/12/62/53/126253971294887139914666902206830198041/Seko_languages.pdf

Mahrul, R. (2017, July 7). *Mengenal Masyarakat Adat dan Budaya Lokal di Kabupetan Mamuju Tengah.* Tanggou News. http://rahmienmahrul.blogspot.com/2017/07/mengenal-masyarakat-adat-dan-budaya.html

McAdams, D. P. (1996). Personality, modernity, and the storied self: A current framework for studying persons. *Psychological Inquiry, 7*(4), 295–321.

Penghapusan Diskriminasi Ras dan Etnis, Pub. L. No. 40, Undang-Undang Republik Indonesia (2008).

O'Reilly, A. (2004). *Toni Morrison and Motherhood: A Politics of the Heart.* State University of New York Press.

Parekh, B. (2006). *Rethinking Multiculturalism: Cultural diversity and political theory* (2nd ed.). Palgrave Macmillan.

Putro, Y. A., Atmaja, H. T., & Sodiq, I. (2017). Konflik Rasial Antara Etnis Tionghoa Dengan Pribumi Jawa di Surakarta Tahun 1972-1998. *Journal of Indonesian History, 6*(1).

Sewang, A. (2018). *Bunga Rampai Bahari Mandar.* Wineka Media.

SIL International. (2023a). *Budong-Budong.* Ethnologue. https://www.ethnologue.com/language/bdx/

SIL International. (2023b). *Panasuan.* Ethnologue. https://www.ethnologue.com/language/psn/

SIL International. (2023c). *Topoiyo.* Ethnologue. https://www.ethnologue.com/language/toy/

Sopu, S. (2016). *Prospek Budaya Lokal Kabupaten Mamuju Tengah untuk Pembangunan Daerah.*

Valkama, K. (1987). Unhas-SIL Sociolinguistic Survey: Kabupaten Mamuju. *South Sulawesi Sociolinguistic Surveys 1983-1987,* 99–117. https://www.sil.org/resources/archives/37657

Waite, S. G. (2022). Islandness as Narratives of Relation. *Shima, 16*(2), 214–232.

Weedon, C. (2004). *Identity and Culture: Narratives of Difference and Belonging* (1st ed.). McGraw-Hill Education.

Yamaguchi, M. (2001). Kedudukan Bahasa Mamuju secara Genealogis dalam Kelompok Bahasa Sulawesi Selatan. *Analisis Tahun II, 3*, 169–188.

The Passive Sentence of Javanese of Indramayu Dialect

Sry Satriya Tjatur Wisnu Sasangka(sstwisnusasangka@gmail.com)
Emma Maemunah(emmamaemunah69@gmail.com) | **Exti Budihastuti**(exti001@brin.go.id)
Sutejo(sute001@brin.go.id)
National Research and Innovation Agency, Archaeological, Language and Literature Research Organization

INTRODUCTION

Javanese is a regional language in Indonesia which is used as a means of Javanese daily communication until today. This Javanese language has the largest number of speakers in Indonesia. Its distribution area also expand to the island of Sumatra, such as in Lampung, Medan (North Sumatra), and Darmasuta (West Sumatra), as well as in transmigration areas on several islands in Indonesia. Javanese is also used by the Javanese and their descendants in New Calidonia and Suriname (Poedjosoedarma, 1979). On the island of Java, Javanese is spoken in Central Java, the Special Region of Yogyakarta, and East Java, while in West Java, Javanese is spoken in Banjar (Banjar Patoman), Losari Kulon, Cirebon, Indramayu, and in Serang (Banten).

The Javanese were able to get to Lampung, Medan, New Calidonia, and Suriname because the Dutch government promised large salaries as contract laborers to work on new land. They were transported by ship by the Dutch government to those places. Arriving at their destination, they were forced to open new land which was still in the form of jungle and then was made into plantation fields. The contracted coolies were forced to plant rubber, coffee and sugarcane in that area. That time, those three commodities were the main commodities for developing the Netherlands foreign exchange which was starting to decline. Along with the development of the people in that place, the Javanese language also developed according to the development of the Javanese community in that area as well. If this is examined, the variations of the Javanese language certainly would be obtained based on various geographical locations.

Like the Javanese language in Indramayu, it developed naturally downstream of the Cimanuk River at the end of the Majapahit era. Cimanuk River was the border of the territory of the Javanese and the Pasundan kingdom in the past (Kasim, 2019). Tome Pires in Armando Ed. (2018) stated that the people in the eastern part of the Cimanuk River used Javanese, while in the west of the Cimanuk River the people used Sundanese. Even so, transactions between sellers and buyers can take place without trouble. Then, during the Mataram era, Indramayu was made a rice barn for the Mataram army when it was about to drive out the Dutch from Batavia. The influence of the two great rulers at different times had an impact on the emergence of a distinctive form of the Javanese language in the Indramayu area. As a result, the Javanese language in Indramayu has its own characteristics compared to the Javanese outside Indramayu. The uniqueness can be seen at the level of sounds, words, or sentences. Kasim (2020) mentions that the Indramayu Javanese language is one of the dialects of the Javanese language used by the Javanese people in the Indramayu region and its surroundings. He further explained that the Javanese language in Indramayu was different from the Javanese outside Indramayu. Even so, these differences can still be understood by Javanese people outside Indramayu.

At the sound level, for example, the Javanese Indramayu dialect--hereinafter abbreviated as BJDI--does not recognize prenasal or prenasalized sounds, like the Javanese outside the Indramayu dialect (hereinafter abbreviated as BJLI) or Javanese in general. The words Bandung, Demak, Jatiwangi, and Gresik, for example, are still pronounced /bandung/, /demak/, /jatiwangi/, and /gresik/ and are not pronounced /mbandung/, /ndemak/, /

njatiwangi/, and /nggresik/ like usually spoken by the BJLI speaking community.

At the word level, BJDI still retains archaic forms, such as *kita* 'me', *luru* 'looking/looking for', *batur* 'friend', *manjing* 'enter', and *kuwen* 'that' which in BJDI the word is equivalent to *aku* 'me', *golek* 'search', *kanca* 'friend', *mlebu* 'enter', and *kuwi/iku* 'that'. Meanwhile, at the sentence level, BJDI also has its own characteristics, as shown in the example below.

(1) *Tarling ditonton kita/reang mau bengi.*
tarling dilihat saya tadi malam
'Tarling kulihat tadi malam'
Tarling was watched (by me) last night

(2) *Buku baru kuwen wis diduweni reyang!*
buku baru itu sudah dimiliki saya
'Buku baru itu sudah kumiliki!'
The new book had been owned by me

(3) *Buku kiyen ditulis sira kapan?*
buku ini ditulis kamu kapan
'Buku ini kautulis kapan?'
This book, when was written by you?

The equivalent sentences in BJLI for the three BJDI sentences (1-3) above can be seen in sentences (4-6) below.

(4) *Tarling taktonton mau bengi.*
'Tarling saya lihat tadi malam'
Tarling, I watched it last night.

(5) *Buku anyar iku wis takduweni!*
'Buku baru itu sudah kumiliki.'
The new book had been owned by me

(6) *Buku iki koktulis kapan?*
'Buku ini kautulis kapan?'
This book, when was written by you?

The example above shows that there is a difference in form between sentences (1-3) which are BJDI and sentences (4-5) which are BJLI even though they both speak Javanese and are used to express the same meaning. The above differences are likely due to different geographical locations. The Indramayu region is located on the western part of the North Coast of Java Island or located on the North Coast of West Java which is far from the negari (the center of the Javanese kingdom), both during the era of the Pajang Sultanate and the Mataram Sultanate.

Because it is far from the center of government, the Indramayu Javanese language develops naturally so that innovations that occur in the center of government experience obstacles or have not yet reached the Indramayu area. Such conditions gradually gave birth to a new geographical variety. Language varieties that arise due to geographical differences are commonly called dialects (Ayatrohaedi, 1979).

Indramayu Javanese had been studied by Kartika et al. (2007) titled *Penelitian Kekerabatan dan Pemetaan Bahasa-Bahasa di Jawa Barat dan Banten.* However, Kartika saw Indramayu only from a dialectometric point of view to calculate the degree of kinship of regional languages in West Java and Banten. Meanwhile, Kasim (2020) in his book entitled *Bahasa Jawa Indramayu: Latar Sosiolinguistik, Dialektologi, Politisasi, dan Pemertahanan Bahasa* explicitly stated that Indramayu language is one of the dialects of the Javanese language that is developing on the North Coast of West Java. The two authors, both Kartika and Kasim, did not discuss grammatical aspects at all, both morphology and syntax, more over discuss BJDI passive sentences.

In relation to the explanation above, this paper would sufficiently describe the form of BJDI passive sentences, both in the form of *bagongan* (ngoko) and *bebasan* (krama). Therefore, the author used a qualitative approach by utilizing descriptive, comparative, and inferential methods so that it was hoped that a sufficient description of the passive form of the Indramayu dialect of Javanese which is different from other Javanese dialects could be obtained.

1. Passive Sentence

Passive sentences are sentences which its predicate is a passive verb and the subject acts as a sufferer or becomes the target of an action (Sasangka, 2014: 22). This is in line with the opinion of Wedhawati et al. (2001: 436-437) which stated that passive sentences are sentences which the verbal predicate requires a subject to act as a sufferer or recipient. Here are some examples.

(7) *Wahyono dinasehati atasannya karena sering lupa mengisi daftar kehadiran.*
Wahyono was advised by his boss because he often forgot to fill in the attendance list.

(8) *Kaki gadis itu terjepit pintu KRL Jakarta--Bogor dua hari yang lalu.*
The girl's leg was pinched in the door of the Jakarta-Bogor KRL two days ago.

(9) *Mur dan baut ini dibuat di Tegal.*
These nuts and bolts are made in Tegal.

The sentences above are passive sentences because the predicates in the three sentences, namely advised (7), pinched (8), and made (9) are passive verbs. In addition, the subjects in the three sentences, namely Wahyono (7), irl's feet (8), and nuts and bolts (9) are the targets of the act or become sufferers. According to Sasangka (2014), Javanese passive sentences can be divided into five types, namely passive sentences which its predicate uses the affixes below.

(i) *dak-/tak-* + basic verb + *-i/-kan*
(ii) *ko/kok* + basic verb + *-i/-kan*
(iii) *di-* + basic verb + *-i/-kan*
(iv) *ke-* + basic verb
(v) *ka-* + basic verb
(vi) *-in-* + basic verb

This is in line with the opinion of Slametmuljana (1955: 120-124) and Dardjowidjojo in Purwo (1986). The use of passive sentences in Javanese can be seen in the following examples of sentences.

(9) *Omah iku wis daktuku.*
'Rumah itu sudah kubeli.'
The house has been bought by me.

(10) *Blangkon iki arep kokenggo kapan?*
'Blangkon ini akan kaugunakan kapan?
When will the blangkon be used by you?

(11) *Herman digoleki Warsi wiwit wingi.*
'Herman dicari Warsi sejak kemarin.'
Herman was looked for by Warsi yesterday.

(12) *Negeri iku ketekan musuh saka mancanegara.*
'Negara ini kedatangan musuh dari luar negeri.'
This country has been attacked by an enemy from abroad.

(13) *Tumindak ala lan becik bakal kacatet malaikat.*
'Perbuatan baik dan buruk akan dicatat malaikat.'
Good and bad deeds will be noted by angels.'

(14) *Katresnan iku ora bisa tinumbas arta.*
'Kasih sayang itu tidak bisa dibeli dengan uang.'
'Love can't be bought with money.'

Cartier (1979) argued that in general passive has an active equivalent and vice versa. Thus, the passive sentence above can be returned to the active form or can be traced to its original form as shown in the following changes.

(9) a. *Omah iku wis taktuku.*
'Rumah itu sudah kubeli.'
The house has been bought by me

b. *Aku wis tuku omah iku.*
'Saya sudah membeli rumah itu.'

I have bought that house.

(10) a. *Blangkon iki arep kokenggo kapan?*
'Blangkon ini akan kaugunakan kapan?
When will the blangkon be used by you?

b. *Kowe arep ngenggo blangkon iki kapan?*
'Kamu akan memakai blangkon ini kapan?'
When will you use the blangkon?

(11) a. *Herman digoleki Warsi wiwit wingi.*
'Herman dicari Warsi sejak kemarin.'
Herman was looked for by Warsi since yesterday

b. *Warsi nggoleki Herman wiwit mau.*
'Warsi mencari Herman sejak tadi.'
Warsi looked for Herman since yesterday.

(12) a. *Negeri iku ketekan musuh saka mancanegara.*
'Negara ini kedatangan musuh dari luar negeri.'
This country has been attacked by an enemy from abroad.

b. *Musuh saka mancanegara nekani negeri iku.*
'Musuh dari luar negeri mendatangi negeri itu.'
An enemy from abroad has attacked that country.

(13) a. *Tumindak ala lan becik bakal kacathet malaikat.*
'Perbuatan baik dan buru akan dicatat malaikat.'
Good and bad deeds will be noted by angels.'

b. Malaikat bakal nyathet tumindak ala lan becik.
'Malaikat akan menncatat perbuatan buruk dan baik.'
Angels will note good and bad deeds '

(14) a. *Katresnan iku ora bisa tinumbas arta.*
'Kasih sayang itu tidak bisa dibeli dengan uang.'
'Love can't be bought by money.'

b. *Arta ora bisa numbaskatresnan iku.*
'Uang tidak bisa membeli kasih sayang.'
Money cannot buy love.

Sentences (9a) and (10a) are actually not original passive sentences, but are peripheral passive sentences (Sasangka 2014) because the passive form of sentences (9a) and (10a) should be (9c) Omah wis dituku (dening) aku and (10c) *Blangkon iku arep dienggo kowe kapan?* However, sentences (9c) and (10c) in standard Javanese are considered ungrammatical, instead the grammatical ones are passive forms as seen in sentences (9a) and (10a) above.

Passive sentences which its predicate is in the form of a verb, which use the affix ke-, and which express an accident also cannot be returned to their original form.

(15) a. *Sikile Yanto kecepit lawang sepur.*
'Kaki Yanto terjepit pintu kereta.'
Yanto's leg was pinched in the train door.'
b. *Lawang sepur nyepit sikile Yanto.*
'Pintu kereta menjepit kaki Yanto.'
'The train door pinched Yanto's leg.'

Syntactically sentences (17a) and (17b) are grammatical sentences, but semantically there are fundamental differences in meaning. Sentence (17a) Yanto suffers from *kecepit lawang sepur* (being pinched by the train's door) because of the train door's being accidentally closed, while (17b) Yanto suffers because *lawang sepur* (train's door) deliberately pinch *(nyepit)* Yanto's leg *(sikile Yanto).*

2. Form of Passive Sentence of BJDI

BJDI passive sentences, both the *bagongan* variety and the *bebasan* variety, have their own characteristics compared to BJLI. This uniqueness is not only seen in the diction used, but also in the sentence structure. The uniqueness of diction can be seen in the following examples of sentences. The (a) is the *bagongan* variety (ngoko) and the (b) is the *bebasan* variety (krama).

(16) a. *Sira ditinggal batur-batur kabeh?*

b. *Sampeyan ditilar rencang-rencang sedaya?*
'Kamu ditinggal teman-teman semua?'
You were left by all your friends?

(17) a. *Buku kiyen ditulis mama kapan?*
b. *Buku puniki diserat Bapak kapan?*
'Buku ini ditulis Bapak kapan?'
When was this book written by Bapak?

(18) a. *Endhase bocah kuwen ditotok bapane.*
b. *Sirahe lare puniku ditotok bapane.*
'Kepala anak itu dijitak ayahnya.'
The child's head was hit by his father.

(19) a. *Runtah ning pinggir dalan dirubung laler.*
b. *Runtah teng sisi margi dirubung laler*
'Sampah di tepi jalan dikerumuni lalat.'
The trash by the side of the road was swarmed with flies.

(20) a. *Kunir dibebek mimi sampe alus.*
b. *Kunir dibebek mimi ngantos alus.*
'Kunyit ditumbuk ibu sampai halus.'
The turmeric was pounded by mother until smooth.

The sentences above are passive sentences because the word *ditinggal* 'were left' in (16a) and *ditilar* 'were left' in (16b), *ditulis* 'was written' in (17a) dan *diserat* 'was written' in (17b), *ditotok* 'was hit' in (18a and 18b), dirubung 'was swarmed in (19a and 19b), as well as *dibebek* 'was pounded in (20a and 20b) are *di-* affixed passive verbs which function as the predicate of the sentence. Whereas the word *sira* 'you' in (16a) and *sampean* in (16b), *buku kiyen* 'this book' pada (17a) and *buku puniki* in (17b), *endhase bocah kuwen* 'the child's head' in (18a) and *sirahe lare puniku* (18b), *runtah ning pinggir dalan* 'trash by the side of the road' in (19a) and *runtang teng sisi margi* (19b), as well as *kunir* 'turmeric' in (20a dan 20b) are nouns or noun phrases which function as subject and become the target of the actions. On the oyher side, *batur-bature kabeh* 'all your friends' pada (16a) dan *rencang-rencang sedaya* (16b), *bapak* 'bapak' in (17a) and *bapak* 'bapak' in (17b), *bapane* 'his father' in (18a and 18b), *laler* 'fliest' in (19a and 19b), and *mama* 'mother' in (20a and 20b) are nouns or noun phrases which function as as complements and become actors of the sentence's actions.

If the sentences are returned to their original forms, the sentences will change into the following: (a) is a passive sentence and (c) is an active sentence.

(16) a. *Sira ditinggal batur-batur kabeh?*
'Kamu ditinggal teman-teman semua?'
You were left by all your friends?
c. *Batur-batur kabeh ninggal sira?*
'teman-teman semua meninggalkanmu?'
All your friends left you.

(17) a. *Buku kiyen ditulis mama kapan?*
'Buku ini ditulis bapak kapan?'
When was this book written by bapak?
c. *Mama nulis buku kiyen kapan?*
'Bapak menulis buku ini kapan?
Bapak menulis bukui ini kapan?

(18) a. *Endhase bocah kuwen ditotok bapane.*
'Kepala anak itu dijitak ayahnya.'
The child's head was hit by his father.
c. *Bapane notok endhase bocah kuwen.*
'Bapaknya menjitak kepala anak itu.'
His father hit the child's head.

(19) a. *Runtah ning pinggir dalan dirubung laler.*
'Sampah di tepi jalan dikerumuni lalat.'
The trash by the side of the road was swarmed with flies.
c. *Laler ngrubung runtah ning pinggir dalan.*
'Lalat mengerumuni sampah di pinggir jalan.'
The flies swarmed the trash by the side of the road.

(20) a. *Kunir dibebek mimi sampe alus.*
'Kunyit ditumbuk ibu sampai halus.'

The turmeric was pounded by mother until smooth.

c. *Mimi mbebek kunir sampe alus.*
'Ibu menumbuk kunyit sampai halus.'
Mother pounded the turmeric until smooth.

When they are compared to BJLI, there is no difference in the *di-* affixed passive structure in BJDI. The following is the comparison of it. The (a) is BJDI and the (d) is BJLI.

(21) a. *Sira ditinggal batur-batur kabeh?*
d. *Kowe ditinggal kanca-kanca kabeh?*
'Kamu ditinggal teman-teman semua?'
You were left by all your friends?

(22) a. *Buku kiyen ditulis mama kapan?*
d. *Buku iki ditulis bapak kapan?*
'Buku ini ditulis bapak kapan?'
When was this book written by bapak?

(23) a. *Endhase bocah kuwen ditotok bapane.*
d. *Endhase bocah kuwi dikethak bapake.*
'Kepala anak itu dijitak ayahnya.'
The child's head was hit by his father.

(24) a. *Runtah ning pinggir dalan dirubung laler.*
d. *Uwuh ing pinggir dalan dirubung laler*
'Sampah di tepi jalan dikerumuni lalat.'
The trash by the side of the road was swarmed with flies.

(25) a. *Kunir dibebek mimi sampe alus.*
d. *Kunir didheplok emak nganti alus.*
'Kunyit ditumbuk ibu sampai halus.'
The turmeric was pounded by mother until smooth.

The analysis showed that *sira* 'you' (21a) and *kowe* 'you' (21d), *buku kiyen* 'this booki' (22a) and *buku iku* (22d), *endhase bocah kuwen* 'the child's head' (23a) and *endhase bocah kuwi* (23d), *runtah* 'trash' (24a) dan *uwuh*

(24d), as well as *kunir* (25a and 25d) are nouns or naouns phrases which function as subject and become the sufferer or target.

The words *ditinggal* 'were left' (21a and 21d), *ditulis* 'was written' (22a and 22d), *ditotok* 'hit' (23a) and *dikethak* 'hit' (23d), *dirubung* 'swarmed' (24a and 24d), as well as *dibebek* 'pounded' (25a) and *didheplok* (25d) are *di-* affixed verbs which function a predicate. On the other side, words *batur-batur kabeh* 'all friends' (21a) and *kanca-kanca kabeh* (21d), *Bapak* 'bapak' (22a) and *bapak* 'bapak' (22d), *bapane* 'his father' (23a) and *bapake* '(23d), *laler* 'flies' (24a and 24d), as well as *Ibu* 'mother' (25a) and *emak* (25d) are nouns or nouns phrase which function as compliments and also become the doer of the actions in those sentences.

Meanwhile, *kapan* 'when' (22a and 22d) are questioner pronoun which function as adverb, while *sampe alus* 'until smooth' (25a) and *nganti alus* (25d) are prepositional phrase which function as adverb. Therefore, the structure of passive sentence between BJDI and BJLI are the same, which is the structure of S-P-Pel as seen in the sentence of (21a and 21d), (23a and 23d), dan (24a and 24d; the structure of S-P-Pel-K as seen in the sentence of (22a and 22d) dan (25a and 25d).

Meanwhile, the uniqueness of the passive sentence structure of BJDI can be seen in the following examples.

(26) *Novel Dermayu kiyen sira tulis kapan?*
'Novel Dermayu ini kautulis kapan?'
When was Dermayu Novel written by tou?

(27) *Buku kuwen durung kita baca.*
'Buku itu belum saya baca.'
The book has not been read by me.

(28) *Perjanjian kiyen wis dheweke setujuni?*
'Perjanjian ini sudah dia setujui?'
The agreement has been agreed by him.

(29) *Kesepakatan kiyen wis wong-wong iku weruhi?*
'Kesepakatan ini telah mereka ketahui.
The deal has already been known by them.

(30) *Ketekaan rombongan kuwen ora kita-kita weruhi.*
'Kedatangan rombongan itu tidak kami ketahui.'
The arrival of the group hasn't been known by us.

The analysis showed that *sira tulis* 'you wrote' (26), *durung kita* baca 'has not been read' (27), wis *deweke setujuni* 'has been sgreed' (28), *wis wong-wong iku weruhi* 'has been known by them' (29), and *ora kita-kita weruhi* 'we havenot known' (30) are verb phrase which is pronoun + verb without affix functioning as predicate. Whereas *Novel Dermayu* 'Dermayu Novel' (26), *buku kuwen* 'that book' (27), *perjanjian kiyen* 'this agreement' (28), *kesepakatan kiyen* 'this deali' (29), and *ketekaan rombongan kuwen* 'the arrival of the group' (30) are noun phrase which function as subject and becpme the target of the actions. Meanwhile, *kapan* 'when' (26) is the questioner pronoun which function as adverb. Even though the predicate is pronoun + verb without prefix and *di-* prefixed, those sentences are still passive sentences because the subjects of those become the target of the actions.

Even though the predicate in the sentence of (26—30) do not use di- affixed verbs, the sentences can be returned into the active forms, as follows.

(31) *Sira nulis Novel Dermayu kuwen kapan?*
'Kamu menulis Novel Dermayu ini kapan?'
When did you write Dermayu Novel?

(32) *Kita durung maca buku kuwen.*
'Saya belum membaca buku itu.'
I haven't read that book.

(33) *Dheweke wis nyetujuni perjanjian kiyen?*
'Dia telah menyetujui perjanjian ini?'
He has agreed to the agreement.

(34) *Wong-wong iku wis meruhi kesepakatan kiyen?*
'Mereka telah mengetahui kesepakatan ini?'
They knew the deal.

(35) *Kita-kita ora meruhi ketekaan rombongan kuwen.*

'Kami tidak mengetahui kedatangan rombongan itu.'
We didn't know the arrival of the group.

The uniqueness of BJDI sentences will be clear if sentence (26) above is compared with BJLI, especially with standard Javanese or the Javanese language used in Surakarta and Yogyakarta as below. Which (a) is BJDI and (b) is BJLI.

(26) a. *Novel Dermayu kiyen sira tulis kapan?* (S-P-K)
b. *Novel Dermayu iki koktulis kapan?* (S-P-K)
'Novel Dermayu ini kautulis kapan?'

f sentences (26a—26b) are examined, it appears that BJBI and BJLI do not show structural differences, that is, they both have the S-P-K structure, but the difference lies in the form of the verb which is the predicate in the sentence. In BJDI the predicate is in the form of a second singular pronominal + verb (sira + tulis) as in (26a), whereas in BJLI it is in the form of a proclitic second singular pronominal + verb (*kok* + *tulis*) as in (26b). This shows that BJDI does not recognize the *kok-* form as a proclitic second person singular pronoun as commonly used in BJLI. However, the passive sentence (26a) has another variant as shown in sentence (26c) below.

(26) c. **Novel Dermayu kiyen kok tulis kapan?*
'Novel Dermayu ini ditulis kamu kapan?'
When was Dermayu Novel written by tou?
d. *Novel Dermayu kiyen ditulis sira kapan?*
'Novel Dermayu ini ditulis kamu kapan?'
When was Dermayu Novel written by tou?

Meanwhile, in BJLI—associated with the predicate in the form of a singular first person pronoun used as a passive verb marker—sentence (26b) does not have other variants as in BJDI above so sentences (26d) and (26e) below are forms that are not accepted in BJLI.

(26) d. **Novel Dermayu iki kowe tulis kapan?*
'Novel Dermayu ini kamu tulis kapan?'
e. **Novel Dermayu iki ditulis kowe kapan?*
'Novel Dermayu ini ditulis kamu kapan?'

Thus, BJDI active sentences changed into passive *Sira nulis Novel Dermayu kuwen kapan?* 'Kamu menulis Novel Dermayu ini kapan?' is (i) *Novel Dermayu kiyen sira tulis kapan?* 'Novel Dermayu ini kautulis kapan?and (ii) *Novel Dermayu kiyen ditulis sira kapan?* 'Novel Dermayu ini ditulis kamu kapan?' both sentence a and b are both accepted in BJDI.

The other uniqueness of BJDI sentence will clearly appear if sentence (27) above compare to BJLI, specially with the Javanese of Surakarta dan Yogyakarta as below.

seperti di bawah ini; (a) is BJDI and (b) is BJLI.

(27) a. *Buku kuwen durung kita baca.* (S-P)
'Buku itu belum saya baca.'
b. *Buku kuwi durung takwaca.* (S-P)
'Buku itu belum kubaca.'

If sentences (27a) and (27b) wre examined, it appeared that between BJBI and BJLI did not show structural differences, that is, they both have an S-P structure, but the difference lies in the form of the verb which becomes the predicate in the sentence. In BJDI the sentence predicate (27a) is in the form of the first singular pronoun + verb (kita + baca), whereas in BJLI the sentence predicate (27b) is in the form of the first singular pronoun + verb (tak + tulis). There is another interesting thing, namely that in Indramayu sentence (27a) above has another variant as shown below.

(27) c. *Buku kuwen durung tekbaca.* (S-P)
'Buku itu belum kubaca.'
d. *Buku kuwen durung dibaca kita/reang.* (S-P-Pel)
'Buku itu belum dibaca saya.'

Some of the data above shows that sentences (27a), (27c), and (27d) are acceptable forms and productively used in Inderamayu. This shows that the BJDI passive sentence—associated with a predicate in the form of a single personal pronoun used as a passive verb marker—has three forms, namely (i) *tek + verb,* (ii) *kita/reang + verb,* and (iii) *di- + verba + kita/reang.*

Meanwhile, in BJLI—associated with a predicate in the form of a single personal pronoun used as a passive verb marker—sentence (27b) does not have other variants as in BJDI above so sentences (27e) and (27f) below are forms that are unacceptable in BJLI, especially in standard Javanese (Surakarta and Yogyakarta).

(27) e. **Buku kuwi durung aku waca.* (S-P)
'Buku itu belum saya baca.'
f. **Buku kuwi durung diwaca aku.* (S-P-Pel)
Buku itu belum dibaca saya.'

Thus, the passivity of active sentences in BJDI *Kita durung maca buku kuwen* 'Saya belum membaca buku itu' is (i) *Buku kuwen durung kita baca* 'Buku itu belum kubaca', (ii) *Buku kuwen durung tekbaca* 'Buku itu belum kubaca', dan (iii) *Buku kuwen durung dibaca kita/reang* 'Buku itu belum dibaca saya.' All three forms are equally acceptable in BJDI.

On the other hand, the uniqueness of the BJDI sentence will become clear if sentence (28) above is compared to the BJLI as shown in the following sentence, which (a) is BJDI and which (b) is BJLI.

(28) a. *Perjanjian kiyen wis dheweke setujuni?* (S-P)
'Perjanjian ini sudah dia setujui?'
b. *Perjanjian iki wis disetujoni dheweke?* (S-P-Pel)
'Perjanjian ini sudah disetujui dia?'

If sentences (28a) and (28b) are examined, it appears that between BJBI and BJLI there are structural differences, sentence (28a) has an S-P structure while sentence (28b) has an S-P-Pel structure. The form of the verb that becomes the predicate is also different. In BJDI the predicate is in the form of a third person singular pronoun + verb + -i (*dheweke* + *setujuni*) as in sentence (28a), whereas in BJLI the predicate is in the form of a verb with an affix di- -i + third person singular pronoun (*disetujoni* + *dheweke*) as in sentence (28b). There is another thing that needs to be said, namely that in Indramayu sentence (28a) has the following variant (28c).

(28) c. *Perjanjian kiyen wis disetujuni dheweke.*
'Perjanjian ini telah disetujui dia.'

However, outside Indramayu, especially in areas where standard Javanese is spoken, sentence (28b) above does not have any other variants, so sentence (28d) below becomes unacceptable.

(28) d. **Perjanjian iki wis dheweke setujoni.*
'Perjanjian ini telah dia setujui.'

Thus, passivity of active sentence BJDI *Dheweke wis nyetujuni perjanjian kiyen*? '*Dia telah menyetujui perjanjian ini*?' is (i) (i) *Perjanjian kiyen wis dheweke setujuni?* 'Perjanjian ini sudah dia setujui?' and (ii) *Perjanjian kiyen wis disetujuni dheweke*. 'Perjanjian ini telah disetujui dia.' Both forms are equally acceptable in BJDI.

On the other hand, the same thing is also found in the case of passive sentences with a pronoun + verb predicate, both affixed and unaffixed, as in sentences (29a—29b) and (30a—30b) below. Which (a) is BJDI and (b) is BJLI.

(29) a. *Kesepakatan kiyen wis dheweke kabeh (wong-wong iku) weruhi?* (S-P)
'Kesepakatan ini telah dia (orang-orang itu) ketahui?'
b. *Kesepakatan iki wus diweruhi dheweke kabeh?* (S-P-Pel)
'Kesepakatan ini telah mereka ketahui?'

(30) a. *Ketekaan rombongan kuwen ora kita-kita weruhi.* (S-P)

'Kedatangan rombongan itu tidak kami ketahui.'

b. *Ketekan rombongan iku ora dingerteni awake dhewe.* (S-P-Pel)

'Kedatangan rombongan itu tidak kami ketahui.'

If the sentences above are examined, it appears that between BJBI and BJLI there are structural differences, sentences (29a) and (30a) have an S-P structure, while sentences (29b) and (30b) have an S-P-Pel structure. The form of the verb that becomes the predicate is also different. In BJDI the predicate is in the form of a third personal pronoun plural + verb + -i (*dheweke kabeh* + weruhi dan *kita-kita* + *weruhi*) as in sentences (29a) and (30a), whereas in BJLI the predicate is in the form of a verb with an affix di- -i + personal pronoun the three plural (*diweruhi* + *dheweke* dan *dingerteni awake dhewe*) as in sentences (29b) and (30b). In addition, in Indramayu sentences (29a) and (30a) have the following variants (29c) and (30c).

(29) c. *Kesepakatan kiyen wis diweruhi dheweke kabeh (wong-wong iku)?* (S-P-Pel)

'Kesepakatan ini telah diketahui mereka (orang-orang itu) semua?'

(30) c. *Ketekaan rombongan kuwen ora diweruhi kita-kita.* (S-P)

'Kedatangan rombongan itu tidak diketahui kami.'

Outside Indramayu, especially in the area of standard Javanese users, sentences (29b) and (30b) above do not have other variants so if there are sentences (29d) and (30d) below, it can be ascertained that these sentences are not acceptable sentences.

(29) d. **Kesepakatan iki wus dheweke kabeh weruhi?* (S-P)

'Kesepakatan ini telah mereka ketahui?

(30) d. **Ketekan rombongan iku ora awake dhewe ngerteni* (S-P)

'Kedatangan rombongan itu tidak kami ketahui.'

Thus, the passivity of the active voice of BJDI *Wong-wong iku wis meruhi kesepakatan kiyen*? 'Mereka telah mengetahui kesepakatan ini?' is (i)

Kesepakatan kiyen wis dheweke kabeh (*wong-wong iku*) *weruhi*? 'Kesepakatan ini telah diketahui mereka (*orang-orang itu*) semua?' and (ii) *Kesepakatan kiyen* wis diweruhi dheweke kabeh (*wong-wong iku*)? 'Kesepakatan ini telah diketahui mereka (orang-orang itu) semua?' Meanwhile, the passivity of active sentence *Kita-kita ora meruhi ketekaan rombongan kuwen*. 'Kami tidak mengetahui kedatangan rombongan itu.' was (i) *Ketekaan rombongan kuwen ora kita-kita weruhi.* 'Kedatangan rombongan itu tidak kami ketahui.' and (ii) *Ketekaan rombongan kuwen ora diweruhi kita-kita.* 'Kedatangan rombongan itu tidak diketahui kami.'

CONCLUSION

Based on the explanation above, the structure of the BJDI passive sentence is somewhat different from that of BJLI. This difference is evident in passive sentences derived from active sentences whichc subjects are first, second, or third pronouns, both singular and plural. When formed in passive, the subject pronoun in the active sentence will become the predicate in the form of a pronoun + verb (both affixed and unaffected verbs) in the passive sentence. The pronouns in the predicate, only those in the form of a singular first person, which can be changed into a bound form (*tek-*), not *tak-*'ku-', like Javanese in general, while the others are not shortened, but whole in the form of pronouns + verbs. The first singular pronouns in BJDI are *kita* dan *reang*, while the clitic forms of these pronouns are *tek-*. Meanwhile, the second singular pronoun form in BJDI is *sira* not *kowe* and BJDI does not recognize the clitic form of the second singular pronoun *kok-* or its variant *koen-* as in BJLI. Even so, BJDI passive sentences are more varied than BJLI.

References

Ayatraohaedi. 1979. Dialektologi: *Sebuah Pengantar.* Jakarta: Pusat Pembinaan dan Pengembangan Bahasa, Departeman Pendidikan dan Kebudayaan.

Cartier, Alice. 1979. "Kalimat Berverba Transitif yang Mengalami Pemudaran Diatesis di dalam Bahasa Indonesia Ragam Formal". Dalam Bambang Kaswanti Purwo (Ed.). 1989. *Serpih-Serpih Telaah Pasif Bahasa Indonesia.* Yogyakarta: Penerbit Kanisius.

Cortesao, Armando. (Ed.). 2018. *Suma Oriental Karya Tome Pires: Perjalanan dari Laut Merah ke Cina dan Buku Fransiscao Rodrigues.* Yogyakarta: Penerbit Ombak.

Dardjowidjojo, Soenjono. 1986. "Benang Pengikat Wacana" dalam Bambang Kaswanti Purwo (Ed.). 1986. *Pusparagam Linguistik dan Pengajaran Bahasa.* Jakarta: Arcan.

Kartika. 2007. *Penelitian Pemetaan dan Kekerabatan Bahasa-Bahasa di Wilayah Jawa Barat dan Banten.* Bandung: Balai Bahasa Jawa Barat.

Kasim, Supali. 2020. *Bahasa Jawa Indramayu Latar Sosiolinguistik, Dialektologi, Politisasi, dan Pemertahanan Bahasa.* Indramayu: Rumah Pustaka.

Moeliono, Anton M. dkk. 2017. *Tata Bahasa Baku Bahasa Indonesia Edisi Keempat.* Jakarta: Badan Pengembangan dan Pembinaan Bahasa, Kementerian Pendidikan dan Kebudayaan.

Poedjosoedarmo, Supomo. 1979. *Tingkat Tutut Bahasa Jawa.* Jakarta: Pusat Pembvinaan dan Pengembangan Bahasa.

Purwo, Bambang Kaswanti (Ed.). 1989. *Serpih-Serpih Telaah Pasif Bahasa Indonesia.* Yogyakarta: Penerbit Kanisius.

Sasangka, Sry Satriya Tjatur Wisnu. 2014. *Kalimat Pasif Bahasa Indonesia dan Bahasa Jawa Suatu Kajian Pembandingan.* Yogyakarta: Azza Grafika.

Slametmuljana. 1955. *Kaidah Bahasa Indonesia* II. Jakarta: Penerbit Djambatan.

Wedhawati dkk. 2001. *Tata Bahasa Jawa Mutakhir.* Yogyakarta: Penerbit Kanisius.

Cultural Values of Rote Ndao Folklore Telukaman Lailona Dan Hakaman Nepedae

Erwin Syahputra Kembaren(erwi015@brin.go.id) | **Syaiful Bahri**(syai008@brin.go.id)
Dian Susilastri(dian067@brin.go.id) | **Erlinda Rosita**(erli008@brin.go.id) | **Yulia Fitrina**(yuli052@brin.go.id)
National Research and Innovation Agency, Archaeological, Language and Literature Research Organization

INTRODUCTION

The diversity of ethnic groups and oral traditions in East Nusa Tenggara makes this province rich in oral traditions interesting to study. Oral tradition occupies an important position in social life. Folklore, another term for oral tradition, is a collective culture that is spread and passed down traditionally from generation to generation in different versions, in oral form or in examples accompanied by gestures or memory aids, Danandjaya (1991). Oral literature is one part of the oral tradition. Oral literature is a variety of verbal utterances that have characteristics as literary works in general, which include poetry, prose, singing, and oral drama, Taum (2011). Oral literature is an invaluable wealth for society. However, this wealth is now endangered. At the beginning of oral literature thrived in the midst of society, it was not difficult to hear and enjoy traditional literature. However, along with the development of the times, it has become difficult to enjoy oral literature circulating in society. For this reason, in addition to the need for the maintenance of oral literature, it is also necessary to revitalize and document oral literature, so that the oral literature in the speaking community continues to survive.

Folklore can be classified into traditional literature. Traditional literature consists of several types, such as myths, legends, folklore, fables, folk songs, and others, Nurgiyantoro, (2010).. Folklore itself develops without the author knowing. Furthermore, it was spread orally from one generation to the next until today. The immortality of ancient stories cannot be separated from the role of the supporting community. One form of preservation of these regional stories is by passing them on to the younger generation. Many young people in the area are not interested in listening to folklore. Whereas in ancient times, people who were good at telling stories or good at oral literature were people who were considered to have intelligence and had a high social position in a village.

One of the wealth of oral literature in East Nusa Tenggara Province, especially in the Rote area is folklore. As with other areas, the Rote people have a wealth of very diverse folklore. Folklore that exists in the Rote community, is not just a story that has an entertaining function, but the folklore has moral, cultural and religious values for the Rote people in living their lives, Mboeik, (1985). One of the well-known folktales in Rote Ndao Regency is Telukaman Lailona and Hakaman Nepedae which became stories in the beliefs of the ancient Rote people. The story has a deep message that is so important for the life of the Rote people. This can mean that folklore is not just an ordinary story or an empty story without meaning, but is full of the values contained therein.

Research of cultural values in folklore in various regions of the archipelago has been researched, one of which is entitled Cultural Values in West Kalimantan Folklore of Arue Birds and Talokot Birds, Febrianti, (2018). The researcher describes the cultural values contained in folklore using a literary anthropological approach. The cultural values contained in West Kalimantan folklore are gratitude to God, keeping promises and trustworthiness, the value of compassion, patience, and brotherhood. The second researcher who examines cultural values is Ratnawati, (2019) who researches cultural values in Toraja folklore using a cultural anthropological approach. In folklore it is described that the values contained in the folklore are influenced by the Auk To Dolo belief which includes the relationship between humans and creators, nature, and others and oneself.

The approach used in studying cultural values in folklore is carried out through a literary anthropological approach. The literary anthropology approach is the study of literary works that emphasizes the cultural heritage of the past. Therefore, cultural values in a work of oral literature, folklore will be described through an ethnographic approach. In relation to this, Endraswara, (2015) states that an anthropological analysis of literature should reveal things, including the following.

1) Oral traditions in the past which were repeated over and over again in a literary image. Ancestral habits of doing things such as meditating, chanting rhymes, reciting mantras, telling folk tales, and so on are the focus of research..
2) Revealing the roots of tradition or sub-culture and the beliefs of a writer reflected in literary works. In this regard, traditional themes passed down from generation to generation will be of particular concern.
3) Any research can be directed at aspects of ethnographic literary connoisseurs, why they are so obedient in carrying out the messages contained in literary works.
4) Researchers also need to pay attention to the process of inheritance of traditional literature from time to time in an area.
5) The research is directed at the ethnographic or cultural elements of the society surrounding the literary work.

The method used in this research is qualitative. According to Moleong, (2000) qualitative research is a research procedure that produces descriptive data in the form of written or spoken words from people and their behavior can be observed. The object of this research is the folklore of Telukaman Lailona and Hakaman Nepedae in Mokdale Village, Lobalain District, Rote Ndao District. The data collection technique for this research was field data collection using free interviews and directed interviews. Structured/directed interviews, namely asking questions that have been prepared beforehand to get a complete and in-depth picture (in-depth interview), Taum, (2011) and using recording techniques. Recording technique is a data acquisition technique by recording using a tape recorder. After the story data is obtained in the form of a recording, then the data is transcribed. After obtaining written data, the data was translated by translators of the Rote regional language, then the data was analyzed using the hermeneutic theory.

From this background, it can be concluded that this study aims to describe cultural values in the folklore of Telukaman Lailona and Hakaman Nepedae through an analysis of literary anthropology. Furthermore, the results of this study are hoped that the community can preserve the folklore of Telukaman Lailona and Hakaman Nepedae in particular, and other oral literature in the Rote Ndao area and that the community can apply and know the noble values of each of these stories, oral literature and oral traditions. on Rote Island.

DISCUSSION

This story presents two important figures who represent the early beliefs of the Rote people. Telukaman Lailona as the Highest Being who is referred to as the Ruler of the sky and the universe. Meanwhile, Hakaman Nepedae as the ruler of the earth who is entrusted with maintaining and managing crops.

Telukaman Lailona and Hakaman Nepedae are two characters who are emulated by the people who own the story. Telukaman Lailona is a person who is used as a role model because of his power and greatness, as well as his forgiving attitude which is a sign of a harmonious relationship between the creator and his creatures. Likewise, Hakaman Lailona is set as an example because of his persistence and hard work in supporting life. Another example of life is Hakaman's awareness of the power and greatness of the Lord of the sky, so with humility he gives the best offering of the results of his hard work.

It is in this view and belief that the people of Rote will not forget to give offerings to the Lord of the heavens and the universe. They believe in this because the offering is a prayer and an expression of gratitude to Telukaman Lailona (Lord of the Sky) who has given them life and blessings.

1. Synopsis Folklore of *Telukaman Lailona dan Hakaman Nepedae*

In the beliefs of the ancient Rote people, Telukaman Lailona was the ruler of the sky and the universe, while Hakaman Nepedae was the ruler of the earth. Between the two there is an agreement that Hakaman Nepedae as the ruler of the earth must pay tribute to Telukaman Lailona after he has harvested his crops. This agreement was eventually betrayed by Hakaman. Hakaman thinks of Telukaman as a lazy person, who wants to make it easy for him.

Hakaman Nepedae is a rich man. His wealth is abundant thanks to his own hard work. Every time when Hakaman was about to leave, he promised his wife and children, if someone asked for something to eat or drink, then I was not allowed to give it to them. If we give it once then they come asking for it continuously. They have hands, they have legs to work for them, they have a life for their wife and children, don't just make it easy.

One day Telukaman Lailona visited Hakaman's house. He asked about processed products that Hakaman had not offered to him. But what Hakaman said made Telukaman hurt. Hakaman arrogantly flaunts all his wealth. He also said that Telukaman did not know himself, did not work hard but asked whatever he wanted. Telukaman became angry because of Hakaman's arrogance.

When Telukaman returned to the sky, where he lived, he said not to rain for 3 years. But Hakaman thought that it was just an ordinary greeting. He also continues to work to collect as much wealth as possible.

The days continued to pass, the months continued to circulate, the years did not seem to continue to pass. The expected drop of dew and rain did not come. Earth is getting hotter. The grass died, the livestock all died, the food ran out, hunger hit Hakaman, disease befell him. Nature is wrathful, humanity is helpless.

Three years passed. Hakaman is weak, his body is sick, treasures are lost, animals die. Hakaman is destitute. In agony, he came to his senses, remembering Telukaman's warning. Telukaman is hurt by Hakaman's arrogance. Hakaman regrets. He begged for mercy, but it was too late.

Then in a low voice he said: "Servant begs forgiveness, thousands of pardons Your Majesty." I am very sinful, I am arrogant, stubborn and forget myself to offer what I have got, even a little bit. Have mercy on your servant, Your Majesty. Now I believe that Your Majesty is the ruler of heaven and earth, who can do anything for those who don't believe. Therefore please and have mercy on this servant of yours."

Then gently Telukaman held his friend and said: "Come on friend, wipe your tears and wake up, the most important thing is that you are aware and want to repent. I'm going home, get ready, it's going to rain. Goodbye, work hard and see you soon."

Telukaman rushed away and not long after, it started to rain heavily. The water is there, the grass is starting to grow, Hakaman is starting to work as hard as he can.

2. Analysis of Cultural Values in Folklore *Telukaman Lailona dan Hakaman Nepedae*

Within the scope of this research, value is seen as an important characteristic and is embodied in the human heart as a standard of beauty that is appropriate, valuable and can affect the lives of people who have these values. The analysis in this study also refers to cultural values that cover all aspects of human life. This includes life in relation to God, fellow human beings, and nature. Next will be discussed as follows,

2.1. Human Relations With God

Humans as creatures created by God, are very closely related to the Creator. The manifestation of that relationship can be in the form of prayers or ceremonies. Likewise for the Rote people in the folklore of Telukaman Lailona and Hakaman Nepedae. The community believes that God or also called the Supreme Being (Telukaman Lailona) has a very important role in their lives. According to the local community, Telukaman Lailona (God the creator) is evident in their way of life. Because of the awareness that everything in this universe has a creator.

Neme mamahelek hataholi latek, lelekndia mahahuluna, Telukaman Lailona anahou basa-basa manalain ma basa-basa daebafoka masodak lalaen. Kada Hakaman Nepedae anahou kadi daebafok.

(In the beliefs of the ancient Rote people, Telukaman Lailona was the ruler of the sky and the universe, while Hakaman Nepedae was the ruler of the earth.)

Based on the early beliefs held by the people of Rote, Telukaman Lailona is the Ruler of the Sky and Hakaman Nepedae is the ruler of the earth. Humans as intelligent living beings certainly realize that he and everything in this universe was created by someone who has power over everything.

In ancient times, the people of Rote did not know religion. But they believe that there is someone who has power over this nature. They believe there is something that gives life and everything it needs. They call this figure Telukaman Lailona. The word Telukaman means having three powers or authorities. The three powers include creating, giving blessings and judging. The word Lailona means that which comes from above. Meanwhile, the so-called ruler of the earth is Hakaman Nepedae. The word Hakaman means he who is entitled to the four corners of the world or the earth. The word Nepedae means that which is below. Therefore, he was ordered to inhabit and cultivate the land for his life.

Hataholi kaduak ialah lahelulahalak fo Hakaman Nepedae ana kuasa nai daebafok ia ana baefe kamasuin luma neu Telukaman Lailona ana tungasanga basaso hahambu neme sosota.

(Between the two there is an agreement that Hakaman Nepedae as the ruler of the earth must pay tribute to Telukaman Lailona after he harvests his crops.)

In the early part of the story, Telukaman Lailona and Hakaman Nepedae are involved in a mutual agreement. The agreement must be carried out by Hakaman. Hakaman Nepedae, who acts as the ruler of the earth, is obliged to make offerings to Telukaman Lailona. The offering was in the form of produce that Hakaman had to offer to the Lord of Heaven.

The relationship between humans and God in the texts of the stories Telukaman Lailona and Hakaman Nepedae is symbolized by offerings in the form of produce from the fields/fields. For example: rice, sweet potatoes, corn and other rice yields obtained. The offering ordered by Telukaman was a simple offering. Even though Telukaman is a figure of the Most High, he does not demand lavish offerings. The results of rice fields / fields that are obtained by humans are received with open arms.

According to the Rote people, one form of worship and exaltation to the Creator is by giving offerings in the form of crops that have been obtained. As described in the second paragraph, Hakaman Nepedae is obliged to make offerings to Telukaman Lailona. This means that the people of Rote believe that everything in this world belongs to the Creator. Because everything we have received from the Creator must be given as gratitude for His gift.

In the life of the Rote people, giving offerings to the Creator is something that must be done. The offering is a form of expression of gratitude to the Creator who has bestowed life on earth. Not only the breath of life, but also because He has fulfilled all needs, giving strength and health to process these natural products well. The Creator, who pours rain, gives growth to every plant and animal, so that humans can make good use of all of them. Therefore, it is fitting for the Creator to accept offerings from mankind's primary produce on earth.

Until now, things like that are still maintained and upheld by the people of Rote. After they know religion very well, then they understand more about the purpose of giving offerings to the Creator. Giving offerings or commonly called tithing is mandatory. The offering or tithe can be in the form of money or other crops. Such as rice, corn, sweet potatoes and other crops. The people of Rote believe that by giving offerings, one day the Creator will repay their kindness with an abundance of crops.

Telukaman Lailona is a figure who is exalted and glorified because He is the Ruler of the universe who created everything. In addition, his very friendly figure makes him close to humans on earth. Telukaman is a just, patient, gentle and forgiving figure.

The feature of Telukaman Lailona is that he is very fair. For anyone who disobeys and obeys him, a reprimand is deservedly accepted. Like Hakaman who no longer makes offerings, he is given a proper reprimand. All of this is for the good so that Hakaman can repent and return to being a human being who always obeys the Creator.

The following is a quote that indirectly describes the justice of Telukaman:

> *Nae tolanoe mamanene ma masanenedak. Neme faik ia mai au ta oke o babae bali tunga o dudua afin, te hu neme faik ia lasa teuk telu manamaik, ia udan ta ma dinis ta tuda leo daebafokamai, Telukaman ana helu Hakaman.*
> *'Brother, listen and remember carefully, from now on I will not demand any more offerings according to your wishes, but from today until three years from now, there will be no rain or dew that will drip onto the earth," said Telukaman.'*
> *Basa lelesu aelah nai lain au kenasa boema au fe ledo katabikan lae daebafok teuk telu lalaen, Telukaman ana kokolak no Hakaman. Boema Telukaman falileo lalaia neu mamasa leleon na neu.*
> 'I will close all the floodgates in the sky and the hot sun will fall on you for three years, continued Telukaman, then returned to Telukaman to the sky, to his residence.
> The warning given to Hakaman was not a joke. Moreover, the warning is very threatening human life on earth. Telukaman is a fair figure. That justice illustrates that he deserves to be called a ruler. This means that Telukaman does not side with anyone. He judges fairly those who do evil.

Next, the nature of Telukaman is patient and gentle. Patience and gentleness is what Telukaman does when he hears words that are against and belittles himself. He remained calm and patient to hear every word from Hakaman. Hakaman said that Telukaman did not know himself, was lazy to work but wanted to demand profit sharing. But even so Telukaman can be patient and gentle. The nature of this Telukaman can be used as an example, that anger should not be answered with anger.

His meek nature is seen when Hakaman confesses to each of his sins. Telukaman gently approached his friend and forgave his mistake. Telukaman is not indifferent but on the contrary he really cares about Hakaman. This can be seen in the quotation below.

> *Boema no halakokola kokoe nae foaleo, "sadia faledalen mao bertobat. Au sanga fali hundia sadialeo te ndana anakona Telukaman natea anafali tao ueledis maheleo, losa tatonggo seluk."*
> Then gently Telukaman held his friend and said: "Come on friend, wipe your tears and wake up, the most important thing is that you are aware and want to repent. I'm going home, get ready, it's going to rain. Goodbye, work hard and see you soon.

Apart from some of the attitudes above that should be used as examples, Telukaman is also a very forgiving person. This is evidenced from the quotation below.

> *Hakaman dalena hedis mamanene halanatanek neme Telukaman mai nakando. Hakaman anaki nasokahedu nasaneda anatabisaso.*
> 'Hakaman was very sad to hear Telukaman's question. He wept bitterly at the memory of his powerlessness.'
> *Boema no aon nahala, "ata noke fe ampun lai lifun neu mana houanasodak. Ata dosana neunaseli. Ata hataholi mana koaok, langgabatuk analilihena aoiman fo baefe ata tungga sangan luma neu manalain mae bibiana lain hambu. Suemala atamafa manahau masodak. Neme ia mai ata namahele manahau masodak nai lalaia ma daebafoka, nae hambu tao sudi hata soaneu tamanehelek. Ndia tulufali mala, ata dei."*
> 'Then in a low voice he said: "Servant begs forgiveness, thousands of pardons Your Majesty." I am very sinful, I am arrogant, stubborn and forget myself to offer what I have got, even a little bit. Have mercy on your servant, Your Majesty. Now I believe that Your Majesty is the ruler of heaven and earth, who can do anything for those who don't believe. Therefore please and have mercy on this servant of yours.'

Boema no halakokola kokoe nae foaleo, "sadia faledalen mao bertobat. Au sanga fali hundia sadialeo te ndana anakona Telukaman natea anafali tao ueledis maheleo, losa tatonggo seluk."

'Then, Telukaman held his friend and said: "Come on friend, wipe your tears and wake up, the most important thing is that you are aware and want to repent. I'm going home, get ready, it's going to rain. Goodbye, work hard and see you soon.'

In the quote above, it can be seen that when Hakaman begged for forgiveness for each of his sins, Telukaman did not remain silent. Telukaman did not let Hakaman continue to suffer. When Hakaman begs for forgiveness for the sins he has committed, Telukaman is very concerned. He forgave all the sins that Hakaman had committed. According to Telukaman, Hakaman has suffered enough for three years. This moment is the turning point in life that Hakaman should have lived. Hakaman has realized and repented. It's not good if a second chance is not given to him. In addition, Telukaman also granted all of Hakaman's requests. Not long after the rain came down to earth.

Humans as created beings should always obey and obey the Creator. One of them with obedience to give offerings. In addition, respect is also a human awareness that the Most High must always be worshiped. In the folklore of Telukaman Lailona and Hakaman Nepedae, a Hakaman also acts like that. Even though Hakaman behaved inappropriately, he still believed that Telukaman Lailona was "The Most High". This can be seen in the following quotation:

Telukaman, o ta maefa neu oaoinan manaa mudak, ta tao hata-hata ma o moke – moke au sasatanga bae fe o.

'Your honour Telukaman, you are indeed an ignorant person, you are very lazy, you only come begging'.

When Hakaman became emotional and opposed the agreement that had been made, he still called Telukaman "Your Majesty". This means that Hakaman still has respect for Telukaman:

Faikluma Telukaman mai natonggo no tolanoe nai daebafok.
"Tolanoe," Telukaman Nahala.
Talobe betamu taouleding, ledo demaleaso?
"Noke ampun neu ia mana kuasa, ata tabisa tao hata-hata so."
"Leobe naibe o soka-soka hadela laibe, ulek-ulek tuanasu nouk omaka duduluk laibe?"
"Noke ampun neu ia mana kuasa, hatataso ndoesa lasau."
"Bafi-bafi noli besi ma manu-manu ngain lilo mbilas laibe?"
"Talobe oo mamahedi? Omae hataholi balakaik hataholi kamasuik atu-atuk?"
Hakaman dalena hedis mamanene halanatanek neme Telukaman mai nakando.
Hakaman anaki nasokahedu nasaneda anatabisaso.
'One time Telukaman came to visit his best friend on earth.
From far away Telukaman called Hakaman.
"Brother, why haven't you gone to work yet, the sun is already this high?"
"Beg Your Majesty's mercy, helpless servant."
"Oh yes ..., where are your rice granaries, where are the many pots of sugar?"
'Beg your Majesty's mercy, everything was long gone due to a famine.'
"Where are your pigs with iron teeth and chickens with golden spurs?"
"Why are you sick? Are you not a strong and rich man who is always in abundance?"
Hakaman was very sad to hear Telukaman's question. He wept bitterly at the memory of his powerlessness.'

In the quote above it is told that when Hakaman was suffering, he really realized that Telukaman was the only figure in power. In his helplessness his attitude of respect is clearly seen in the quotation below. He called Telukaman with the greeting "Your Majesty".

Boema no aon nahala, "ata noke fe ampun lai lifun neu mana houanasodak. Ata dosana neunaseli. Ata hataholi mana koaok, langgabatuk analilihena aoiman fo baefe ata tungga sangan luma neu manalain mae bibiana lain hambu. Suemala atamafa manahau masodak. Neme ia mai ata namahele manahau masodak nai lalaia ma daebafoka, nae hambu tao sudi hata soaneu tamanehelek. Ndia tulufali mala, ata dei," Hakaman no hala maganau ma hihina.

'Then in a low voice he said: "Servant begs forgiveness, thousands of pardons Your Majesty." I am very sinful, I am arrogant, stubborn and forget myself to offer what I have got, even a little bit. Have mercy on your servant, Your Majesty. Now I believe that Your Majesty is the ruler of heaven and earth, who can do anything for those who don't believe. Therefore please and have mercy on this servant of yours.'

Likewise in the quote above, Hakaman realizes that he is a "servant" who should not have sinned against Telukaman. The awareness of calling himself a "servant", means that he believes that Telukaman is the Supreme Being. A servant should be obedient and loyal to his master. Likewise humans are creatures of God's creation. Humans should realize that only He is always exalted and glorified. Because without the deeds of His hands humans are only weak creatures.

2.2. Human Relations With Others

Humans are social creatures. Human life on earth will never be separated from other humans. In relations with fellow human beings, both parties need each other, cooperate with each other, help each other, respect, and appreciate. Humans are the highest portrait of God, so that closeness between people must be fostered in order to create a harmonious relationship.

In the folklore of Telukaman Lailona and Hakaman Nepedae, it is described that the expression of gratitude to the Creator is not only through offerings of crops. Besides that, gratitude to the Creator can be in the form of an attitude of mutual help to others. The attitude of giving help to others is a commendable trait. Because by helping people directly carry out God's love in the form of love for others.

In the folklore of Telukaman Lailona and Hakaman Nepedae, human relations with others are symbolized by the provision of food and drink. Food and drink are very important needs for human life. Likewise the importance of human relations with each other.

Hakaman Nepedae nda hataholi kama suik atuk-atuk. Hataholi dia kamasuik nan seli, Hakaman Nepedae dia ana helu sawana ma anan nae hataholi mai noke naha nininuk do bana manu ma au tanga uma na ta bisa fe, te ita fen lai esa ma ana mai noke-noke nakando. Te hatama sila kaeik ma kalimak, de ala bisa tunga sanga soa neu sila la'a linu malada de boso fee sa. Hakaman Nepedae ana helu sawana ma anan leo ndiak.

'Hakaman Nepedae is a rich man. His wealth is abundant thanks to his own hard work. Every time when Hakaman was about to leave, he promised his wife and children, if someone asked for something to eat or drink, then I was not allowed to give it to them. If we give it once then they come asking for it continuously. They have hands, they have legs to work for them, they have a life for their wife and children, don't just make it easy'.

At the beginning of the story, the character Hakaman is an arrogant person. All the wealth he earned was not offered to the Creator. He enjoys the results of his hard work alone and does not share it with others in need. He ordered his wife and children not to give food and drink to those who came asking. Because of his arrogance and malice, in return, Telukaman did not send down rain for three years.

After three years had passed and all his wealth was gone, Hakaman regretted it. At the end of the story, when Telukaman is recovering his life, Hakaman does not forget to always share with others in need. Hakaman realized that the neighbors he had rejected were also suffering because they were deprived of food. As is the case with all that Hakaman has experienced at this time, he too has suffered the same as them.

Telukaman nasalempo falileo tadok udan ankona belana seli. Besaka oeneuka dadi, nama moli, banala lasoda, Hakaman Nepedae naue naledi soa neu ndia adinan ma sawo anan masoda.

Hakaman Nepedae nafada sawo anan nae neme faik ia mai hataholi noke hata na musi fesa, inafalu, anamak ala main na fesa la'a linu ma alafali na haifesa fo ala lua neu aluna fo lini lo umanaleu.

'Telukaman rushed away and not long after, it started to rain heavily. The water is there, the grass is starting to grow, Hakaman is starting to work as hard as he can. Hakaman Nepedae told his wife and children, "from now on, people who are in need come and give them food and drink, also when they come home give them the results of our efforts'.

The same goes for interpersonal relationships held by the Rote people. Wherever and whenever social relations with others must be properly fostered. Mutual help, respect should be an obligation in maintaining and maintaining harmony among people. Because the manifestation of love for the Creator is loving others. Loving means sharing and being ready to help others who are suffering. Apart from that, lightening the burden on other people's lives is a commendable deed before God.

This is also used as an example for the people of Rote in living their lives. A human cannot live alone without each other. In work, for example, alone can not do very much work. The power possessed is not able to get the job done quickly and well. He needs other people to be able to share and jointly do the work. The strengths and weaknesses possessed by each individual complement each other in working.

For the Rote people, differences are not a barrier in sharing love. Although they have no family ties, they have a very close relationship. In everyday life, they always call each other as tolanoe which means brother. Anyone who is met every day is always greeted like that. The term tolanoe describes a close brotherhood. This attitude is manifested in everyday life by helping each other.

In the life of the Rote people, such as rice fields, there needs to be an attitude of mutual assistance between people, from planting to harvesting. All of that of course requires the energy of several people. The attitude of sharing with others is also manifested in the customs of the people of Rote today, namely Tu'u Belis (collecting money together for families whose children are getting married). Every family that comes to provide assistance will also receive the same assistance. The same is true when a family experiences a bereavement event. Other families were there to feel and also to lighten the family's burden by working physically or helping materially, such as donating rice and livestock. This is what the people of Rote have been doing since the beginning. The attitude of brotherhood among people is always maintained and upheld in social life.

2.3. Human Relations With Nature

Humans are the only living things created to control and manage everything on earth. Human life on earth will never be separated from nature. Humans must always live in balance with nature which always provides crops to be managed to support their lives. Human life will be influenced by nature and natural life will also be affected by human existence. It is clear that man cannot live without food, water, air and sun. Likewise with nature. Humans are a factor for the continuity and preservation of nature's life, which in the end nature also provides for the preservation of life for humans. But humans can also be the cause of damage or destruction of nature.

The Rote people in their daily lives are very dependent on nature. They are always working, cultivating crops to support life. One form of gratitude to God is to process crops well and wisely. This is also reflected in the folklore of Telukaman Lailona and Hakaman Nepedae".

> *"Nau malada-malada, au tu'u bei balakain ma akatu'u afoa boema ledo ha au ma udan tetau tunga-tunga faik neme fafain ndia losa leonaso. Adiu mbuse ma au mbusengga tete autao daeaenga mateena ndia naemdadik-dadik mesan," Hakaman duduan nemedalu dalenai.*
>
> 'I am the one who works my bones, I don't know the scorching heat burning my skin, I don't know the rain that soaks my body from morning to sunset. The whole body is wet with sweat to cultivate the land. Eh… he's just waiting for it to happen," said Hakaman to himself'.
>
> *Te au lima boang makambi, ma bitiboa manutolonga dei de au kamasuinga henuhenu o mete au kampaga, sampila, bafila, bi'ila, manula, sokala henuk no hade, au suinga basan tesa.*
>
> 'Just look, I have big, toned hands and big round leg calves. I have full wealth, just look, buffalo, cows, pigs, chickens, goats, sheep, and rice full of barns, all complete. This is me having tired energy every day to work my bones to have

wealth, not from above that is for my love'.

The relationship between humans and nature in this story is symbolized by land. Soil is the origin of life. Humans are formed from the ground, so can plants grow on the ground. Anything that is planted on the ground can thrive. This is what humans must do as a form of gratitude to God who has provided a good place for cultivation in the form of land to be managed.

Hakaman Nepedae is a hard worker. In order to support his life he worked hard to cultivate the land or soil. He faced all the obstacles. Fatigue and fatigue he uses as a trigger in work. His enthusiasm never stops making him continue to work to collect treasures on earth. Strength and expertise in producing preparations is the main capital for him.

Telukaman laoelan, Hakaman ana dudua leo nae nama hele boema tanama hele hala kokola Telukaman.
"Isinaka halo kokolan Telukaman leo belaka, ana ancam au, te hu talobe de naloe hala kokolana", Hakaman duduan neme dalendalemai. "Ndia malolena au tao ueleding au tao daengga no au manggatunga fo au suingga bae lamanou."
'After Telukaman died, Hakaman hesitated between believing and not believing Telukaman's words. Earlier, Telukaman's words were in the form of a threat, but why did you convey it so gently, "Hakaman wondered to himself. "Ah... it's better if I continue to work diligently to cultivate this land, so that my wealth will increase," Hakaman said'.

Even though Hakaman is an arrogant person, there is one thing that is exemplary from his figure. Hakaman's enthusiasm and hard work at work really helped him to support his life and family. The different nature of Hakaman's personality has become a role model for today's Rote people. They realize that thanksgiving to God is to make the best use of all that has been given. Nature and all its wealth must be managed properly to sustain life. If nature is left alone without cultivating it, it will be of no use at all. It is better if nature is managed very well it will prosper human life.

Like the people of Rote today. Their daily life is always filled with work.

From morning to late evening spent processing natural products. Among them is slicing palm wine (tapping palm leaves). The work of tapping lontar is carried out in the morning. An atmosphere that in Rote is called fua fanu tapa deik, malelo afe take tuk (getting up almost noon and standing straight, aware and sitting quickly), symbolizing hard work starting from the morning. The same is true for other jobs, namely farming. This type of work also requires hard work. Starting from opening new land, plowing fields, planting, harvesting to selling it to the market. All of that is done diligently to support daily life.

In addition, the relationship between humans and nature does not end here. There is another connection regarding the belief that nature has powers that cannot be accepted by human reason. But that was the belief of the ancient people before they got to know religion. They believe that mountains, boulders, the sun, stars, moon and such things have power. Therefore it must always be worshiped. This belief is called dynamism.

In the folklore of Telukaman Lailona and Hakaman Nepedae, it is described that when Hakaman opposes Telukaman, nature is angry. For more details, see the quote below.

> *"Nae tolanoe mamanene ma masanenedak. Neme faik ia mai au ta oke o babae bali tunga o dudua afin, te hu neme faik ia lasa teuk telu manamaik, ia udan ta ma dinis ta tuda leo daebafokamai, Telukaman ana helu Hakaman.*
> 'My friends… listen and remember carefully, from now on I will not demand any more offerings according to your wish, but from today until three years from now, there will be no rain or dew dripping on the earth," said Telukaman'

The rain and dew that fall to earth is a blessing from the Creator. Rain brings life and makes nature green. But because nature became angry, all of that increasingly threatens the existence of humans on earth. By order of Telukaman, it did not rain for three years. Not even a drop of dew will fall to the earth. Such is the wrath of nature for the sins that have been committed by humans.

Faila laok lakondo, bulak-bulak laok lagagatik, teuk-teuk talomeda. Dinis ma udan lamahenan te ala ta titi mai. Daebafok ana boe-boe natobi. Naula mate basan, banala mate basan, saila mombo basan-basan, ndoesa lau na Hakaman Nepedae. Tanatetu, daebafoka male, hataholila, talabei.

'The days continued to pass, the months continued to circulate, the years did not seem to continue to pass. The expected drop of dew and rain did not come. Earth is getting hotter. The grass died, the livestock all died, the food ran out, hunger hit Hakaman, disease befell him. Nature is wrathful, humanity is helpless'.

The sun was angry, until the scorching heat seemed to burn and obliterate everything on earth. Soil cannot be cultivated. Animals are thirsty, plants dry up and finally humans are stricken with hunger and disease. Victims fall. Humans are powerless against the ferocity of nature.

Such wrath cannot be avoided by man. As a creature that is weak and has many limitations, humans should obey and obey the decrees of the Creator. Nature can prosper human life but nature can also destroy life when all things can no longer be relied upon.

CONCLUSION

Based on the description of the discussion, it can be concluded that the cultural values contained in the folklore of Telukaman Lailona and Hakaman Nepedae are as follows:

1. Human Relations with God

The folklore of Telukaman Lailona and Hakaman Nepedae tells about the relationship that exists between humans and the Creator. They believe that life in this world is regulated. Telukaman as the Ruler of the Heavens and the Universe must always be worshiped and also obeyed. One form of obedience is to always give offerings as thanksgiving for all that the Almighty has given to mankind. Such a relationship is closely symbolized by giving offerings in the form of agricultural products (rice fields or fields).

Likewise in the life of the Rote people today, they believe that God has power over everything. Whatever you try to do will not work without His intervention. Therefore, the results obtained must be offered as thanksgiving for God's blessings and grace. This is what the people of Rote have always done until now.

2. Human Relations with Others

In this life humans must always care and want to help others. The attitude of giving help to others is a commendable trait. The same is true for the relationships that exist in the stories of Telukaman Lailona and Hakaman Nepedae. This relationship is symbolized by the provision of food and drink, as a good deed between people. Food and drink are very important for the body, as well as human relationships with each other. Living alone would be meaningless without the presence of others. Mutual help, respect should be an obligation in maintaining and maintaining harmony among people. Because the manifestation of love for the Creator is loving others. Loving means sharing and being ready to help others who are suffering. Apart from that, lightening the burden on other people's lives is a commendable deed before God.

3. Human Relations with Nature

Human life on earth will never be separated from nature. Humans must always live in balance with nature which always provides crops to be managed to support their lives. Like Hakaman who always works hard cultivating the land to support his life and family. The relationship between humans and nature, in the story texts Telukaman Lailona and Hakaman Nepedae is symbolized by land. This is because land is a symbol of life. The Rote people in their daily lives are very dependent on nature, which always provides land to manage. They realize that thanksgiving to God is to make the best use of all that has been given.

References

Danandjaya, J. 1991. Indonesian Folklore, Gossip Science, Fairy Tales and Others. Jakarta: Pustaka Utama Grafiti Publisher.

Endraswara, Suwardi. 2015. *Literary Anthropology Research Metodology.* Yogyakarta: Ombak Publisher.

Febrianti, B.K. 2018. *Nilai-Nilai Budaya dalam Cerita Rakyat Kalimantan Barat Burung Arue dan Burung Talokot.* Jurnal Sirok Bastra. Vol.6, Nomor 2: hlm.171—184.

Mboeik, S.J. dkk. 1985. *Oral Literature of Rote.* Indonesian Literary Language Research Project and the NTT Regional Center for Language Development and Development, Ministry of Education and Culture.

Moleong, L.J. 2000. *Qualitative Research Methodology.* Bandung: Remaja Roda karya.

Rahmawati. 2019. *Cultural Values of Toraja Folklore.* Jurnal Mabasan. Vol.3, Nomor 2: hlm. 48—65.

Nurgiyantoro, B. 2010. *Fiction Research Theory.* Yogyakarta: Gadjah Mada University Press.

Taum, Y.Y. 2011. Oral Literature Studies: History, Theories, Method, and Approaches Accompanied by Example of Their Application.Yogyakarta: Lamalera Publisher.

Teeuw, A. 1984. *Literature and Literary Science.* Jakarta: Pustaka Jaya Publisher.

Language Style in Sinlirik Bosi Timurung

Rahmawati(rahm053@brin.go.id) | **Binar Kurniasari Febrianti**(bina003@brin.go.id)
Syaifuddin(syai007@brin.go.id) | **Nursyamsi**(nurs012@brin.go.id) | **Suyadi**(suya014@brin.go.id)
National Research and Innovation Agency, Archaeological, Language and Literature Research Organization

INTRODUCTION

Literary works exist because of the ability to combine ideas, views, experiences, feelings, and human imagination (literati) using language. Someone who has a knack for playing with words makes literary works as a medium for overflowing feelings and emotions. In the hands of literati, language is the raw material for expressing oneself and conveying thoughts (Wellek and Warren, 1990). Like food ingredients that are still in the form of raw materials, it takes a touch of qualified skill and expertise to present it as a delicious and nutritious meal. Works that manifest in the form of literary texts mixed in a language that matches the impression or effect to be highlighted. Compared to non-literary texts, the peculiarities of language in literary texts have the following characteristics: (1) literary language predominantly uses feelings rather than thoughts; (2) literary language refers more to connotative meaning; (3) literary language is imaginative work; (4) the language is characterized by distorted pronunciation; and (5) literary language uses certain elements to achieve beauty (Hyland in Nurgiyantoro, 2014).

Language style or style is limited as a way of expressing thoughts through language in a distinctive way that shows the soul and personality of the writer (language user) (Keraf, 2009). This opinion is in line with Ratna (2009) who explains that language style is a way of using the language medium distinctively so that a goal (aesthetic, ethical, and pragmatic) can be achieved optimally. Functionally, literary language conveys thoughts through styled language to produce all possible impressions of language (Asmuth and Berg Ehlers cited by Junus, 1989). Lexical and figurative speech options are part of the language style. Lexical choice refers to the use of certain words deliberately chosen by the author. The decision to use a certain word in his work is based on certain considerations to obtain a certain effect, the effect of accuracy (aesthetic). The problem of accuracy is related to form and meaning related to whether diction is able to support the aesthetic goals of the work concerned, able to communicate meaning, messages, and able to express ideas as intended by the author (Nurgiyantoro, 2009). Figurative speech is part of the language style used in the form of certain word choices in accordance with the intention of the author or speaker in order to obtain beauty (Ratna, 2009).

One of the varieties of Makassar regional literature whose language use is remarkably interesting is Sinrilik. Sinrilik is present as a story that is arranged in a poetic rhythmic (prose-lyrical) manner, the content is in the form of amorous songs, songs of mourning or lamentation for the dead and there are also times in the form of heroic songs that tell the courage and officer-ship of someone. Based on its content and way of delivery, Sinrilik are divided into two types, namely Sinrilik *kesok-kesok* and Sinrilik *bosi timurung* (hereinafter abbreviated as SBT). The narration of *kesok-kesok* is accompanied by a pretentious musical instrument while SBT is not accompanied by a musical instrument. The existence of SBT becomes a medium of expressing emotional expression related to (a) attraction to a girl; (b) a young man's longing for a lover; (c) lamentation of disappointment over failure; and (d) grief due to the abandonment of loved ones such as husband or wife (Basang in Saputri and Marwati, 2017).

Sinrilik *Bosi Timurung* manifests itself in Makassar regional language speech which is an expression of feelings by speakers or certain people who are asked to speak SBT. The language used has the power of having a soul so that it attracts and touches feelings. The use of interesting language can be seen from the use of lexical choices and figurative speech as a revealer of the speaker's intent. Word for word can arouse the emotions of both speakers and listeners. The narrative form resembles poetry or verse with the right selection and combination of words and repetition of lyrics (Mumtaz, 2021). The use of lexical and figurative speech choices into linguistic means that become the language style of SBT delivery helps clarify the meaning or intent of speech and can arouse the feelings and emotions of readers. Lexical choice or diction is the ability to distinguish precisely the nuances of meaning from the idea to be conveyed, and the ability to find a form that fits with the situation and taste values of the listening community (Keraf, 2009).

The expression of sadness, sorrow, longing, and disappointment conveyed by language in SBT narration can arouse the listener's emotions until the listener feels deep sadness until tears are filled. The expression of sadness and sorrow is expressed by the diction of *majeknek mata mami* 'crying pilu', *makrau-raumo* 'wailing', *makkuring-kuring* 'sad, languishing' as synonyms of the word *angngarru* 'crying'. A person who *makrau-raumo* 'wailing' does not just cry but cries while talking, about something sad. Crying is usually accompanied by complaints and screams. The lexical selection of *majeknek mata mami*, *makrau-raumo*, and *makkuring-kuring* not only presents a picture of a person who is crying because of sadness but is also able to describe the state of a person whose heart is so broken that crying incessantly, screaming, and wailing because of feelings of loss and grief that are very deep.

Sinrilik *bosi timurung* is a medium of expression or outpouring of hearts of speakers who are present not only as aromatherapy of the soul that is running but also to ground several moral messages that are important in building soul character. Speakers of oral literature can be likened to novelists or poets who construct long stories in line with a complex special imagination and sensitivity, which arises from the intense stimuli between the play of natural and human forces. The urgency of observing oral literature is related to its function as a container of traditional wisdom that contains conventions, value systems, customs, and various norms that apply in the society that owns oral literature (Taum, 2011). Language styles in SBT related to lexical and figurative speech choices are studied using stylistic theory. Stylistics is the study of stiles (Leech &; Short, 1981). Stylistic studies can be aimed at several types of language use, not limited to literature (Chapman quoted by Naurgiyantoro, 2009) in the form of studies on the form of linguistic performance, especially those found in literary works. However, stylistics are more often associated with literary language. Literary language cannot be understood without a sincere appreciation of the way ordinary language functions (Leech &; Short, 1981).

Unfortunately, nowadays SBT narration is rarely done. Makassarese who can say SBT are rarely found. In fact, many people are not familiar with SBT at all, especially from among the younger generation. This situation makes SBT marginalized and can eventually disappear from Makassar's ethnic life. Protection efforts made so far are still limited. One of them is the documentation of SBT texts carried out by Salma Djirong (1997), namely collecting SBT texts in *lontara* manuscripts, then transcribed, translated, and recorded. The same effort needs to be made to document and publish other SBT texts that are still contained in lontara manuscripts or that are still stored in the memories of old people.

Research on sinrilik has been done by researchers before. Oktaharapan (2021) examines *Sinrilik Art as a Communication Media in Gowa Regency*, Machmud (2011) examines *Communication of Makassar Ethnic Local Wisdom through Sinrilik* in Media Warisan Sinlirik (Sinrilik Heritage Media), Hafid (2012) *Sinrilik Recitation Art in the Context of Makassar Tribe Marriage Traditional Ceremonies in Gowa Regency, South Sulawesi (An Ethnomusicological Study)*, Mumtaz (2021) *The existence of Sinrilik in the Makassar Tribe,* and several other studies. Research specifically examining sinrilik Bosi Timurung was conducted by Saputri and Marwati (2017) examining *The moral values contained in Sinrilik Bosi Timurung* by Djirong Basang, Rahmadani (2021) *Moral Values* in Sinrilik *bosi timurung in*

Gowa Society through a Literary Sociology Approach, and Larigau (2021) research related to Meaning Pappasang in Sinrilik Bosi Timurung in Galesong Community. Research related to language style in SBT has not been found by the author.

Based on the above background, researchers are interested in examining the use of language in SBT with the theme of sadness and longing based on lexical choices and figurative speech with the following formulation of research problems.

1. How is the style of language in SBT themed sadness and longing theme viewed from lexical choices?
2. How is the style of language in SBT themed sadness and longing theme viewed from figurative speech?

Discussions related to the use of lexical options in SBT belong to the realm of stylistics. Stylistics and style are related to language issues (Junus, 1989). Stylistics (style) is the study of language style; *style* comes from the root *stylus* (Latin) which originally meant 'a pointy-tipped tool used to write on a wax-coated field. The discussion of stile elements is carried out by following the analysis of Leech and Short (1981), namely identifying lexical and figurative speech elements in literary works. For the purposes of analyzing the lexical choice of a literary work can be identified by word type. Questions that can be asked related to what type of words are used? And then followed by the following questions. (a) Noun, simple or complex? abstract or concrete? if abstract refers to what meaning, event, perception, process, moral quality, or social? If concretely refers to what, for example, objects, creatures, or people?; (b) verb, simple or complex, transitive or intransitive, meaning referring to a statement, action, event, or otherwise?; (c) adjectives, to describe what, for example, something physical, psychic, visual, referential, emotive, or evaluative?; (d) the word number, necessarily or indefinitely, and to explain what?; (e) the word task, what it exists, e.g. *dan (and), atau (or), lalu (then), kemudian (later), pada (on), tentang (about)*, which is often grouped into conjunctions and prepositions.

For literary communication, in accordance with the nature of literature related to human feelings, other types of words with connotations are needed. The first time, it is considered to cause a certain feeling when used. It may arouse anger, hatred, and pity.

Figurative speech is part of the language style that is widely used in literary works. Its existence makes a literary work more meaningful, memorable, and raises the imagination. Figurative speech is interpreted as a way of describing a way, equating it with something else *(KBBI (Big Dictionary of Indonesian Language)* V). Figurative speech is a certain choice of words according to the intention of the writer or speaker to obtain aspects of beauty. Figurative speeches are divided into four kinds; a) affirmation figurative speech (apheresis, aphorism, alonin, anagrams, anticlimax, apophasis, enumeration, repetition, climax, etc.), b) comparative figurative speech (allegory, allusion, antonomasia, dysphemism, epithet, eponym, euphemism, eponym, hyperbole, litotes, metonymy, metaphor, etc.), c) opposition (anachronism, antithesis, contradiction, oxymoron, occupation, paradox, etc.), and d) satire (antiphrasis, inuendo, irony, wordplay, sarcasm, cynicism, etc.) Traditionally, these four figurative speeches are also called stylistics. However, according to modern literary theory, figurative speech is part of the style. Figurative speech appears as a support that serves to complement the language style (Ratna, 2009). The figurative speech that will be described in this section are only those found in SBT. Explanations and examples of figurative speech refer to the opinion of Keraf (2009) as follows:

a) Repetition is a repetition of a sound, syllable, word, or part of a sentence that is considered important to emphasize in an appropriate context. Example: *atau maukah kamu pergi bersama serangga-serangga tanah* (or want you to go with the earth bugs), *pergi bersama* kecoak-kecoak (go with cockroaches), *pergi bersama mereka yang menyusupi tanah, menyusupi alam* (go with those who infiltrate the soil, infiltrate nature).
b) Metaphor is a kind of analogy that compares two things directly, but in a short form e.g., *bunga bangsa (hero), buaya darat (playboy),*

cindera mata (souvenir) (Keraf, 2009). In a narrow sense, namely figurative speech that compares an object with other objects while metaphor in a broad sense, encompasses all forms of allusion, the use of language that is considered "deviant" from the standard language (2008). Example: *orang itu buaya darat (That person is a playboy).*

c) An equation or simile is an explicit comparison that directly states something is equal to another. Usually use the word *seperti, bagaikan, laksana, etc.* Example: *Kakinya seperti kepiting batu (his legs are like stone crabs).*

d) Personification is a kind of figurative style of language that describes inanimate objects or lifeless items as if they possess human properties.

e) Tautology or pleonasm is a speech that uses references that use more words than are necessary to express a single thought or opinion. Example: *Saya telah mendengar hal ini dengan telinga saya sendiri (I have heard this with my own ears).*

The existence of Sinrilik as a literary work of Makassar region has been going on since the reign of the Gowa Kingdom. Sinrilik is played by a man who acts as a storyteller called *pasinrili* (Parawansa in Saputri, Widyanti, 2017). Two types of sinrilik, namely sinrilik *pakesok-kesok* and sinrilik bosi timurung, are distinguished based on the tools used. It is called sinrilik pakesok-kesok because it uses a musical instrument called *kesok-kesok.* The SBT is spoken or read by someone who is good at carrying SBT without using any tools. The content of synergy is related to folklore, love stories or information to find out a history that contains elements of education, advice, criticism, social control, entertainment and delivery of information (Djirong, 1999). While the content of SBT is an emotional expression such as sadness, longing, love, and so on. In addition, there is also sinrilik *bosi timurung* which is an *ammaca kitta* activity carried out after the *tadarus* (reading) of the Quran on the nights after the death of a person. The content is related to the description of the situation in the afterlife. The afterlife becomes the last place to account for all the actions that have been done in the world. Usually, sinrilik *bosi timurung* is spoken in a quiet atmosphere, for example in the middle of the night when the people around him are asleep.

Sinrilik lives together with various other Makassar regional literature such as (1) *rupama*, fairy tales that are usually told in leisure time; (2) *pau-pau*, is a kind of folklore commonly told to children growing up; (3) *Patturiolong*, a kind of admonition and narration of the ancients who usually told about the genealogy of a king who once ruled, the manner of his government, and his characteristics; (4) Sinrilik, a song that depicts the ups and downs of one's struggle and heroism. There are two kinds of sinrilik, namely, sinrilik *bosi timurung* which is usually performed with emotion and sinrilik *pakesok-kesok* which is usually delivered with a vibrant rhythm because it tells about one's heroism and courage; (5) *Royong*, ritual chants as an expression of prayer to *batara*; 6) *Doangang*, a kind of poem containing prayers or mantras; (7) *Aru*, an oath or pledge of allegiance of a person pronounced before a king, for example when the soldiers of the Kingdom of Gowa are about to leave for battle; (8) *Pakkio* bunting, a series of sentences chanted when welcoming and calling the bride and groom to go up or enter the house; and (9) *Kelong*, which is a type of Makassarese literature that uses a language that is neatly arranged to form beautiful and meaningful compositions of Kelong verses (Daeng Dalam Nensilianti, 2011).

This research is qualitative descriptive research. The research data are SBT texts themed sadness and longing. Data is sourced from the book *Prosa dalam Sastra Makassar (Prose in Makassar Literature)* compiled by Salmah Djirong. The material for the preparation of the book comes from the *book Makassarche Christomotie* by Dr. B.F Matthes. *Prosa dalam Sastra Makassar* compiled by Salma Djirong contains several sinrilik bosi timurung themes of sadness, longing, falling in love, and others. This research focuses on the theme of sadness and longing.

Data analysis techniques are carried out with the following steps: (1) carefully reading SBT texts (2) identifying stylistic use, especially the use of lexical choices and SBT figurative speech themed sadness and longing; (4) analyze language usage data in SBT; (5) draw conclusions on the use of lexical and figurative speech options in SBT.

DISCUSSION

Lexical Choices in Sadness-Themed *Sinrili Bosi Timurung*

Sinrili *bosi timurung* with the theme of sadness tells the story of the sadness experienced by a wife because a very beloved husband died. The wife's grief was expressed by reminiscing about the togetherness that had been passed together, revealing the condition of herself and other family conditions that were increasingly fragile after being left behind. Sadness is expressed by lexical choices that evoke mood and express sadness.

The noun *saribattang* 'your brother', balu '*widow*', *anak kukang* 'orphan' are some of the concrete nouns that adorn SBT. These words serve as clues to understanding anyone who feels sadness. The departure of the head of the family who had overseen earning a living, being a protector, and other important roles became a great ordeal for the family left behind. Usually, the aura of a family left dead by the head of the family will decrease and show poverty. The wife with the status turned into a widow, her children become orphans, and her poor brother will lose the grip and lose the hopes that have been built.

Furthermore, there are nouns that state the cardinal directions of the *anraik* 'east', kalauk 'west', *timborok* 's outh', and *uarak* 'north'. These nouns authorize the despair, confusion, and heartbreak of the deceased wife's loss of her life partner. The departure of her husband made the deceased's wife lose her direction in the sense of not having enthusiasm and motivation in her life. The feeling of losing hope makes sadness even more suffocating. The use of the name of the cardinal directions is seen in the following sentence.

(1) *Kupakgulingimi matangku anraik, kalauk, timborok, uarak annu taenamo natakrumpakki matangku.*

'I cast my gaze around, north, west, south, east, but I couldn't find yourself in my eyes.'

Furthermore, in data (2) the following are verbs that refer to death events such as *jammeng* 'dead, died', *maklabbak* 'merantau', and *mamo-*

rong ri jajarannu 'make crossings'. These verbs describe events that make the whole family sad. The incident was to the death of one of the family members. The use of different words for the same meaning makes the delivery of sentences more varied, more interesting, and more flexible, so there is no impression of monotony. *Anja* is the name for the afterlife which is the destination for *tumateya* 'deceased people'. In the realm of the *verb of death* which is equated with a person who is away wandering the *maklabbak* 'merantau' implies the hope of the family left behind that someday the deceased will return. Even though the family understands that the deceased is gone for good, this hope is presented to compensate for the grief felt. In the phrase *mamorong ri jajarannu* is stored the understanding that the afterlife is a place to move after the period of human service in the world ends. Moving to the afterlife is likened to a person crossing from one place to another. The use of verbs is seen in the following data.

(2) *Kaddek naniak ballianganna anjaya. Na angka todong poteranganna tumateya. Kusuro kioji anja berua maklabbak. Nakukana kana jammenna paleko bedeng mamorong ri jajarannu.*

'Cloudburst. If the word can be repatriated the person who goes to the anja (afterlife). And the dead can also be returned. I told him to call the new dead. And tell him about the death of the person who crossed (died).'

Futhermore, verbs that express actions include lexical choices found in SBT texts on the theme of grief. The actions in the verbs *makkiok-kiok* 'calling', *makngambo-ngambo, angkere jeknek matangku* 'wipe/wipe my tears', *makrera-rera, makrau-raumo* are knee-jerk reactions to a feeling of sadness felt by his family. Repetition of the word *akkiok becomes makkiok-kiok, rera* becomes *makrera-rera, rau* becomes *makrau-raumo* expressing intensity (strengthening meaning). A word that has a neutral meaning for the verb *angngrru* 'to cry'. In *KBBI (Big Dictionary of Indonesian Language)* V, *crying* is interpreted as giving birth to feelings of sadness (disappointment, regret, and so on) by shedding tears and making sobbing sounds, screaming. The verbs *makrau-rau* and *makrera-rera* both mean to cry. However, *makrau-*

rau and *makrera-reramo* are crying activities carried out while issuing sad remarks or complaints over the memories of the deceased and its merits. The word *makrau-rau* is also commonly used to refer to the sound of dogs howling prolongedly. Its use can be seen in the following data.

(3) *Makrau-raumo balu nisorong bokonu. Makrera-reramo anak kukang ninanronu.*
'Roar over the widow (balu) you left behind. 'Weep the orphan you left behind.'

Next, the verb that means hope that happiness continues to overshadow the deceased is the closing text of SBT with the theme of sadness.

(4) *Kuretomami limangku, nakupatara kuangkamami bongga kananna kulantukku. naku makpalak ri karaeng tinang tuna, naku manganro ri lebang tinang salasa nusunggulalo ri empoang maknassa;*
'I just ring my finger and face up. I only lifted the right thigh of my knee. Then ask God for Always Glorious. And begging the happy never wretched (unlucky).'

Kuretomami limangku, nakupatara 'I face up', *kuangkamami bongga kananna kulantukku* 'I lift the right thigh of my knee', *naku manganro* 'asking to God' to be a verb that refers to the activity of praying. The form of a wife's love for her husband is marked by always wishing the best for her husband. Prayers for the husband to always find happiness and forgiveness constantly arise from his mouth. Prayers offered to the Almighty become repentance and encouragement of the heart facing grief. The verb meaning hope in SBT is seen in the sentence.

The deterioration and helplessness due to the pain experienced by the wife of the deceased after the death of her husband is illustrated from the verbs that refer to the actions of *mattrinro* 'sleeping', *nanatungkusuk* 'wrap', *angkere, makgeleng, manyengo, maktayang, tanaassengmo, lanaboya*. The departure of her husband made the wife lose her enthusiasm and passion for life so that she seemed to have no energy to move. The presence of the adverb *mamak* only accompanies several verbs in functioning to strengthen or affirm the actions or deeds committed by the wife of the deceased. The wife's behavior is like a person who is confused, does not know what to do, and seems to not believe the situation that is being experienced.

(5) *Mattrinro mamak, nanatungkusuk bongonna, makmenang maniak nanreto karemenna. Matinro mamak, angkere jeknek matangku, makgeleng mamak, manyengo, nangammang kana. Maktayang rannumo, tanaassengmo apa la-naboy, takballe jeknek tanakullemo narappung tappu tasakbe tanaassengmo natoddok.*

'I just slept, veiled, encrusted, (ringed) my fingers. I just slept while swept away tears. I just turned away, turned my head, was about to say something. The excitement was gone, not knowing what to look for. Water spilled, can no longer be lifted. The prayer beads are broken, they can no longer be pierced.'

The position of the adverb *mamak* only accompanying some of the verbs in the above serves to strengthen or affirm the actions or deeds done by the deceased's wife such as only sleeping, only veiling the hood, only encrusting, and only turning away no other activities.

In addition, another lexical option that also expressly gives shades of sadness is the presence of lexical adjectives with respect to emotions. Some of them are *sino* 'silent', *nakku* 'longing', *garring* 'sick', *tuttulu* 'pain', and *dodong* 'lethargic'. The adjective describes the grieving condition experienced by the family of the deceased, especially his wife. The adjective that describes the situation that has become habitual is seen in the use of the word sino 'silent' in the sentence *Masino bonena tuntung lebonnu* 'silent is your place that usually crowded.' The *silent* and *crowded* adjectives in this sentence describe two opposite conditions. The deceased used to feel crowd and it became a habit. The lively atmosphere, full of cheerfulness, and happiness that felt in the family turned into silence after the death of the deceased. Crowds are not only related to boisterous (flares, sounds) or festive atmosphere but crowded to the existence of enthusiasm, joy, and happiness because of the presence of someone who is loved and always dependable. The word *tuttulu* 'crushed' accompanied by *bukubukungku* 'my bones' expresses grief so deep that even the bones feel crushed and helpless.

Lexical Options in Sinlirik Bosi Timurung of Longing

SBT with the theme of longing talks about the feeling of longing experienced by a man for a woman. Longing often brings grief because there is no clarity on the time to be able to meet again. Concrete nouns include the dominant lexical choice used SBT text. Nouns refer to places, natural phenomena, jewelry, and nouns meaning dead people. The words *jandela* 'window,' *bilik* 'room', *loteng* 'attic', and *ri jajarannu* 'meeting place' are some nouns that refer to places in the form of part of the house of women who are being missed. The urge to meet physically or meet in person is very desirable when longing is dominating feelings. To reduce it, a person will look for a cure for longing by looking at something related to the person who is missed. One of them is by seeing the residence of a lover even if it is seen from a distance. The man put his hope on the wind that blew over the attic and windows to leave his lover's message.

Furthermore, there are concrete nouns that refer to jewelry such as *intang* 'diamond', *jamarro* 'emerald', and *bulaeng* 'gold'. These three objects become symbols of love, beauty, privilege, and luxury. Next, there are two lexical that refer to natural phenomena such as bosi 'rain' and *kilat* 'lightning'. Natural symptoms that occur affect mood. Hot weather makes us more excited while rainy weather conditions bring feelings of sadness and gloom. The lightning and rain in the SBT text cause longing to become more intense, making the heart more eager to meet the sweetheart. Memories with someone who is meaningful in our lives but already in a distant place. Another case with *kilak* 'lightning' whose appearance often brings anxiety and fear. The occurrence of several events that claimed lives caused fear and anxiety when it began to rain, signs that there would be lightning. In the SBT text, the *kilak* that is present flashes makes a feeling of shuddering at the thought of someone who cannot be met.

(7) *Turung minne bosi makkunakku-nakku. Takbewe monne kilak makkadinging-dinging. kakdek naniak anging sallatang, makring kusuro, naaniak todong*

anging barak lolo kunjung mange kusuro erang-ji nakku, makmole-moleku,
'This rain brought longing. Lightning flashed with coldness. If only the south wind could have told me to. And there was also a westerly wind going there. I told you to bring my unrelenting longing.'

The Use of Figurative Speech in Sinrilik *Bosi Timurung* Theme of Sadness

Figurative speech includes language facilities used in SBT. The use of figurative speech makes SBT speech able to present imagination, become more interesting, and more memorable and present nuances that are in accordance with the theme of sinrilik such as sadness, longing, disguise, etc. The comparative values in SBT are metaphor, personification, and simile. The use of figurative speech metaphor in SBT text on the theme of grief is seen in the following data.

(8a) *Majai nakku nubolik makpilannassi.* 'Many longings thou hast left astonished'.

(8b) Malowe *enrong nunanro, makparutusang* 'Many desires you keep are troublesome'.

The sense of longing and desire felt by the family of the deceased is present because of the good memories or services of the deceased to the people around him. During his life, the figure of the deceased did goodness to others so that his passing left deep sorrow. His figure is present as a reliable figure when family and relatives are experiencing difficulties, a figure whose presence makes people happy because of his personality, cheerfulness, and friendliness. The kindness he planted during his life made not only close relatives feel lost, but others also felt lost, always remembered, and expected his presence to always be with them in everyday life. The amount of kindness that the deceased sowed during his life is emphasized in the metaphor *Numammoli songo bauk ri rasakrinnu* 'You left fragrant sweat by his side'. *Songok bauk* 'Fragrant sweat' is a metaphor for all the hard work that the deceased has done during his life to be used by his relatives.

Furthermore, the affirmation figurative speech in SBT is in the form of repetition of words located at the beginning of the sentence (anaphora). In SBT, longing reps give an effect of emphasizing the pain felt by someone who is harboring longing. This repetition confirms that the absence of a lover beside him makes him restless so that all the activities he does feel torturous. The repetition of the adverbial *sikedde* 'slightly' in the data (9a) and (9b) makes clear the helplessness of someone who is grieving.

(9a) *Sikeddeka jammeng kugilinna paklungangku.* 'A little bit I die, when I turn my pillow'.

(9b) *Sikeddeka soleng kupinrah tinroku.* 'A little bit I die, when I change my sleep'.

Looking back at the data (8a) and (8b) it appears that the use of figurative speech of tautology in the words *majai* and *malowe* which means "many", the words *nakku* and *enrong* which means 'to have the desire to meet' includes two synonymous words. The phrases *majai nakku* and *malowe enrong* mean that the deceased left many memories that made him always missed. In data 9a) and (9b) the words *jammeng* and *soleng* are synonymous words that mean 'died, fall, dead'. Tautologies make SBT narratives more varied and interesting. The tautology is also seen in the following data.

Kakdek naniya sambeanganna, naangka todong suleanna tumatea; kakdek inakke erok ri olo lingka ri anja; anna kalengkujammeng numempo ri lino.
'If it can be replaced or it can be exchanged for a dead person. If I could, I wanted it to feel like I died first. Let me die, and you sit in the world.'

Kata *kaddek* 'if', 'in case' is used to describe the weight of accepting the fact of being abandoned by the deceased so that if he could, his wife would be willing to take the place. This assumption arises from a sense of loss, deep sorrow, and loss of family hope so that it can make a person lose a clear mind. This sense of loss is reinforced by the wife's desire to replace her husband's turn to the grave. His wife felt that her husband was not yet the time to leave, the age was still young to carve more good memories. This gives a moral message to other humans that age does not look at age. When death comes, there will be no bargaining to win it. Therefore, every breath deposited by the Creator must be filled with benevolent deeds as a provision for life in the hereafter.

The Use of Figurative Speech in Sinrilik Bosi Timurung Theme of Longing

Metaphors include figurative speech that also decorate the SBT of longing. Its existence appears in the following noun phrases.

(10) *Jamarro Kulebangannu* 'Emerald My Longing'.

Emerald is a type of gemstone that has high value. In *KBBI (Big Dictionary of Indonesia Language)* V, emerald is interpreted as a green gemstone like moss, as a mineral founded especially in limestone layers in Colombia. This gemstone is special and dreamed of by everyone. However, the exorbitant price makes it only owned by rich people. Longing is a feeling by someone special such as parents, lovers, friends, and others who are mentally attached. The desire to meet in person becomes a potent longing cure. In SBT, longing reigns supreme in a man's heart for someone special. A lover of the heart who is very loved and highly expected to be a life partner. In the metaphor *jamarro kulebangannu* implied a man's promise to protect, guard, make his sweetheart happy, and make his lover a special person.

Furthermore, the use of figurative speech of simile is also seen in the following data.

(11a) *Kontu intang kungainnu* 'Like a diamond in my love for you'
(11b) *Kuntu bulaeng kubolikmu ri pakmaik* 'Like gold I keep in my heart.'

Love is equated with diamonds and the woman he loves is equated with gold. Diamond and gold became a symbol of sincere love, longing, and a man to the woman he yearned for. As jewelry that has a high value because of its beauty, jewelry becomes something special. For a woman, besides being able to support appearance, jewelry can also add confidence as well as investment. Expensive jewelry that is only owned by these rich people will be taken care of as well as possible. It is stored in a secure storage area and only used at important times. This means that the woman he adores is a special person both in terms of her beauty and the height of her morals and ethics. A man who loves his woman wholeheartedly will give her special treatments such as respecting, appreciating, protecting, treating softly, making her an excellent work partner so that they can jointly build a happy family in the afterlife.

Furthermore, figurative speech of personification comes by assuming *anging* 'wind' as an animate object that can help convey the message of longing to the idol. Its use is visible in the following data.

(12) *Kakdek naniak sallatang, makring kusuro. Na niak rodong barak lolo kunjung mange, kusuro erangji nakku, makmole-moleku, kusuro kangkangji enrong maklao ulengangku, ikau anging! anging! pakbattui mange, ikau barak, baliki ri dallekanna,*

'If only the south wind could have told me to. And there was also a westerly wind going there. I told you to bring my unrelenting longing. I told him to hold my desires back and forth.'

The presence of wind can be felt through its gusts. The gust gives a cool and calm feeling. The coolness of the breeze is expected to be felt by the lover so that the feeling of longing can be treated. For that the man will tell the wind to convey the feeling of longing that he is feeling. In the word "sending the wind" implies the meaning of the commanding effort to do work. It is implied that the hope that the message of longing can be conveyed as soon as possible because the wind includes objects that move quickly and can be felt anywhere.

In data (12), there are also repetitions, namely the words *kusuro* 'kusuruh' and *ikau'kau'* emphasize that men who are longing will make various efforts so that their lovers know the longing they feel, including by telling the wind.

CONCLUSION

Sinrilik *bosi timurung* is present as a Makassar regional literature in the form of speech that can drain emotions or psychological reactions of listeners such as sadness, emotion, longing, and love. This reaction is present as an effect of the choice of lexical and figurative speech that is appropriate and in accordance with the meaning that the speaker wants to convey. Lexical choices in grief SBT use concrete noun types in the form of parties who feel grief because of the loss of the deceased, nouns that express directions that inform the condition of confused families such as people who lose grip. The verb used refers to the event of death, action, or reaction of a bereaved relative and wishes for the happiness of the deceased. The adjective word class is present with respect to the emotions felt by the party feeling lost. The lexical choices in SBT longing include word classes, nouns refer to places (parts of the dwelling of people who are dugling), natural phenomena (rain and lightning that bring sad atmosphere), and nouns that mean dead people. There is a concrete noun that refers to jewelry (diamond, emerald, gold) as a symbol of love. The possibilities seen in SBT sadness and longing include metaphor, personification, simile, tautology, and repetition. There is a metaphor of longing and desires to make sweet memories. There is a jewelry metaphor to symbolize love, the personification of the wind as a conveyor of longing. There are many uses of tautologies to reinforce meaning. The presence of figurative speech adds to the beauty of language, and the emotional expressiveness of every word.

References

Badan Pengembangan dan Pembinaan Bahasa. (2019). *KBBI Daring*. Diakses tanggal 2 Maret 2023 dari https://kbbi.kemdikbud.go.id/entri/ gaya bahasa.

Djirong, Salma. 1999. *Prosa dalam Sastra Makassar*. Jakarta: Pusat Pembinaan dan Pengembangan Bahasa. Departemen Pendidikan dan Kebudayaan.

Junus, Umar. 1989. *Stilistik Satu Pengantar*. Kuala Lumpur: Dewan Bahasa dan Pustaka. Kementerian Pendidikan Malaysia.

Keraf, Gorys. 2009. *Diksi dan Gaya Bahasa*. Ende: Nusa Indah.

Larigau, M. Yusuf. 2021. *Analisis Makna Pappasang dalam Sinrili Bosi Timurung di Kalangan Masyarakat Galesong*. Skripsi. Makassar: Universitas Muhammadiyah. https://digilibadmin.unismuh.ac.id/upload/14503-Full_Text.pdf

Mumtaz, Muh. Mughniz. 2021. *Eksistensi Sinrili pada Suku Makassar*. Skripsi. Makassar: Universitas Hasanuddin.

Nensilianti. 2011. *Sistem Klasifikasi Prosa Naratif Masyarakat Bugis dan Makassar: Studi Komparatif*. Disertasi (Tidak terbit). Makassar: Universitas Hasanuddin.

Oktaharapan, Manuri. 2021. *Kesenian Sinrili sebagai Media Komunikasi di Kabupaten Gowa*. Skripsi. Makassar: Universitas Negeri Makassar.

Leech, Goofrey dan Michael H. Short. 1993. (diterjemahkan oleh Umar Junus). *Gaya dalam Cerita Rekaan. Penerapan Linguistik dalam Prosa Cereka Inggris*. Selangor: Dewan Bahasa dan Pustaka.

Nurgiyantoro, Burhan. 2009. *Teori Pengkajian Fiksi*. Yogyakarta: Gajah Mada University.

Rahmadhani, Ismi. 2022. Nilai Moral dalam Sinrilik Bosi Timurung pada Masyarakat Gowa Melalui Pendekatan Sosiologi Sastra. *Jurnal Aksara Sawerigading*. Vol. 1, No.1, http://ojs.unsamakassar.ac.id/jas/article/view/111

Ratna, Nyoman Kutha. 2009. *Kajian Stilistika Bahasa, Sastra, dan Budaya*. Yogyakarta: Pustaka Pelajar.

Saputri, Widyanti., dan Marwati. 2017. Nilai Moral dalam Sinrili *Bosi Timurung* Karya Salmah Djirong. Bastra. Vol. 1 (4).

Taum, Yoseph Yapi. 2011. *Studi Sastra: Sejarah, Teori, Metode, dan Pendekatan Disertai Contoh Penerapannya*. Yogyakarta: Lamalera.

Wellek, Rene dan Austin Warren. 1990. *Teori Kesusasteraan*. (Diterjemahkan oleh Melani Budianta). Jakarta: Gramedia

Local Wisdom in Minahasan Folklore as a Character Degradation Mitigation Recommendation

Nontje Deisye Wewengkang(deisy020912@gmail.com) | **Lefrand Rurut**(lefrandrurut@yahoo.co.id)
Sri Diharti(sridiharti1973@gmail.com) | **M.P. Handoko**(muaw001@brin.go.id)
Sjane F.Walangarei(sjan001@brin.go.id)
National Research and Innovation Agency, Archaeological, Language and Literature Research Organization

INTRODUCTION

Literature presents—for the most part—the realities of human life that greatly influence human life itself. Literary works portray the civilization carried out by humans including how humans arrange human relations with humans, human relations with nature, even humans with themselves. Literary works have an important function for humans. It presents the reality of human life which then influences people in living that life. Through literary works the author seeks to convey truth, including historical and social truth. Taum (2011: 6) revealed that literature is an existential knowledge field that is important to study as an effort to find and find human truth because literature is a description of human experiences and perceptions that have personal and social dimensions.

Taum (2011: 6) states that literature is an existing field of knowledge that is important to be studied as an effort to find and find the truth of humanity because literature is a dynamic description of human experiences and perceptions both personally and socially. A literary work, whenever it is created, always has a useful meaning for man. Literary works have always dealt with man and his attempts to conform. Widijanto (2016: 8) states that literature grows from the existence of human natural needs that strive to achieve at least three values, namely the value of truth, the value of beauty and the value of goodness. It gives birth to the eternal objects of thought in literary texts, namely man, life, and truth. Widijanto (2016: 10) also continued his opinion that today's literary text is present as a discourse that becomes a history mentality that displays cultural reality.

The author of a literary work is someone who conducts deep contemplation through his sensory experiences and even through his inner experiences to bring out the noble truths that humans believe in a time. Through literary works the author seeks to convey truth, including historical and social truth. Hegel and Taine (in Yoesoef, 2007: 18) even view literary works as monumental social documents, as transparent images of the conditions of an era. Yoesoef (2007: 18) also cites Lukacs' opinion which states that literary works are not only mirrors that reverse the imagination of objects located in front of them but also a knowledge of reality that actually exists before we know it in the form of thoughts. In other words, literary works reflect not only the forms of reality but also the knowledge of that reality.

The literature we know today actually originated from an earlier development in the past. Literary works in the past are known today as folklore, riddles, proverbs, and folk songs (Dananjaja, 1994: 5). Some people call literary works in the past oral literature, some call it oral tradition. No different from today's literary works, oral literature is also a medium of understanding and inheritance of cultural values believed by society. Oral literature is a monument of the values of society in a region, which was recognized long ago. Even oral literature has for centuries served as the basis of communication between creators and society.

Folklore as a form of oral literature is also a momentum for the value system of the owner's society. The thoughts contained in folklore represent the thoughts of the people. Some systems that exist in modern society can still be traced to the system that has been implemented by society in the past. Even when modern thought began to be doubted, people then returned to the thinking at the beginning of civilization and began to formulate new meanings according to the needs of society. This is in line with Sibarani (2004: 149) who explained that the search for new meanings of cultural values in tradition is motivated by the needs of society that have previously exceeded the modern stage and are basically also the personal needs of every human being. That is why the excavation of the noble thoughts of the people in the past contained in folklore needs to continue.

The problem is the narrower space for folklore in the hearts of the people who own it, especially the youth, teenagers, let alone children. This assumption is based on observations made by Alex John Ulaen (in his introductory note to the discussion of bacirita folklore, 14 November 1998) in three villages of the Bantik ethnic group, Tombulu, and Tonsea. These observations show that it turns out that people of youth, adolescents, and children are more familiar with cartoons than folklore. In fact, there are children who do not know any folklore from their own region at all. They are even more familiar with folklore from western countries such as Snow White than folklore from their own region, North Sulawesi, such as Keke Panagian. Umar Junus (1981: 79) explained that the habit of modern society placing folklore as children's reading is a mistake. Placing folklore as children's reading makes it lose its serious value. It no longer has the power to express philosophy except moral values alone. For example, by making Malin Kundang's story a mere children's story, with certain moral gifts by "parents", Malin Kundang's story can only be interpreted in one mere relationship, namely bad luck that befalls a child because he disobeys his mother. The possibility of other interpretations is ignored and even closed. In-depth analysis is no longer carried out so other meanings are no longer unearthed.

This fact is certainly very unfortunate considering that folklore has cultural meaning, as described at the beginning, which can establish our identity as a nation. Folklore is a mine of noble value that is very valuable to society. The noble value that can be found in folklore is the wisdom of society in the past that is still relevant and can even guide the meaning of various human relations in the present. And these values will only be buried if today's generation no longer reads folklore. That is why the author needs to explore noble values in folklore in North Sulawesi.

These thoughts raise questions that need to be investigated more deeply, namely what local wisdom is contained in folklore in North Sulawesi? The research objective is to explore the noble values which are the local wisdom of the people of North Sulawesi in folklore in North Sulawesi. The benefits of this research are directed at two things, namely theoretical goals and practical goals. Theoretically, this research is important to formulate local wisdom in North Sulawesi folklore. And practically it can be a recommendation for the formulation of North Sulawesi regional policies.

To obtain the formulation of local wisdom in North Sulawesi folklore, researchers will conduct a study with a content analysis model. Endraswara (2004: 160) explained that content analysis in the field of literature is classified as an effort to understand works from extrinsic aspects, namely matters concerning moral/ethical messages, didactic values, philosophical values, religious values, historical values, and so on. Content analysis is a strategy for capturing the message of a literary work to make inferences obtained through identification and interpretation. One of the goals of content analysis is to capture the meaning of literary works that are useful for humans to build better characters.

In simple terms it can be said that folklore is a story that belong to the people, the content is related to the real life of the people who own the story. Folklore is usually spread from one person to another through oral, therefore usually folklore has other versions. This has also been revealed by Danandjaja (1994: 3) the folklore has characteristics such as its spread and inheritance is usually oral and therefore has several versions, it is not known who first created the story.

Above it has been mentioned that folklore can have several versions because it is spread orally. We can imagine that one story told orally by two people will certainly be different, some are different in one part and in the other part may increase. Not only that, the situation that makes a person then tell a story, both the story he hears from others and the story he creates himself, it also varies. And therefore, the delivery of stories has different purposes as stated by Danandjaja (1994: 4) that folklore has a function as a tool of education, solace, a tool of social protest, and projection of pent-up desires. Even the folklore demands that Danandjaja (1994: 4) is prological, that is, it has its own logic and sometimes does not conform to general logic and is plain and straightforward so that it seems rude.

Along with the times, many are then interested in rewriting folklore obtained from various sources, both those heard through other people's narratives and those read from other people's writings. Discussion rooms were even held to collect folklore, research related to folklore was also carried out, finally the initial understanding that folklore was spread orally became debunked. But we cannot then eliminate that part because that is the original reality. And that's also what distinguishes folklore from short stories or other types of prose.

This section is still necessary not to overlook that there are groupings of folklore. The folklore still has a group. In this paper the author quotes the opinion of Willem R. Boscom (in Danandjaja, 1984: 50) who divides folklore into three groups, namely mites, legends, and fairy tales.

a. Mite

Mite is a folk prose story that is considered to have actually happened and is considered sacred by the community that owns the story. The characters in the mite are gods or demigods. The setting of the story takes place in another world, not the world we live in today.

b. Legends

Legends have traits similar to mites. This folklore in the form of legend is considered by the community of its owner as a real kisa that has actually happened. The difference with mite, legends are not considered sacred, more secular in nature. Characters in legends are human and sometimes these human characters have miraculous properties. The place where it happens is in the world we live in today. Legends are often considered historical and are also migratory in nature, that is, they can move around. Legends are often spread in the form of groupings called cycles, which are groups of stories that tell about a certain time, character, or event.

c. Fairy Tales

A fairy tale is folk prose that is not expressed and is not considered to have actually taken place by the society of its owner. Fairy tales are not bound by time and place. A fairy tale is a collective story told for entertainment purposes although there are also many fairy tale types that have ideas whose truth can be accounted for, contain lessons and satire. Danandjaja (1984: 86) cites the opinion of Anti Srose and Atith Thompson who divide fairy tales into four groups, namely animal tales, ordinary fairy tales, jokes or anecdotes, and formulaic fairy tales.

1. Content Analysis in Literary Studies

Endraswara (2004: 160-162) explained that content analysis is used if researchers want to uncover, understand, and capture the message of literary works. This understanding relies on rigid literary interpretation. This means that the researcher has built a concept to be revealed, just entering the literary work.

According to Endraswara, basically content analysis in the field of literature is classified as an effort to understand literary works from extrinsic aspects. Aspects that are beyond the aesthetics of the structure of the literary work are dissected, lived, and discussed in depth. There are quite a lot of literary aesthetic elements that attract attention to content analysis, including moral/ethical messages, educational/didactic values, philosophical values, religious values, historical values, cultural meanings, and so on. In simple words, the use of content analysis is when you want to reveal the content of certain values in literary works. The emergence of content analysis is based on the view that a literary work necessarily contains positive messages for its readers. However, of course, it must still be remembered in a balanced manner that there are also negative things contained in a literary work.

The study of content analysis in the field of literature departs from the axiom that the author wants to convey a hidden message in literary works. The meaning contained in a literary work is usually implied or wrapped in symbols. This is quite reasonable because every use of language by the writers contains symbols that contain meanings that must be traced.

Thus, it can be concluded that content analysis in literary works departs from a conclusion that literary works are a phenomenon of disguised message communication, in which they contain content that is very valuable to readers. This kind of literary study, epistemologically, is research that makes use of positivistic ideas. Another important thing to remember in applying content analysis theory to review a literary work is how the results of the study can be implied to anyone. The reviewer examines who can benefit from the study.

2. Local Wisdom

To understand about local wisdom, we certainly cannot be separated from the meaning of these two words. Wisdom comes from the root word 'arif' which in KBBI means wise, ingenious, clever, understanding, understanding. Wisdom means (in KBBI) wisdom, intellect. And the word 'local' means somewhere, unevenly; local. Thus, it can be said that local wisdom is wisdom, ingenuity, intelligence, and understanding that is believed and carried out by the community somewhere.

Pratama (Kompas.com 25/11/2020) states that local wisdom relates specifically to certain cultures and reflects the way of life of a particular community. Pratama also in his article quoted the opinions of Meinarno, Widianto, and Halida who said local wisdom is a method and practice developed by a group of people derived from their deep understanding of the local environment formed from living in the place for generations. They also explained that local wisdom arises from the community itself, is disseminated informally, and is owned collectively by the community concerned. In addition, local wisdom is also developed over generations and embedded in the way of life of the people concerned as a means to sustain life.

Sambowadile et al (2012: 8) explained that local wisdom includes ideas, values, local views that are wise and full of wisdom and good value that are followed by community members. From the description above, it is very clear that local wisdom belongs to one community group. It also means that each community group has its own wisdom. Local wisdom is not static but very dynamic following the development of community civilization along with the change of generations. In an article published on dosensosiologo.com (December https://dosensosiologi.com/kearifan-lokal/, 2022), it is stated that local wisdom is a view of life and science, as well as various life strategies that are manifested in a number of activities carried out by local communities in overcoming various problems in meeting their needs. Local wisdom is a firm knowledge that emerges from the dimension of a long time and is created through a repeated process, using the meaning of internalization and interpretation of religious and cultural teachings that are socialized in the form of social norms, then used as guidelines in daily life for the local community.

It is clear that local wisdom is formed due to human needs as social beings. Humans need interaction but regular interaction. Kaunang (2015: 2) said that to ensure their survival, humans need other people who have the same spirit, have rules, customs that are reflected as unwritten laws and norms and values of living together.

It can be said that actually local wisdom is the essence of the meaning of culture that lives in society. According to Firth in Lyons (1994: 607), the essence of meaning is its overall contribution to the sustainability of life patterns in a society where a person lives, gets a role, and acquires his identity. Culture is a way of life that develops, and is shared by a group of people, and passed down from generation to generation. Furthermore, Rahyono (2009: 53) everything related to the implementation of human life is within the scope of culture. Culture is not just a work of art, not just a custom, not just a tradition or things of a traditional nature. Culture covers all aspects of human life which includes the relationship between man and the Creator, the relationship between man and others, the relationship between man and nature, and the relationship between man and himself.

As stated at the beginning that this study uses a content analysis model. The research procedure with the content analysis model is as follows.

a. Determination of units of analysis

This part is carried out as an exploratory stage. to the problem and availability of research materials. After that, the researcher determines the object of study and related parties that need to be contacted for research purposes.

b. Sampling

This stage is carried out by determining what folklore is suitable to be used as research data to answer this research question. Researchers determine the type of data to be collected and data collection techniques.

c. Data recording/logging

At this stage, the data determined is what folklore will be told by the source. The data collection techniques are as follows.

1) Communication

Communication is a data collection technique carried out by communicating both orally and in writing between data collectors and data providers (Soepardi, 2004: 117). For oral communication, the research team used semistructured interview techniques and for written communication, the research team will use correspondent techniques.

2) Document analysis

Document analysis is a data collection technique by studying books or documents related to the problem under study.

d. Data Presentation Techniques

The presentation of data is carried out in a decomposed manner. Every folklore found, prosecuted, then analyzed and formulated the local wisdom of each story.

DISCUSSION

1. Toar and Lumimuut

It is said that a long time ago there was a princess in the northern kingdom who was considered to have committed a great offense, so she was washed into the sea in a large boat that had been filled with food. According to their belief, if the princess died in the great ocean, it meant that she was really guilty. A few weeks later, the princess's boat washed up on a beach. He was very grateful. He descended and entered the plain which he later knew as Malesung (now Minahasa). He then meets a woman named Karema. The princess introduces herself as Lumimuut. They agreed to walk together. Karema took Lumimuut to Wulur Maatus mountain to meet two other parents named Sumendap and Sumolang. The three of them lived on the plain after the plains were hit by the flood. They considered that Lumimuut was the messenger of Opo Empung (God) to continue life in the land of Malesung. They then asked Lumimuut to worship Opo Empung in order to get offspring. Lumimuut agreed. With the strength of these three people, Lumimuut was confronted to the North, South, East, and West respectively with the request that Lumimuut be given a child. The three elders solemnly performed the wish ceremony, finally their wish was granted. Lumimuut conceived and gave birth to a son and was named Toar. Toar is taken from the word Touari meaning human of unknown origin. Karema adopted him as a child. Toar grows very quickly. In a short time, he had become a stout and burly young man.

One day Karema took two sticks. One comes from the stem of tiwoo (tares) and one comes from the stem of tuis (cardamom). He summoned Toar and Lumimuut and gave each of them a staff. They were told to surround Wulur Maatus mountain from the direction with the message that if one day they met someone who was also carrying a stick, they should equalize the stick. If it is not of equal length, it means that the person must be brought down facing Karema. As they walked around the mountain, they finally met, but they did not know each other because their stature had changed. They equate the cane they carry and as a result the stick is not the same length. They went to Karema and Karema married them both. They then got offspring makatelu sio (three times nine), makarua pitu (twice seven), and Pasiowan telu. Their descendants continue to grow until now, they are the ones who occupy the land of Minahasa until now.

The local wisdom contained in the story is as follows.

a. Wisdom as an individual being.

Fortitude. When Lumimuut was accused of guilt, he steadfastly accepted it. Even when he was thrown away, washed into the sea he was steadfast in living it. He did not give up hope and continued to live his life path even though there seemed to be no hope.

Brave. Lumimuut is stranded on an unknown land. He remained brave even he got out of his boat and walked into the plain.

His courage finally led to good results and even a good future.

Obedient. Lumimuut obediently accepted the punishment imposed on him even though he felt he had done nothing wrong. Even when his life began on a land where he was stranded, Lumimuut and even Toar were at the direction given by Karema as their parent, as their leader

b. Human wisdom as a social being

The need for friends. Lumimuut was stranded on a deserted land after weeks alone on the high seas. Karema also lived alone on the land after the land was hit by the flood. When they met, they decided to walk together. They need each other both to express love and for other individual abilities.

Each generation gives birth to another generation.

Karema, Sumolang, Sumendap, and Lumimuut are the remaining generations of Malesung people after the country was hit by disaster. The future life of the land is in their hands and is their responsibility so they actively sought it with the help of Lumimuut they finally succeeded in connecting the descendants of the land.

c. Human wisdom as God's creature

Prayer and effort. Human desires and ideals can be achieved if they are recognized sincerely and prayed for more earnestly. When Karema wanted to continue the descendants of Malesung Country through Rahim Lumimuut, he did so earnestly. Karema knew that it was impossible because Sumendap and Sumilang were very old. But he still has strong hope. He led the journey to his hope, performing ceremonies and praying fervently to the Creator. Several times Karema failed, but she prayed even more fervently. Finally Karema's request was granted.

Resignation to God. Resubmission to God the creator is a quality of faith that is needed by everyone. Praying and working must be accompanied by resignation. Lumimuut is innocent but he has no power to fight the accusers. He just resigned. Confidence that God would save him and reveal the truth. According to the belief of the people in the kingdom of Lumimuut, a person accused of guilt, who is thrown into the sea, if he survives, he means he is innocent. But if he is swallowed by the ocean, it is true that he is guilty. Lumimuut survived. It was God who declared him innocent.

2. Pingkan and Matindas

In ancient times, in Minahasa there lived a pair of lovers, namely Pingkan and Matindas. Pingkan was the daughter of a Tonaas. They are both the best young men and women in their village. After Pingkan's father died, Matindas immediately proposed to Pingkan. The intention is that he can help make a living for Pingkan and his mother. Pingkan's mother agreed to Matindas' proposal so that the marriage could be smoothly carried out.

A few months after marriage, Matindas planned to go to sea for quite a long time. Before he made his intentions to Pingkan and Mother, Matindas first carved two statues, one resembling himself and the other resembling Pingkan. It was time for Matindas to make his point. Although it was hard, Pingkan and his mother allowed Matindas to leave. Before Matindas left, he handed over a statue that resembled himself to Pingkan and a statue that resembled Pingkan that he took him to sea.

A few weeks later news came that Matindas and his friends had an accident at sea. The storm hit their boat. Matindas and his friends are lost in the ocean. Pingkan and his mother were very sad. They continued to pray to God for Mattoppress' salvation. Pingkan every day goes to the beach to wait for Matindas. Meanwhile, Matindas was stranded in a fishing village quite far from his village. He was cared for by a family of fishermen who found him. The Pingkan statue brought by Matindas has been found by a fisherman from Bolaang Mongondow. The fisherman brought the statue to the king and the king liked the statue very much. The king immediately sent his guards to find the whereabouts of the woman in the statue.

Elsewhere Matindas had returned home. He was greeted with great happiness by the villagers, especially Pingkan and his mother. Almost at the same time, the King's bodyguard also arrived at the village and saw Pingkan, the woman who looked like the statue. Those bodyguards directly reported Pingkan's whereabouts. The king was very happy and immediately sent a messenger to propose Pingkan to be his wife. Pingkan of course rejected the proposal because she already had a husband. The king insisted on revising Pingkan, eventually there was a battle between the king and his guards with the villagers and even assisted by other villagers. The king was killed, Pingkan and Matindas were killed. Many also became victims.

The local wisdom contained in the story is as follows.

a. Human wisdom as an individual

Work ethic. Matindas is someone who is very diligent at work. He was skilled at catching fish in the sea, diligently working on his garden, planting various kinds of plants. His family is not short of food. He doesn't like to be lazy. Every day he always went to work. Pingkan is also a woman who likes to work hard. She does all the chores at home: cooking, washing, cleaning the house, even helping her husband work in the garden.

Steadfast and faithful. When Matindas was reported missing at sea, Pingkan was devastated but he still strengthened his heart. She still believed that her husband was still alive. She remained faithful every day to come to the beach to see when her husband came home. Pingkan also remained faithful to maintain her love for Matindas even though she received a proposal to become the king's wife who would certainly be full of wealth. He was not tempted in the slightest. In fact, she fought to the death beside her husband.

Honesty. Pingkan told him all the king's offers. She did not lie to her husband in the slightest.

b. Human wisdom as a social being.

Filial piety to parents. It is a matter of pride for parents if their children are not only beautiful and dashing but also diligent in helping parents. Pingkan and Matindas are children who can be proud of because they have the qualifications to be proud children. They are obedient and diligent in helping the elderly. That is why they always get a retu from parents. It was the blessing of his parents that finally saved Matindas even though he was hit by a fierce storm.

c. A soul mate in God's hands.

Pingkan and Matindas believed that their soul mate was in God's hands. They get along well and naturally because they believe that. Even though they have loved each other but they still do all the stages recognized by society. Parents remain the most instrumental to the continuity of their relationship.

d. Social solidarity.

The king came about to pick up Pingkan by force. Pingkan was obviously unwilling and had already rejected the king's proposal. The neighbors didn't just watch the romance drama. Seeing that there were parties who wanted to be harmed, neighbors from neighboring villages even volunteered to help Pingkan and Matindas fight against arbitrariness. Those neighbors did not take their safety into account.

3. Centipede and Conipus

It is said that a long time ago there lived two brothers named Centipede and Conipus. They have been abandoned by both their parents. They live loving each other, helping each other in the face of life's difficulties. The elder brother, Centipede is in charge of tapping sap water and collecting firewood in the forest. Meanwhile, the younger brother, Conipus hunted forest animals to be their food. One day Conipus came home from hunting, during a heavy rain, he was cold and wanted to warm his body with a little sap. He called his brother but there was no sahutan. It turned out that Centipede was leisurely enjoying sap and was a little drunk. Conipus became annoyed to see him, especially since Centipede did not leave sap for him. Eventually they quarreled and even fought. They put out all their skills until days of fighting, no one wants to budge. They chased each other and finally came to a plain called Rumoong. Conipus was very thirsty, so he ran towards the water source. Not being careful, he slipped, and his hand rested tightly on a large rock so that on the surface of the stone a hand image was formed. Conipus then told his brother that this signature symbolized the breaking of their brotherly relationship.

The local wisdom contained in the story is as follows.

a. Human wisdom as an individual.

Work ethic. A firm division of labor in a group will make it easier for group members to complete their respective tasks. Centipedes and conipus have their own duties in an effort to continue life. They are both responsible for their respective tasks. They work earnestly.

Humility. Not feeling or showing that one is stronger than the other, not underestimating the work and duties of others, is a good gesture from Conipus.even when they fought, Conipus tried to give in and avoid so that the battle could end quickly.

b. Human wisdom as a social being.

Liquor can undermine common sense. The affection developed since childhood between Centipede and Conipus disappeared in an instant just because Centipede drank more sap than usual. And only because of that sap, they broke the bonds of brotherhood between them even they attacked each other and lusted after defeating each other.

Everyone has their share, don't take other people's share. The centipede was captivated by the sap part of his brother. The cold air due to the rain had enlarged his lust and forgotten the brotherhood between him and his sister. He drank all the sap, sat back and forgot about his only family. Centipedes begin to think selfishly and feel more important than others. That attitude led to disaster in the end. Everything that was built together was eventually destroyed.

CONCLUSIONS

The conclusion of this paper is that local wisdom contained in Minahasa folklore is (1) human wisdom as an individual creature including work ethic, frugal life, fortitude, honesty, loyalty, humility. (2) Human wisdom as a social creature includes filial piety to parents, parental love for children, mutual respect for one another, democratic deliberations of liquor undermine common sense, each has its own part. And (3) Human wisdom as God's creature which includes recognition of God Almighty, obedience to worship, fervent prayer, submission to God, and always giving thanks.

References

Ahimsa-Putra, Heddy Shri. 2013. *Sastra dan Pembangunan Karakter Manusia.* Yogyakarta: Gama Media.

Danandjaja, James. 2007. *Folklor Indonesia.* Jakarta: Pustaka Utama Grafiti.

Endraswara, Suwardi. 2004. *Metodolong Penelitian Sastra.* Yogyakarta: Pustaka Widyatama

Junus, Umar. 1981. *Mitos dan Komunikasi.* Jakarta: Sinar Harapan.

Kaunang, Ivan R.B. 2015. *Minahasa, Epistem Kebudayaan.* Yogyakarta: Graha Cendekia.

Lyon, David. 1994. *Postmodernity.* Minneapolis: University of Minnesota Press.

Penulis Materi Sosiologi. dosensosiologo.com. 2022. *Pengertian Kearifan Lokal, Ciri, Fungsi, dan Contohnya* https://dosensosiologi.com/kearifan-lokal/.

Pratama, Cahya Dicky. 2020. "Kearifan Lokal: Definisi, Ciri-Ciri, dan Contohnya". Jakarta: Kompas.com https://www.kompas.com/skola/read/2020/11/25/150459069/kearifan-lokal-definisi-.

Rahyono, F.X. 2009. *Kearifan Budaya dalam* Kata. Jakarta: Wedatama Widya Sastra

Sibarani, Robert. 2004. *Antropolinguistik: Antropologi Linguistik, Linguistik Antropologi.* Medan: Penerbit Poda.

Sambowadile Pitres, dkk. 2012. *Kearifan Lokal Kaitannya dengan Pembentukan Watak dan Karakter Bangsa di Kabupaten Bolaang Mongondow Selatan.* Yogyakarta: Kepel Press.

Soepardi. 2004. *"Teknik Pengumpulan Data" dalam Kumpulan Materi Pelatihan Metode Penelitian Tingkat Nasional.* Jakarta: Litbang, Diknas.

Taum, Yoseph Yapi. 2011. *Studi Sastra Lisan: Sejarah, Teori, Metode dan Pendekatan, disertai Contoh Penerapannya.* Yogyakarta: Lamalera.

Ulaen, Alex John. 1998. *Catatan pengantar diskusi bacirita folklore.*

Yoesoef, M. 2007. *Sastra dan Kekuasaan.* Jakarta: Wedatama Widya Sastra.

Interpreting Unen-unen Semut Ireng Anak-anak Sapi with an Intertext Approach

Sri Haryatmo(haryatmosri@yahoo.com) | **I Made Budiasa**(budiasaimade1963@gmail.com)
Pardi(tarunayes@yahoo.co.id) | **Ricky A. Manik**(rickymanik@gmail.com)
National Research and Innovation Agency, Archaeological, Language and Literature Research Organization

INTRODUCTION

Koentjaraingrat (1974:19) divides culture into three dimensions. First, culture is a complex of ideas, values, norms, and regulations. This culture's existence is in the community's minds, but it can also be in the form of writings and essays. Second, culture is a complex of activities patterned in society. This form of culture is in the form of a social system in the community concerned. Third, culture is an object created by man. This third type is in the form of genuine culture, visible physically because it is the work of the community concerned.

As social creatures, humans always establish communication relationships with one another. In communication, messages in the form of norms, ideas, ideas, and regulations can be conveyed through language directly or indirectly. In Javanese culture, indirect message delivery can be done through signs, symbols, or symbols (Satoto, 1990, p. 12). In other words, communication between people can also use symbols. Even the delivery of messages through this symbol in Javanese culture seems dominant through the medium of language and other objects.

According to Padmosoekotjo (1960:107—134), symbolism in Javanese language and literature, among others, is seen in riddles (*wangsalan* and *parikan*), proverbs (*paribasan, bebasan, saloka*), *sengkalan, sanepa, isbat,* and *pralambang*. Furthermore, Padmosoekotjo (1960: 73—88) divided symbols into five types, namely 1) symbols in the form of images, 2) symbols in the form of goods, 3) symbols about colors, and 4) symbols in the form of language. Symbols conveyed through language or words can be broken down into symbols of the virtue of character and behavior, symbols of the era, symbols of praja, symbols in songs, and others. Concerning this talk, *uran-uran* 'dendangan' "*Seant Ireng Anak Sapi*" (SIAS) is included in the *pasemon* 'pre-emblem conveyed through language. This type of symbol is written in one stanza of the *Dhandhanggula* song.

The primary data of song are two manuscripts entitled (1) "*Uran-uran Semut Ireng Anak-anak Sapi*", library collection of Reksa Pustaka Mangkunnegaran Surakarta by number A.44a and (2) "*Uran-uran Semut Ireng Anak-anak Sapi*" library collection of Reksa Pustaka Mangkunnegaran Surakarta by number A.44b. In addition, the SIAS text is also found in *Ngengrengan Kasusastran Djawa II* (1960: 135) by S. Padmosoekotjo.

The discussion of SIAS has been conducted by Herusatoto (2010). In the rubric "Mekar Sari" (published by *Kedaulatan Rakyat*) (2010:10), Herusatoto gives the meaning *semut ireng anak-anak sapi* as a black ant that bears a calf. This inferior person has an educated child (student)". Meanwhile, R. Tumenggung Sastranagara (tt:4) gives meaning *semut ireng anak-anak sapi* as *pasemon* 'symbol' of Dewi Sapudi or Dewi Wandan Kuning symbol which was married by Prabu Brawijaya then had a son named Lembu Peteng (compared to Padmosoekotjo, 1960: 89). It becomes the reason for choosing the data. Besides, SIAS is an interesting expression to study its meaning. Thus, the problem that arises is (1) what is the meaning contained in each of these 'expressions'? (2) How to explain the relationship between objects and reality or between signifiers and signifiers through Peirce's semiotic theory? (3) What is the meaning of these *unen-unen* if it is related to the B text of the *Babad Majapahit dan Para Wali*?

As explained in the background, Javanese people conveyed messages through symbols or symbols in the form of words or language. The messages conveyed through language symbols, or words can be figurative language or figurative language. According to Altenbernd (1970:15), figurative language relates something by relating it to something else. Pradopo (1989:62) states that one type of figurative language is a metaphor, that is, figurative language such as comparison, but does not use comparison words: *bagai, laksana, bak, seperti*, which means like or as. Becker (1978:317) states that metaphor is seeing something in comparison with other objects. In contrast, Altenbernd (1970:15) expresses that a metaphor is to express something as the same thing or as costing something else that is not the same.

Further, giving meaning to "*Uran-uran Semut Ireng Anak-anak Sapi*" requires a semiotic theory of Peirce's model. According to Peirce, an interpreter is a researcher, observer, and reviewer of the objects he understands. In studying, he understands that Peirce develops a typology of signs. In this case, the relationship of reality to the object includes icons, indexes, and symbols (North, 1995, pp. 44-45). An icon carries out a function as a sign similar (similar) to the shape of its object; an index performs a function as a sign hinting at its signifier. A symbol carries out a function as a sign that, by convention rules, has been commonly used in society. Thus, a semiotic theory is needed to describe the structure and meaning of each word in the *uran-uran*, focusing on icons, indexes, and symbols as sign science.

Furthermore, to give more profound meaning, intertext theory is needed. It is intended to acquire a sharper meaning because it is associated with other texts as its hypogram. Riffaterre (1978:11, 23) states that the literary work is meaningful to other works. The text that is the setting of creation is called the hypogram, while the text that absorbs the hypogram is called the transformation. Transformations are often accompanied by opposition or alteration to the text, part of the text, or part of the transformed text (Fokkema dan Elrud Ibisch, 1992:99—100). Kristeva (in Culler, 1975:139) states that each literary text is a mosaic of quotations and is an absorption and transformation of other texts. The meaning of a text can usually only be understood if the work is connected or contradicted with other works.

Meanwhile, Teeuw (1983: 65) states that literary works do not essentially arise from a cultural vacuum, but there is influence from the work that precedes them. The point of Kristeva's statement is that each text takes good things from other texts based on its responses and reprocesses them in its work or texts written by later writers (Pradopo, 1999:227—228). Thus, intertext theory views that a text written more than bases itself on other texts that people have written before. In essence, the four principles of intertextuality above are the same. In understanding literary works, a researcher is not only required to examine the work that is the object of his study but must connect with other works that precede him, which Riffaterre called the hypogram. In this case, the work considered as a hypogram is the work of *Babad Majapahit dan Para Wali.*

The method used is descriptive-analytical, meaning that the data is analyzed based on the theory applied. Metaphors consist of two terms, principal term, and secondary term. The principal term is called tenor, and the secondary term is called vehicle. The principal term or tenor mentions the thing being compared; the vehicle is the thing to compare. For example, the principal is also called the tenor, while the secondary term is called vehicle. The principal term or tenor mentions the thing being compared, while the second term or vehicle is the thing to compare. For example, "this earth is a bitch, who attracts men and hermits, to these perverted swamps." (Sastrowardojo, 1975, p. 9)

In that expression, it is known that "earth" is the principal term, while "bitch" is the second term or vehicle. Furthermore, if the poet directly mentions the second term without mentioning the principal term or tenor, such a metaphor is called an implicit metaphor. The author only displays the second term or vehicle, while the first is the meaning the reader must seek. In Javanese culture, there are quite a lot of expressions in the form of implicit metaphors, one of which is the expression entitled "*Uran-uran Seant Ireng Anak Sapi* ."Thus, the expressions explicitly contained in *Uran-uran Seant Ireng Anak Sapi* are the second term, while the first is the meaning the reader must seek. Furthermore, in interpreting SIAS, it needs to be associated with the previous text, namely the BMPW text, which was used as the basis for creating the SIAS text.

DISCUSSION

The discussion includes the meaning of symbols conveyed by Padmasukatja and Sastranagara, a study based on Peirce's semiotic theory, and is associated with the BMPW text. However, before the study is conducted, the complete text of SIAS is presented as follows. The text is taken from a manuscript entitled "*Uran-uran Semut Ireng Anak-anak Sapi*" library collection of Reksa Pustaka Mangkunnegaran Surakarta with number A.44a. as follows.

Semut ireng anak-anak sapi	'black ant delivers a calf'
Kebo bongkang nyabrang kali bengawan	'old buffalo crosses Bengawan'
Keyong gondang jarak sungute	'big snail short its sungut'
Timun wuku gotong wolu	'young cucumbers are raised eight'
Surabaya geger kepati	'Surabaya is in an uproar'
Ana wong ngoyak macan	'a person chases tiger'
Denwadhahi bumbung	'included bumbung'
Alun-alun Kartasura	'Kartasura's town square'
Gajah meta cinancang wit sidaguri	'angry elephant is roped with sidaguri tree'
patine cineker ayam	'dead in chicken claws'

Uran-uran 'song' above is written as a macapat song (Dhandhanggula). However, when viewed based on the convention of the song in the form of *guru wilangan*, 'the number of syllables in each line,' the *Dhandhanggula* song needs to be corrected. In certain lines, there is still an excess of one syllable. The lines referred are second line (*kebo bongkang nyabrang kali bengawan*) has more than one syllable; the third line (*Keyong gondang jarak sungute*) has more than one syllable; the fourth line (*Timun wuku gotong wolu*) have more than one syllable; and tenth line (*patine cineker ayam*) also have more than one syllable. Thus, if adjusted to the *guru wilangan* convention, the Dhandhanggula song should be read as follows.

Semut ireng anak-anak sapi
Kebo bongkang (nya)brang kali bengawan (have more than one syllable)

Keyong gondang (ja)rak sungute (have more than one syllable)
Timun wuku (go)tong wolu (have more than one syllable)
Surabaya geger kepati
Ana wong ngoyak macan
Denwadhahi bumbung
Alun-alun Kartasura
Gajah meta cinancang wit sidaguri
Pati(ne) cineker ayam (have more than one syllable)

1. The Sastranagara and Padmosoekotjo's Meaning of Uran-uran "Semut Ireng Anak-anak Sapi"

Sastranagara (tt) (compared to Padmosoekotjo, 1960:88--90;) gives meaning to *Uran-uran "Semut Ireng*" as follows.

The first line states, "*Semut Ireng Anak-anak Sapi*" 'black ant delivers a calf'—the phrase "black ant" or another name for the disguised figure of Dewi Sapudi. She is from Wandan Kuning area. While anak-anak sapi 'delivers a calf' is a symbol of the Bondhan Kejawan figure or Lembu Peteng.

Therefore, the sentence "*Semut Ireng Anak-anak Sapi*' means that Dewi Sapudi, a booty princess of Wandan (now Banda Island), delivers a boy (named Lembu Peteng) for having an illicit relationship with Prabu Brawijaya in Majapahit.

The second line states *Kebo bongkang nyabrang Kali Bengawan.* The word *kebo* means 'buffalo', while *bongkang* means 'old or very old' for the animal. While the word *nyabrang* ('cross') implies the meaning of "opposite understanding." While the word *kali bengawan* ('Bengawan river') means "life path or life choice." Therefore, "*Kebo Bongkang nyabrang kali bengawan*" means 'the two buffalos named kebo 'buffalo' (Kebo Kenanga and Kebo Kanigara), each of whom chooses the opposite path of life. Kebo Kenanga chooses to follow Seh Siti Jenar's teaching, while Kebo Kanigara retains the old belief in Buddhism.

The third line (*Keyong Gondhang Jarak Sungute*) contains the pseudonym of Jaka Tingkir, or Sultan Adiwijaya figure who manages to become a great king. However, it is short because his ancestor cannot inherit his father's throne. In this case, Jaka Tingkir (Hadiwijaya) is symbolized by the word *keyong*, 'big snail' who lives in water, while *jarak sungute* means 'its short *sungut* or his power is short .'Therefore, *keyong gondhang jarak sungute* means 'big snail.'

In the fourth line (*Timun Wuku Gotong Wolu*), the word *timun* means 'cucumber,' the word *wuku* means 'small,' while the word *gotong* means 'support,' and the word *wolu* means 'eight .'Therefore, *gotong wolu* means 'supported by eight people .'The word *Timun wuku* 'small cucumber,' symbolizes the Panembahan Senapati or Sutawijaya figure. While the word *gotong wolu* means eight people support it. It means that Sutawijaya (Panembahan Senapati) can reign as the king of Mataram because eight significant figures support him.

The fifth line, *Surabaya Geger Kepati*, gives meaning to the occurrence of a big war in Surabaya City during Raja Sultan Agung's throne. This great war caused a considerable death toll.

The sixth line (*Ana Wong Ngoyak Macan* 'a person chases the tiger') describes the rebellion that occurred in Kartasura kingdom by Pangeran Puger. In this case, the *macan* 'tiger' symbol is Pangeran Puger (younger Sunan Amangkurat Agung) raja Mataram. Pangeran Puger is likened to the macan 'tiger' because he is a royal nobleman.

The seventh line, *Denwadhahi Bumbung*, means that the rebellion led by Pangeran Puger can be quickly suppressed by Tumenggung Urawan (Sunan Mangkurat's confidant). Therefore, it is likened to the word "*denwadhahi Bumbung*" or 'inserted in roof 'bamboo tube.' It illustrates how easy it is to capture rebels until they are put in bamboo pieces.

The eighth (*Alun-alun Kartosura*), ninth (*Gajah Meta Cinancang Wit Sidaguri*), and tenth lines (*mati cineker ayam*) depict the rebellion occurring in Kartasura kingdom by one of Demang Sruti's children named Dirana. Because a few people only carry out the rebellion, it is quickly resolved. Dirana is arrested and sentenced to *picis* (death sentence) punishment. The event is not a significant rebellion or war, it aims to prosecute justice for the ruler, but the claimant instead becomes the victim.

2. Pierce's Semiotic Approach and Intertext Perspectives

In the previous part, the *uran-uran* 'song' *SIAS* can be classified as a symbol disguised in metaphor in its expression. The principal term is not mentioned, but the second term is stated explicitly, "*Semut Ireng Anak-anak Sapi*," consisting of ten lines, forming one stanza of the macapat song. In Peirce's semiotic, language (word, phrase, expression) can be categorized as a meaningful sign. *Unen-unen* 'dendangan' "*semut ireng anak-anak sapi*" is a sign that must be searched its meaning. The search for meaning can be applied to semiotic theory, including iconical, symbolic, and indexical relationships. In addition, the study of meaning is then continued by linking with other texts, namely BMPW as hypograms.

a. Iconic-Symbolic Meaning

Previously, it has been explained that *semut ireng* is a metaphor for a girl (Dewi Sapudi) from Wandan. In semiotic theory, *semut ireng* is signed or signified, while the girl (Dewi Sapudi) is signified and must be searched for meaning. Semiotically, the relationship between the signifier and to signified leads to the similarity of shape (iconic). Iconically, the body of *semut ireng*, '*black ant*,' resembles someone who is slim and 'small waisted' but has a big butt like a black ant. In this case, the *ireng* 'black' color iconically illustrates a similarity in color with the person's skin from Eastern Indonesia, Dewi Sapudi, who is faithful as sweet black skin. Therefore, iconically, Dewi Sapudi is symbolized by an ant because the shape and color are similar.

Besides icons, the relationship between sign and signified can be symbolic. *Semut* or ants belong to small animals. Besides being similar, in the Javanese culture, ants mean small or ordinary folk. Therefore, the symbol of ants is the image of a woman who comes from the commoners. It is supported by the BMPW text describing that Dewi Sapudi comes from familiar people. At first, she was a housekeeper serving Ratu Dwarawati, a booty princess from Banda Island, East Indonesia. Because Ratu Dwarawati (her master) is brought to Majapahit as a booty princess, Dewi Sapudi also goes to Majapahit. In the text, it is explained that Putri Wandan is a booty princess who is hired to be a cook at Majapahit place.

Why is the existence of Putri Wandan or Dewi Sapudi necessary? Her existence is vital because she delivers the great kings in Java. Putri Wandan gives birth to a son named Ki Bondhan Kejawan or Lembu Peteng. In history, Lembu Peteng is taken son-in-law by Ki Ageng Tarub, married to Dewi Nawangsih or Rara Kasihan. From that marriage, Ki Getas Pendhawa is born. Ki Getas Pendhawa has a son named Ki Ageng Sela, Ki Ageng Sela has a son named Ki Ageng Ngenis, and Ki Ageng Ngenis has a son named Ki Ageng Pemanahan. Ki Ageng Pemanahan becomes the forerunner of the Islamic Mataram kingdom.

b. Symbolic Meaning

In symbols, the relationship between signifier and signified is arbitrary. A sign that becomes a symbol will be attached to cultural, situational, conditional traits or local, personal, and universal symbols. The symbols in SIAS appear in symbols that refer to Javanese culture, local Javanese, and personal that refer to Javanese culture.

1) Local Symbol

Local symbols are related to cultural properties, which refer to the Javanese cultural context. In this expression, local symbols are found in the word choices such as *sapi* 'cow,' *kebo bongkang* 'old buffalo,' elephant, *timun wuku* 'small cucumber,' and *macan* 'tiger.'

In Javanese vocabulary, the word *sapi*, 'cow,' is synonymous with *lembu*, 'ox .'Concerning the name of the figure, the word *lembu* is commonly used to give the initials or noble figure name. It can be seen in the names of figures such as Lembu Sura (in puppets) or Lembu Ampal (in the history of the Singasari kingdom). In Javanese vocabulary, the word *lembu* is also synonymous with the word *maesa*. Therefore, names such as Maesa Cempaka and Maesa Wongateleng (noble son of the Singasari kingdom) are often found in naming characters. In this context, the word cow symbolizes Lembu Peteng, a son of Raja Brawijaya, Majapahit. Lembu Peteng then brings down kings in Java.

Local symbolic signified can also be seen in the word *kebo* (line two) in the expression "*kebo bongkang nyabrang kali bengawan.*" Like cows, the word *kebo* 'buffalo' is signified (local symbol) by Demak royal nobles named Kebo Kenanga and Kebo Kanigara. The BMPW text explains that Kebo Kenanga and Kebo Kanigara are siblings, both sons of Adipati Andayaningrat (Adipati Pengging). However, both of them determine different paths in life. Kebo Kanigara chooses the old faith by adhering to Buddhism, while Kebo Kenanga adheres to Islam.

The use of the name "elephant" as in the expression "*gajah meta*" 'elephant is angry,' and the word "*macan*" (in line 6) is symbolic. Elephants signify Dirana's figure because of his courage in fighting for his rights, which the ruler (Patih Pringgalaya) usurped during the Kartasura era. Meanwhile, the word "macan" or " tiger " symbolizes Pangeran Puger. The similarity of attitudes can cause the iconic symbol. The courage of the Dirana figure faces Kartasura soldiers as his opponents. Besides, the power of elephants is iconically similar to the power of Dirana's figure. The angry elephant will not be afraid to face anyone. Likewise, Dirana also dares to face thousands of royal warriors. At the same time, the word "chicken" (line ten) symbolizes ordinary people. The important thing from the tenth and eleventh lines is social critics of the ruler's crimes (Patih Pringgalaya), who has misbehaved against the people. The governor usurps the right of Dirana as village chief (replacing his father), and the position is given to others arbitrarily.

Furthermore, *timun wuku* 'small cucumber' symbolically becomes signified (symbolic) of Sutawijaya's figure (first Mataram king), who eventually becomes Panembahan Senapati. Javanese proverbs have the expression "*Timun wungkuk jaga imbuh*" and 'small cucumber as alternatives.' Sutawijaya is symbolized by *wungkuk* cucumber because, in the power struggle from Pajang to Mataram, Sutawijaya is only a backup puppet, not a significant role. After the war, he is asked to become king in Mataram with Panembahan Senapati's title. While the word gotong wolu gives the meaning that Panembahan Senapati can reign as the king of Mataram because of being supported by eight significant figures. The eighth great figures are 1) Ki Ageng Pemanahan, 2) Ki Jurumartani, 3) Ki Penjawi, 4) Ki Jurukithing,

5) Ki Buyut Wirasaba, 6) Tumenggung Mayang, 7) Pangeran Made Pandan, dan 8) Adipati Batang.

2) Personal Symbol

In addition to local symbols (cultural), personal symbols are also found in the expression. The personal symbols are seen in the expressions of *bumbung, gajah meta, ayam*, and *keyong gondang*.

The word *bumbung*, 'bamboo strips that have not been split' (as a symbol of captive traps), is a personal thing. Besides that, *bumbung* is figurative of a trap or prison. Such meanings will be known if the reader is familiar with the social and personal context.

In addition to the word *bumbung* as a symbol of the word trap, the word wit *sidaguri* 'sidaguri grass' is also a personal symbol. Sidaguri becomes the symbol of the banyan tree planted in the town square. The relationship between the banyan tree and *sidaguri* grass can be symbolically-iconically opposed. Its relationship with types or materials can be considered iconic because of its similarity. It is in terms of plant types. In this case, the personal local symbol appears in the word choice of *sidaguri* as the metaphor for the banyan tree in the town square. Therefore, *gajah meta cinancang wit sidaguri* means that the rampaging elephant is caught and handcuffed (rope) with the banyan tree.

Furthermore, personal symbols are also seen in the word "*cineker ayam*" in line *mati cineker ayam*. In this case, the relationship between sign and signified is symbolically personal. *Cineker ayam* gives personal meaning. The chicken belongs to *sembelihan*, or slaughtered animals consumed by humans. However, in this case, the kitchen is used as a symbol of a familiar place. The statement is ironic in that the death of Dirana seems despicable because the people are involved in participating in the death sentence by slicing his body with bamboo blades or *siladan* to death.

3) Indexical Symbol

The symbolic sign referring to the index is seen in the expression *Keyong Godang Carak Sungute*. Indexically, *keyong* becomes a symbol (sign) of

Jaka Tingkir or Sultan Hadiwijaya (Raja Pajang). In BMPW, Jaka Tingkir is narrated to have been born in the Pengging area, which is said to have many water sources. Therefore, he is symbolized as *keong* 'snail,' who used to live in water. In this case, Jaka Tingkir symbolically alludes to the snail because they have much water in the same place to live. Jaka Tingkir comes from Pengging, a place close to the water source. The relationship between reality and object indexically refers to the place of residence. Pengging City has a water source called Umbul Pengging because Jaka Tingkir comes from the Pengging area near the *umbul* 'water source'. He is symbolized as a *keyong* 'snail' who indeed lives near water. While the word gondhang 'big' means that Jaka Tingkir alludes to *keyong gondhang* 'big snail' who has short *sungut* or short antennae). The expression of the antennae's length means that Prabu Hadiwijaya's enthrone as king in Pajang is in a short time. In BMPW, Pangeran Benawa (Brawijaya's son) cannot inherit to be a great king like his father because Sutawijaya or Panembahan Senapati holds his power.

Conclusion

In Javanese culture, expression is conveyed directly and indirectly, but symbols, gestures, and signs hide it. One of them is figurative language. It is classified as a disguised language in *uran-uran 'dendangan' semut ireng anak-anak sapi* (SIAS). SIAS, tied in the Javanese song Dhandhanggula, raises essential events that occurred in the past. The critical event is the birth of Bondhan Gejawan (Lembu Peteng) figure in the Majapahit kingdom, which brings down the kings of Java (Mataram); line two raises the existence of two figures (Kebo Kanigara and Kebo Kenanga) in Demak kingdom era; line three marks the event in Pajang kingdom; line four marks the founding of Mataram kingdom; line five marks the defeat of Kadipaten Surabaya at Sultan Agung era, line six dan seven mark the rebellion in Kartasura kingdom, and line 8,9,10 mark the rebellion in Surakarta kingdom.

Furthermore, based on Pierce's semiotic theory, the signifier-sign relationship between iconic-symbol and symbolic relationships can be seen. The symbolic relationship includes local (Java), personal, and indexical symbols. The iconic relationship is seen in the same reality of base form, including the similarity of the body= (body shape) and skin color. However, the dominant thing is the symbolic relationship. The symbolic relationship is built by local symbols referring to Javanese cultures, such as the word *sapi, kebo, gajah,* and *macan*, which symbolically means a noble figure. Besides that, the relationship between reality and objects is also built by a personal symbol such as the word *bumbung* as a trap symbol, wit *sidaguri* as a symbol of the banyan tree, and chicken as the symbol of ordinary people.

Furthermore, in the indexical symbolic relationship, it is seen that the word choice *keyong* is a symbol of the Sultan Adiwijaya (Jaka Tingkir) figure. The relationship between reality and object is not associated directly. Relating to the text that becomes hypogram, SIAS refers to BMPW text. More comprehensive figures and events need to associate with BMPW as a hypogram.

References

Altenbrend, L. (1970). *A Handbook for the Study of Poetry.* London: Collier-Mac Millan Ltd.

Becker, A.L. 1977. *Linguistik dan Analisis.* Jakarta: Pusat Pembinaan dan Pengembangan Bahasa.

Culler, J., (1975). *Strukturalist Poetics: Structuralism, Linguistic and the Study of literature.* London: Routledge and Kegan Paul.

Fokkema, D.W. (diterjemahkan oleh Praptadiharja dan Kepler Silaban) 1998. Teori Sastra Abad Keduapuluh. Jakarta: Gramedia Pustaka Utama.

Koentjaraningrat. 1974. *Kebudayaan, Mentalitet, dan Pembangunan.* Jakarta: Gramedia.

North, Winfried. (1995). *Handbook of Semiotics.* Bloomington and Indiana Polis: Indiana University Press.

Padmosoekotjo, S. 1960. *Ngengrengan Kasusastran Djawa II.* Yogyakarta: Hien Hoo Sing.

------------------ 1958. *Sarine Basa Djawa.* Yogyakarta: Hien Hoo Sing.

Pradopo, Rahmat Djoko. 1989. *Pengkajian Puisi.* Yogyakarta: Gajah Mada University Press.

Riffaterre, Michael. 11978. *Semiotics of Poetry.* Bloomington & London. Phoenix House.

Santosa, Puji. 1993. *Ancangan Seniotika dan Pengkajian Susastra.* Bandung: Angkasa.

Sastrowardojo, Subagijo. 1975. *Simphoni.* Jakarta: Pustaka Jaya.

Satoto, Budiyono Heru.1990. Simbolisme Budaya Jawa. Jakarta: Bina Ilmu.

Sudjiman, Panuti dan Aart van Voest. 1992. *Serba-serbi Semiotika.* Jakarta: Gramedia.

Suratno, Pardi. 2021. *Transformasi Serat Centhini dalam Novel Indonesia Modern.* Yogyakarta: Lokus Tiara Wacana Group

Bibliographical Information

Anonim, tt. *Uran-uran Semut Ireng Anak-anak* Sapi" (manuskrip) koleksi perpustakaan Reksa Pustaka Mangkunegaran Surakarta dengan nomor A.44a.

Prawirayuda, R. Panji. Babad *Majapahit dan Para Wali.* Diterbitkan Departemen Pendidikan dan Kebudayaan 1988.

Sastranagara, R.T. tt. *Uran-uran Semut Ireng Anak-anak Sapi"* (manuskrip) koleksi perpustakaan Reksa Pustaka Mangkunegaran Surakarta dengan nomor A.44b.

Epilogue
Elevating Language and Literature, Opening the Door to Cooperation between Nations

Koh Young Hun
Hankuk Univ. of Foreign Studies, Korea

The marginalization of language and literature in various cultural areas in the world is unavoidable, when certain cultural groups feel superior or superior to other cultural groups. To provide justification for this act of marginalization, arguments are put forward which state that one cultural product is of higher quality, more complex or more valuable. Meanwhile, other cultural products are below it.

In the lives of people who are under an imperial, royal or sultanate system of government, this dichotomous view is deliberately and necessary to be presented by the authorities to establish socio-cultural power and domination. From here, various kinds of myths were born which substance was to emphasize the legitimacy of the superior image of the authorities. In this way, every fatwa or ruling government is believed to have supernatural powers and anyone who violates this order will receive punishment or curse from the ruling gods of the universe.

Apart from that, another aim of creating these myths is to differentiate between the stratification of the position of the ruler (with all of his superiorities) and the position of the common people, ordinary people, and the peripheral (with all of their inferiorities) from the spectacle of the ruler. The existence of strict boundaries in the structure of social stratification forces the general public or ordinary people to feel the need to have their own cultural products.

From here, artistic products were produced within and for their own circles. In this extend, some myths emerged to describe their lives (ordinary people) issues which later were known as folklore in the oral tradition. Most of these folk tales are modeled after myths or legends with which they are (perhaps) familiar. The creation of folklore is also (almost) always associated with the manners, ethics and social norms that apply among them. Therefore, it is understandable that in most folk tales, superpower figures or other magical figures appear as representatives of the rulers of the universe.

Considering that artistic products, with their various folk tales in oral traditions, are so fluid, easily spread and so widely liked by various groups, there are always efforts to reproduce them. Therefore, it can be understood why folk tales which are claimed and believed to belong to a particular society, also appear in other societies, even though they are geographically very far away. Just as an example, for example, the folk tales of Bawang Merah and Bawang Putih and Ande-Ande Lumut (Indonesia). In Korea, the story of Soy Beans and Red Beans (Gong Jui Phat Jui – 콩쥐 팥쥐) is also known , which in some cases is similar to the two Indonesian folk tales mentioned above, although in Gong Jui Phat Jui also has a falling shoe incident which is also similar to the Cinderella fairy tale.

Of course we will find many folk tales from various regions in Indonesia which have resemblances with stories from other countries, such as the story of Joko Tarub and the Seven Angels, for example, in Korea there is also a similar story, namely the Angel and the Woodcutter (Seonnyeowa Namukkun – 선녀와 나무꾼). We also find similar stories in various countries in the Southeast Asia region. So, the spread of folklore often crosses national and cultural boundaries.

However, people's treatment of folk tales in one particular cultural area and in another cultural area is not the same. There are those who consider them a mere fairy tale, but there are also those who place them as a cultural source of national identity that contains local wisdom. In Korea, folk tales such as Myth And Gun (단군신화) or The story of the origins of the Hang Geul letters (Hun Min Jeong Eum – 훈민정음) is an important story for school children to know. Therefore, the teachers will convey the story along with the meaning and philosophy values behind the story.

***

In relation with the above, various studies on language and literature written by the Indonesian National Research and Innovation Agency (BRIN) researchers in this book show the importance of introducing linguistic and literary issues that live and grow in various regions in Indonesia that tend not to be so well known to Indonesian society as a whole. This message is implied in the title of this book, namely Marginal Language and Literature, which suggests that the 14 research results take language and literature as objects that are marginalized or considered marginal. Thus, this book offers another perspective on language and literature in various regions in Indonesia or ethnic languages and literature that are not yet widely known in their own communities.

The publication of the results of this research in English and published by the Hankuk University of Foreign Studies (HUFS) Publisher is also an effort to expand this introduction to the world community, especially Korean society. More importantly, the publication of the results of this research is the first step to develop more immense research collaboration between BRIN and HUFS researchers. It is certain that this collaboration in the future will not only produce various joint researches between BRIN and HUFS, in particular, but also for the people of Korea and Indonesia.

Seoul, December 2023

Marginal Language and Literature

Author	Badan Riset dan Inovasi Nasional
Edited by	Maman S. Mahayana · Prof. Koh Young Hun
First Printed	2023.12.26
First Published	2023.12.29
Director	Yunsung Koh
Executive Contents Creator	Sunho Shin
Contents Creator	Haejung Jang Jihyun Lee Mihyun Park
Designer	Daewook Kim Jaeyoung Choi
Published by	HANKUK UNIVERSITY OF FOREIGN STUDIES KNOWLEDGE CONTENTS & PRESS 107, Imun-ro, Dongdaemun-gu, Seoul 02450, Korea Tel.) 82-2-2173-2497 Fax.) 82-2-2173-3363 E-mail) press@hufs.ac.kr Online) http://press.hufs.ac.kr
Printed by	Twinbell Tel.) 82-2-2088-1810
ISBN	979-11-7199-075-7 [93830]
Price	23,000 Won